Harmonic Secrets
of
Arabic Music Scales

Fine Tuning
the
Maqams

Cameron Powers

Two Audio CDs Accompany This Book!

Order the Two Audio CD's
"Harmonic Secrets"
for only $19 plus shipping and handling:

Use Internet:

Go to: http://www.gldesignpub.com/HarmonicSecretsCDs.html
1) place order with Credit Card or Paypal
2) Include your Shipping Address

OR

Email for more info: distrib@gldesignpub.com

Harmonic Secrets of Arabic Music Scales: Fine Tuning the Maqams
-- First Edition

Original Copyright © 2012 by Cameron Powers
Published by GL Design, Boulder, Colorado, USA

All rights reserved. No part of this book may be reproduced in any form or by any electronic or mechanical means including information storage and retrieval systems without permission in writing from the publisher, except by a reviewer, who may quote brief passages in a review.

Library of Congress Control Number: 2012937410
ISBN: 1-933983-19-1
ISBN Complete: 978-1-933983-19-6

Introduction

Musicians in the West have been studying the amazing music of the Indigenous Middle East for centuries. This music is microtonal and has traditional roots which go back for countless centuries.

This book provides a clear path into both solving the mysteries of indigenous Middle Eastern music and combining the harmonic theories of modern physics known as *Just Intonation* with the musical traditions of the ancients. Whether you would like to probe the perfect harmonies preserved in the Music of India, China, Turkey, Greece, Persia or other cultures, the information in this book will provide a sound method.

"Quartertone" concepts were refined early in the twentieth century to try and make Egyptian music accessible to Westerners, but the 24-note equal-tempered scale adopted for teaching has never sounded quite right to Egyptian musical masters. They say things like: "That note needs to be a little different or the magic will never happen!"

Musicians who read this book will find themselves deepening their pitch control with a new confidence that they are now using the perceptible harmonic laws of Just Intonation as an internal guide. Now the comments made by the Egyptian and other Middle Eastern musical masters make perfect sense.

Audiences and dancers will likewise find new appreciation for ecstatic potentials as they learn to hear in more deeply refined ways. These paths also lead to discovering new mixtures of uplifting emotions carried by the incredibly rich variety of popular and sacred music scales common in ancient world-music traditions. Spiritual realms open and health benefits can be experienced.

More than One Hundred Fifty Scales are described or mentioned in this book: Eighteen *Basic Scales;* Sixty-Five *Derived Scales* and Sixty-Seven *Closely Related Scales.* Knowledge of these scales and of their building blocks, known in the Arabic language as *"ajnas,"* unlocks a powerful tool for composing in an infinitely varied realm of harmonious musical possibilities.

Once these basic scales and harmonies are understood and mastered, a beautiful simplicity is revealed and these musical territories can become second-nature to the musician.

Contents

Indigenous Middle Eastern Music	1
• Perfect Ancient Harmony	1
Musical Magic: True Harmonic Perfection of Just Intonation	5
Illustrations Below: Waveform Images	7
• Just Harmonic Intervals	7
• Equal Tempered Harmonic Intervals	8
Waveform Illustrations of Various Intervals	9
• Perfectly Harmonious "just" Divisions of an Octave	9
Interval Wave Patterns	10
• Just 5th	10
• Just 4th	11
• Just Major 3rd	11
• Just Minor 3rd	12
• Just Major 2nd	12
• Another Just Major 2nd	13
• Just Half-flat 2nd	14
• Another Just Half-flat 2nd	14
• Just Major 6th	15
Schematic Waveform Diagrams	16
Frequently Heard Comments	18
What Happened to Perfect Harmony in Western Music?	19
Harmony in Arabic Music	19
Quartertones	21
Early Arabic Music History	22
Value of Indigenous Musical Traditions	23
Overtone Analysis and Just Intonation	23
Arabic Maqamat and Just Intonation	26
Note Naming Traditions	28
Classification of Maqamat	31
Practical Tools	33
The Essential Building Blocks of Maqamat: Ajnas	35
Notes on Terminology & Abbreviations Used in the following Tables	36
• Jins Hijaz on D	38
• Jins Kurd on D	39
• Jins Bayat on D	40
• Jins Saba on D	41
• Jins Saba Zamazama on D	42
• Jins Rast on C	43
• Jins Nahawand on C	44
• Jins Nawa Athar on C	45
• Jins Athar Kurd on C	46
• Jins Ajam on Bb	47
• Jins Sikah on E half-flat	48
Indigenous Middle Eastern Modes	49

D-Based Maqams — 49
Hijaz Family — 49
Hijaz and Hijaz Gharib — 49
Closely Related Maqamat: Hijaz Humayun, Ajami, al-Isba'ayn (Tunisia), al-Zayyidan (Algeria), Hijaz al-kabir (Morocco), al-Mathnawi (Iraq).
Hijaz Awji — 52
Closely Related Maqamat: Hijaz, Hijaz Masri, Araba (old name)
Shehnaz — 54
Closely Related Maqamat: Sikah Baladi, Zirgule Hijaz, (Turkey)
Kurd Family — 56
Kurd — 56
Closely Related: Phrygian Mode
Bayyati Family — 59
Bayyati — 60
Closely Related Maqamat: Ushaq (Turkey), Bayati Sultani, Ardibar, Isfahan
Husayni — 62
Closely Related Maqamat: Tahir, Hawzi, Nawa, Kutshuk, Sultani Iraq, Gulizar, Kardan
Saba — 64
Closely Related Maqamat: Isfanak, Dugah, Sipahr, Naziniyaz

C-Based Maqams — 67
Nahawand Family — 67
Nahawand — 68
Closely Related Maqamat and Modes: Nihavent (Turkey), Buselik (Turkey), Natural Minor, Harmonic Minor, Aeolian Mode, Rahawi or Sahili (Algeria), Muhayar Sikah (Tunisia), Isfahan (Persia)
Rast Family — 71
Rast — 72
Closely Related Maqamat: Buzurg, Shawqidil
Suznak — 74
Nawa Athar Family — 76
Nawa Athar — 76
Closely Related Maqamat: Hayan, Nevaser (Turkey)
Athar Kurd — 78
Hijaz Kar Family — 80
Hijaz Kar — 80

Bb-Based Maqams — 82
Ajam Family — 82
Ajam Ushayran (Bb Major) — 82
Closely Related: Huezawi, Ionian Mode

E half-flat-Based Maqams — 85
Sikah Family — 85
Huzam — 86
Closely Related Maqamat: Sikah Arabi
Sikah — 88

F-Based Maqams — 91
Jaharkah Family — 91
Jaharkah — 91
Closely Related Maqamat: Shahwar

- Transposed E half-flat--Based Maqamat ... 93
  - Rahat el Arwah (Huzam on B half-flat) ... 94
- Derived Maqams ... 97
  - Derived D-Based Maqams ... 97
    - Kurd Family ... 97
      - Shehnaz Kurdi ... 97
      - Zawqi Tarab ... 98
      - Lami ... 98
    - Bayati Family ... 99
      - Mohayar ... 99
        - *Closely Related Maqamat: Nahfat*
      - Shuri ... 100
        - *Closely Related Maqamat: Bayati Araban, Ajem Murassa, Karjigar (Turkish)*
      - Bayatayn ... 100
      - Saba Zamzamah ... 101
        - *Closely Related Maqamat: Saba Kurdi*
      - Saba Najdi ... 101
      - Saba Busalik ... 102
      - Sabr Jadid ... 102
  - Derived C-Based Maqams ... 103
    - Nahawand Family ... 103
      - Nahawand Kabir ... 103
        - *Closely Related: Dorian Mode*
      - Nahawand Murassa ... 104
        - *Closely Related Maqamat: Nahawand Rumi*
    - Rast Family ... 105
      - Mahur ... 105
        - *Closely Related Maqamat: Kirdan*
      - Suzdilar ... 106
        - *Closely Related Maqamat: Suzdil 'Ara*
      - Nerz Rast ... 106
        - *Closely Related Maqamat: Nayruz*
      - Rast Beshayer ... 107
      - Dalanshin ... 107
    - Nawa Athar Family ... 108
      - Nakriz ... 108
      - Basandidah ... 108
  - Derived Bb-Based Maqams ... 109
    - Ajam Family ... 109
      - Shawq Afza ... 109
      - Shawqi Awir ... 110
        - *Closely Related Maqamat: Tarz Jadid*
  - Derived E half-flat-Based Maqams ... 111
    - Sikah Family ... 111
      - Awshar ... 111
        - *Closely Related Maqamat: Sha'ar, Mayah, Wajh 'ardibar*
      - Ramal ... 111

Derived F-Based Maqams — 112
Jaharkah Family — 112
Jaharkah Arabi — 112
Closely Related Maqamat: Najdi
Jaharka Turki (Shehnaz on F) — 112

Derived Transposed D--Based Maqamat — 113
Transposed to C — 113
Zanjaran (Hijaz on C with Ajam) — 113
Closely Related Maqamat: Zingaran, Zankulah, Zankhala
Hijaz Kar Kurd (Kurd on C) — 114
Tarz Nawin (Kurd on C with Hijaz) — 114
Transposed to G — 115
Shad Araban (Shehnaz on G) — 115
Sikah Balady (Shehnaz on G with the "old intervals") — 116
Transposed to A — 117
Suzidil (Shehnaz on A) — 117
Shawki Tarab (Kurd on A with Saba) — 118
Busalik Ushayran (Bayati on A) — 118
Nuhuft (Huseyni on A) — 119
Closely Related Maqamat: Huseyni Ushayran
Hijazi Ushayran (Shuri on A) — 119
Bayati Ushayran (Bayatayn on A) — 120
Transposed to E — 121
Qatar (Saba Zamzamah on E) — 121

Derived Transposed C--Based Maqamat — 122
Transposed to G — 122
Farahfaza (Nahawand 1 on G) — 122
Sultani Yaka (Nahawand 2 on G) — 123
Closely Related Maqamat: Rahat Faza
Dilkashidah (Nahawand on G with Bayati) — 123
Yak-Gah (Rast on G) (Rast Nawa) — 124
Yekah (Nayruz on G) — 125
Transposed to E — 126
Busalik (Nahawand on E) — 126
Shiar (Nahawand on E with Bayati) — 127
Transposed to D — 128
Nahawand Kurdi (Nahawand on D) — 128
Ushaq Masri (Nahawand on D with Bayati) — 128
Nishaburk (Nayruz on D) — 129
Hisar (Nawa Athar on D) — 129
Transposed to Db — 130
Midmi (C Hijaz Kar 2nd becomes Tonic on Db) — 130

Derived Transposed F--Based Maqamat — 131
Transposed to D — 131
Zirgulah (Jaharka on D) — 131

Derived Transposed Bb--Based Maqamat — 132
Transposed to D — 132
Nishabur (Ajam on D with Nahawand) — 132
Transposed to C — 133
Ajam on C — 133
Closely Related: C major
Suznal (Shawq Afza on C) — 135
Panjigah (Shawqi Awir on C) — 135
Derived Transposed E half-flat--Based Maqamat — 136
Transposed to B half-flat — 136
Bastanikar (Huzam on B half-flat with Saba) — 136
Closely Related Maqamat: Taz Nuin
Irak (Huzam on B half-flat with Bayati) — 137
Farahnak (Sikah on B half-flat) — 137
Unusual C-Based Ajnas and Maqams — 138
Sazkar and Zawil Family — 138
- Jins Sazkar on C — 138
  - Rast Kabir — 139
  - Sazkar — 139
- Jins Zawil on C — 140
  - Zawil — 141
  - Rast Jadid — 141
  Closely Related Maqamat: Rahawi, Pesendide
Unusual E half-flat-Based Ajnas and Maqams — 142
Mustaar and Mukhalaf — 142
- Jins Mustaar on E half-flat — 142
  - Mustaar — 143
  - Mukhalaf — 143
Unusual B half-flat-Based Maqams — 144
Awj Ara Family — 144
- Jins Awj Ara on B half-flat — 144
  - Awj Ara — 145
  Closely Related Maqamat: Rawnaq Numa

Table A: Note Names of Basic Arabic scale — 147
Table B: Names of Expanded 24-note Arabic Scale — 148
Table C: Most Useful Fifty-Eight Just Notes in 1 Octave — 149
Inverse Symmetry — 151
Measuring Frequency — 152
Tastes of Other Ancient World Music Traditions — 153
- Iraqi Maqam Names and Classification — 153
- Chinese Music — 153
- Persian Music — 154
- Music of India — 156
- Music of Turkey — 157
- Music of Greece — 158

Musical Instruments — 159
- Fretless Stringed Instruments — 159
- "Quartertone" Fretted Stringed Instruments — 161
- Other Fretted Stringed Instruments — 161
- Zithers — 162
- Hammered Zithers: Santur — 162
- Wind Instruments — 163
- Other Wind Instruments — 164
- Keyboards — 164

Glossary of Terms — 165
Acknowledgements — 168
Cameron Powers -- Biography — 169
Bibliography — 170
Other Books by Cameron Powers — 174

List of Harmonic Secrets of Arabic Music Scales CD Tracks:

Tracks by "Saadoun", "Jihad" and "Adif" refer to Saadoun Al Bayati from Baghdad, Iraq, Jihad Ibrahim from Amman, Jordan, and Atef Abd elHameed from Cairo, Egypt.
All "Melodies" were written by the author, Cameron Powers, to illustrate the potential for musical creativity for musicians and composers born and raised in Western civilizations.

Harmonic Secrets CD1 -- 31 Tracks:

1. Introduction
2. Hijaz Gharib in D
3. Hijaz Gharib Melody in D -- Rhythm: 8/8 Tsiftitelli
4. Hijaz Taqasim in D by Jihad
5. Hijaz Vocal Taqasim in G by Saadoun
6. Hijaz Dulab in G by Saadoun
7. Hijaz Awji in D
8. Hijaz Awji Melody in D -- Rhythm: 8/8 Tsiftitelli
9. Shehnaz in D
10. Shehnaz Melody in D -- Rhythm: 4/4 Maqsum
11. Kurd in D
12. Kurd Melody in D -- Rhythm: 10/8 Jurjina
13. Kurd Taqasim in D by Jihad
14. Bayati in D
15. Bayati Melody in D -- Rhythm: 8/8 Dabke
16. Bayati Taqasim in D by Adif
17. Bayati Taqasim in D by Jihad
18. Bayati Taqasim in D by Saadoun
19. Bayati Dulab in D by Adif
20. Husayni in D
21. Husayni Melody in D -- Rhythm: 8/8 Wahda
22. Saba in D
23. Saba Melody in D -- Rhythm: 4/4 Sufi
24. Saba Taqasim in D by Jihad
25. Saba Taqasim in D by Adif
26. Nahawand in C
27. Nahawand Melody in C -- Rhythm: 3/4 Waltz
28. Nahawand Taqasim in C by Adif
29. Nahawand Taqasim in C by Jihad
30. Nahawand Dulab in C by Adif
31. Nahawand Vocal Improv in G by Saadoun

Harmonic Secrets CD2 -- 32 Tracks:

1. Rast in C
2. Rast Melody in C -- Rhythm: 2/4 Ayub
3. Rast Taqasim in C by Jihad
4. Rast Taqasim in C by Adif
5. Rast Taqasim in C by Saadoun
6. Rast Dulab in C by Adif
7. Suznak in C
8. Suznak Melody in C -- Rhythm: 8/8 Wahda
9. Nawa Athar in C
10. Nawa Athar Melody in C -- Rhythm: 5/4
11. Athar Kurd in C
12. Athar Kurd Melody in C -- Rhythm: 8/8 Tsiftitelli
13. Hijaz Kar in C
14. Hijaz Kar Melody in C -- Rhythm: 4/4 Maqsum
15. Hijaz Kar Taqasim in C by Jihad
16. Hijaz Kar Taqasim in C by Adif
17. Ajam Ushayran in Bb
18. Ajam Ushayran Melody in Bb -- Rhythm: 7/8 Greek Kalamatiano
19. Ajam Ushayran Vocal Improv in Bb by Saadoun
20. Ajam Taqasim in C by Jihad
21. Huzam in E half-flat
22. Huzam Melody in E half-flat -- Rhythm: 4/4 Sufi
23. Huzam Taqasim in E half-flat by Adif
24. Sikah in E half-flat
25. Sikah Melody in E half-flat -- Rhythm: 8/8 Baladi
26. Sikah Taqasim in E half-flat by Jihad
27. Jaharkah in F
28. Jaharkah Melody in F -- Rhythm: 4/4 Maqsum
29. Rahat el Arwah in B half-flat
30. Rahat el Arwah Melody in B half-flat -- Rhythm: 9/8 Turkish Karsilama
31. Rahat el Arwah Taqasim in B half-flat by Saadoun
32. Rahat el Arwah Taqasim in B half-flat by Jihad

Text of the Introduction on Track 1 of the First CD:

Related Audio Tracks on Harmonic Secrets CD1:

Track 1. **Introduction**

These CD's are specifically designed to accompany my book, Harmonic Secrets of Arabic Music Scales: Fine Tuning the Maqams. (Also published as Lost Secrets of Perfect Harmony: Ancient Music of the Indigenous Middle East.) It is my hope that musicians in the Indigenous Middle East, especially the Arab world, will benefit from knowing that their ancient music can be in tune in a mathematically perfect way that Western equal-tempered music is not. It is also my hope that English-speaking Western-world musicians and composers will awaken to the vast powerful musical universe which awaits them if they are ready to take a look.

There are 18 basic maqamat, or musical modes, which are presented on these cd's. These are the first ones for a musician to learn to gain control of the vast pallet of musical colors presented in the rest of the book.

I have had some fun composing short melodies in these 18 modes. I have used the ancient fretless Middle Eastern stringed lute, or oud as my primary instrument for composition. I have added tracks which also feature the sound of the ancient Middle Eastern cane flute known as the ney or nay. I have also added the sound from the Turkish fretless banjo known as the cumbus, the sound from the Syrian buzuk and occasionally the sound of my voice. And I have used modern electronic tuning technology and have produced tracks with mathematically perfect tuning from a keyboard. I have also built rhythm tracks from the sounds of modern tunable frame drums. Although I have added short improvisations, or "taqasims" to most of these 18 short melodies, I have refrained from modulating away from the maqam I am demonstrating. I do this for the sake of clarity for the student. But in normal artistic improvisation modulations into related maqamat are usually included. One of the cd's which accompanies my first book, Arabic Musical Scales, is devoted to explaining and demonstrating some of the basic patterns of traditional cross-maqam modulation in Arabic music. Hopefully you will enjoy my 18 short compositions which illustrate how much fun we Westerners can have when we give ourselves access to these ancient universal mathematically perfect and justly intonated musical modes. These mathematically perfect intervals of course underlie all of the great carefully preserved world musical traditions. These have been especially well-documented in India, China, Persia, Greece and Turkey as well as in Egypt, Syria and Iraq. Happily, many modern electronic applications for creating music include dozens of justly intonated scales associated with ancient music traditions as something easily selectable for composition. Younger musicians are rapidly being exposed to these rich possibilities.

To add a more authentic feel I have added tracks of various improvisations or "taqasims" created in many of these maqamat which I have recorded personally from three indigenous Middle Eastern oud players.

Many thanks to:
Adif abd el Hamid from Cairo, Egypt,
Saadoun Al Bayati from Baghdad, Iraq
and Jihad Ibrahim from Amman, Jordan
All three have kindly agreed to allow me to publish these recorded short tracks which they designed to be teaching tools for me to record and publish. Please excuse the street noise in the background of some of these recordings.

Hopefully these CD's will inspire musicians and composers to sharpen their listening and performance skills so we can all enjoy a renewal of justly intonated perfectly harmonious music and experience the way it refreshes the soul to allow these musical vibrations to enter into us. Of course all of these recordings which involve playing on acoustic instruments have a fair share of imperfection and human error. But certain moments of perfect harmony will hopefully stand out all the more clearly and provide inspiration to the world musicians and composers of the future.

Indigenous Middle Eastern Music
Perfect Ancient Harmony

Many things have been gained in our 21st century world, but some precious things have been lost. Whenever I travel in Middle Eastern countries where the ancient ways and ancient wisdoms are still intact, I marvel at the tasty richness of the food! Thousands of years of Mesopotamian and Fertile Crescent farming and cooking expertise have compounded to create this healthy and varied cuisine. The same applies to the music. The modes preserved in these parts of the world offer varieties of spicy flavors found nowhere else.

In-depth and detailed study of this musical tradition yields an amazing discovery: although Westerners are fond of saying that harmony is not a major aspect of Middle Eastern music, the intervals used in the system of ancient Middle Eastern musical scales are frequently actually perfectly in tune from the physicist's point of view. The perfectly harmonic intervals preserved correspond to what musicians call "just intonation" in which waveforms of sound created by different musical notes align in repeating patterns which reinforce and amplify each other. The notes used in modern Western music do not do this. Something important has been lost, just as modern mass-production agricultural techniques have resulted in a certain loss. Ancient indigenous musical traditions which preserve perfect harmony bring us back to potentials for deep ecstatic states. Modern physics tells us that the building blocks of the universe are made of vibrational frequecies. We are made of music! So many music-theory books forget to even mention ecstasy. In this book we will understand the ingredients for high ecstatic musical states. It feels daring, even silly to try to use words and concepts to enter those realms. But a new alchemy is upon us. A new mixture of musical insights, skills and techniques can be consciously assembled.

Drink from the artistic and emotional power of thousand-year-old music traditions! Generations of gifted musicians have built on each others' compositions and improvisations.

Dissolve into and build on the ancient musical elegance of the Nile river valley, the Fertile Crescent, Mesopotamia and beyond.

By refining our musical embellishments we go beyond and create a music which is not just a ladder of notes: music is made of undulating sound filligrees which include all the spaces between the notes. But when we do play a note we can listen and trust that we are playing a *real* note which bears a perfectly harmonious relation to the tonic of our scale.

Stay inside these ancient musical traditions and simultaneously transcend the limitations of equal temperament, the utilitarian but not-quite-in-tune system invented for the piano which has taken over music in the West. We are on solid ground here. These musical secrets have been developed to worship the divine for thousands of years in these ancient civilizations.

Musicians who delve deeply into ancient traditions, whether of the Middle East or India, China, Turkey, Persia or Greece find music built on the basic laws of harmony.

The same happens to musicians who move into the magical realms of overtone singing and explore the perfect harmonic intervals which come out of one voice or from one string. But since music is often made from more than one string, intervals which don't even exist in the overtone series, like the perfect 4th, have to be discovered and understood. And why limit the number of notes to only 12 notes per octave? There are hundreds of harmonious notes in an octave. The Table on Page 149 gives the "most useful fifty-eight."

And what if we move the tonic (or beginning note of a scale) from one pitch to another? Don't all those hundreds of harmonious notes in the rest of the scale move too? Yes they do!

The Arab musical tradition brings elegant knowledge to the art of modulation from one tonic note to the next and then to the next. This is what the dozens of traditional scales from the musical system called "maqam" or "makam" from the indigenous Middle East can offer. We are no longer just appreciating perfect harmony coming from one chosen pitch. We can move the pitch through musical space on ancient fretless instruments or modern highly tuneable instruments with total fluidity.

By combining the acoustic perfection of just intonation and the moveable tonics of Arabic maqamat we enter the magic world of harmonics with the capacity for multiple degrees of freedom.

> *"Because the Arabian tone system is not tempered, the size of an interval can change during the presentation of a maqam, giving rise to a particular characteristic coloring of a tone level and simultaneously eliciting a specific emotional mood in the Arab listener. It is the changeable size of certain intervals in this non-tempered tone system that influences the emotional content of a maqam. Such an emotional content, however, becomes lost as soon as the tone system is artificially changed and organized into intervals of equal size." --Touma 1996*

The hundreds of perfectly in-tune notes per octave curve and intertwine with each other with amazing eloquence in the hands of traditional masters. But sometimes these masters are not even conscious of how they are doing what they are doing! At last it is coming clear that it is possible to explain the ultimate magic of music and place that knowledge in the hands of musicians who are in search of the roots of ecstasy. What exactly are the components of the music which bring listeners and dancers into an ecstatic state?

"Few theoretical works describe the ecstatic role of intonation ... most sources present melodic intervals in terms of the microtonally crude, largely Western-inspired theoretical system of equal tempered half-steps, three-quarter-steps ... derived from a theoretical scale of 24 equal quarter tones per octave. In actual practice however, tarab (ecstatic) music exhibits an intricate and a highly patterned system of intonation." --Racy 2003

The possibilities of endless freedom in music-making can finally be made clear.

"A musical system that calls for harmonically pure intervals at all times is called Just Intonation. It requires that notes have the flexibility to vary in pitch according to the needs of the harmony at any given moment, and this is only possible with voices or on instruments with a capacity to make real time adjustments as the music is being performed." --Duffin 2007

And to think: most music theory books claim that Arabic music "doesn't use harmony" because it is not generally written for a piano-player's hands which are accustomed to holding multiple notes sustained together at once. Harmony in Arabic music is more fleeting: the overlapping and intertwining of multiple instrumental decorations.

"Melody, like language, said Rousseau, was born of an erotic fervor: man's untamed impulses creating release. Springing from the deepest well of hunger, desire, pleasure, and sorrow, original melody imitates the accents of language but it has 100 times more energy than speech itself. Unfortunately, believed Rousseau, along came civilization. As language was perfected, and melody subjected to rules, both lost their primitive powers. Music's raw poetic intensity became stifled through the imposition of artificial conventions." --Isacoff 2001

"In 762 Baghdad became the capital of the Islamic empire in the East… and Cordoba became the capital of the empire in the West. The former was destroyed by Mongols in 1258 and the latter, reconquered by Christians in 1236.

…Arabian literature included not only a voluminous and highly sophisticated collection of works on the art and science of music, but on the precise mathematics of lute tunings as well.

…Baghdad and Cordoba boasted running water, paved and lighted streets, world-renowned architectural monuments, international markets, universities, hospitals, and above all, libraries that contained hundreds of thousands of volumes. If it were not for these libraries, and the care Arabian translators and scholars bestowed on ancient texts, the works of Homer, Hippocrates, Plato, Aristotle, Euclid, Archimedes, Nichomachus and Ptolemy, to name only a few, would probably not have survived."
--Forster 2010

Musical Magic: True Harmonic Perfection of Just Intonation

Arabic music scales offer the musician an amazing discovery: the ancient harmonic intervals preserved in Arabic maqamat can be performed using the very same intervals defined by the laws of physics as perfect harmony. "Just Intonation" is a modern term used by musicians, composers and others interested in the science of acoustics to refer to musical intervals between notes which are "perfectly harmonious." By this term "perfectly harmonious" we mean that the sound waves generated by the two notes which create the musical interval reinforce each other because their peaks and valleys coincide perfectly at regular and frequent intervals which are describable with simple mathematical fractions. To hear a pair of recorded musical intervals and listen for the differences between perfect just harmony and equal temperament go to http://www.innernationals.com/microtonal.html

"Just intonation, or pure tuning, is the universal foundation for harmony which is constructed from musical intervals of perfect mathematical proportions. Pythagoras and other ancient Greek philosophers and mathematicians discovered that musical harmonies arise from mathematical relationships based on whole numbers. The most consonant harmonies are created when two strings or other musical bodies vibrate in simple musical proportions. For example, the two notes comprising an octave have a 2:1 relationship, where the higher note is vibrating exactly twice as fast as the lower note. A perfect 5th is a 3:2 relationship, a perfect 4th is 4:3, a major 3rd is 5:4, a minor 3rd is 6:5, a septimal minor 3rd is 7:6, a whole step is 9:8, and so on. Every different set of whole numbers corresponds to a different set of musical intervals." --Michael Harrison

"When your unison with a string is true, you seem to merge into it, to disappear, and all your fantasies and financial statements disappear too, at least for a breath."
-Mathieu 1997

Was playing in perfect harmony important to musical masters who lived in the ancient times?

> *"The roman orator Quintilian, a frequently cited authority in the mediaeval universities, left us to ponder the sad story of a piper accused of manslaughter. He had played a tune to accompany a sacrifice but used the wrong musical scale, with the result that the person officiating went mad and flung himself over a precipice."* --Isacoff 2001

> *"North American musicians who do not read Arabic, French or German have very limited opportunities to study ancient Arabian music and tuning theory from original sources. Of the treatises on music writtten by Al-Farabi (d. c. 950), Ibn Sina (980-1037), Safi Al-Din (d. 1294), Al-Jurjani (d. 1413), Al-Ladhiqi (d. 1494), and Al-Shirwani (d. 1626), not a single work has ever been translated into English. Furthermore, due to intractable religious, linguistic and intellectual prejudices again Islam, Christian-dominated institutions throughout Europe -- such as Catholic and Protestant churches, schools and universities and craft guilds -- managed by 1600 to completely eradicate the Arabian influence from the history of European music."* --Forster 2010

> *"According to the 12th century writer, Ibn al-Hijari, 'students from all parts of the world flocked to Cordoba to sit at the feet of Arabic scholars.'"* --Forster 2010

Illustrations Below: Waveform Images

Here are some visual aids which help us understand true harmony.

Just Harmonic Intervals

Regularly repeating harmonious mutually re-inforcing patterns:

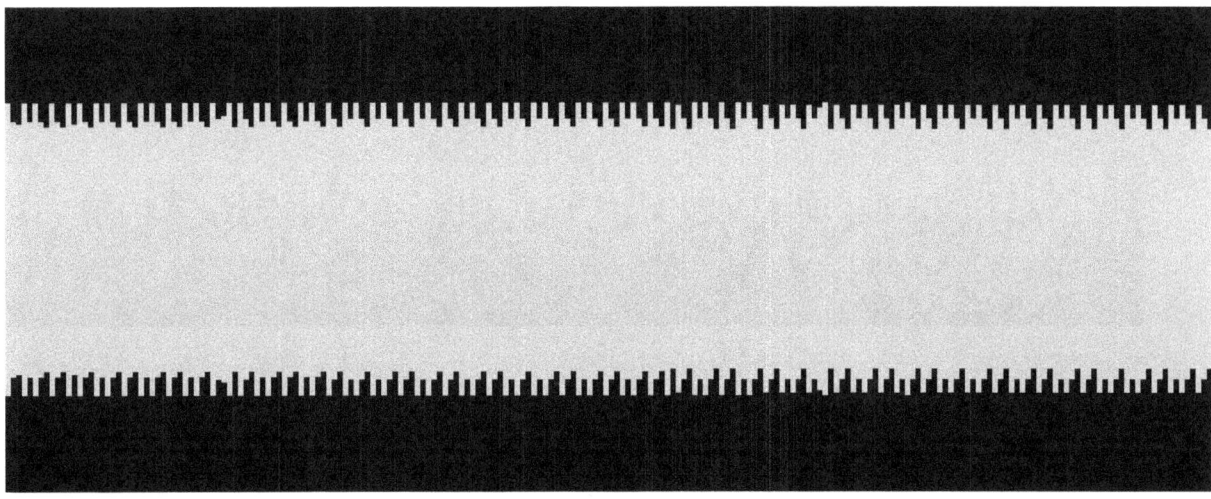

Just intonation utilizes harmonic intervals which are basic multiples and divisions of each other so that the waves generated by two notes frequently coincide and reinforce each others' existence. These perfectly harmonic intervals represented by ratios such as 6:5, 5:4, etc, resonate perfectly and form the basis for truly harmonious "minor thirds," "major thirds" and other intervals found in justly intonated musical scales. Compare these wave images with those on the next page.

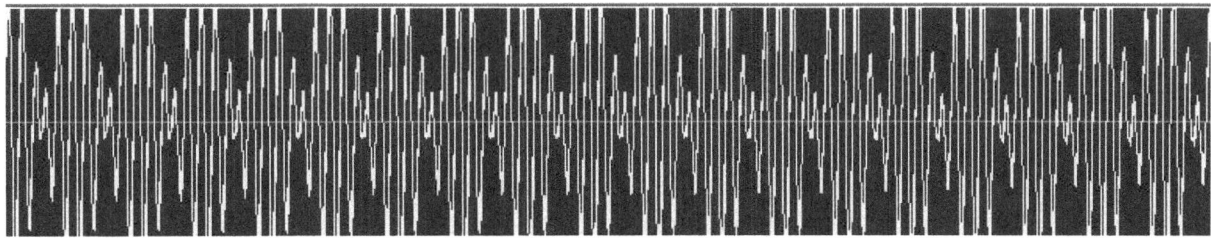

The waveform image above was created on my Moog synthesizer by combining a Just major 3rd with its tonic. You can see that the mixture of the two soundwaves repeats itself with exactly the same pattern which reflects a perfect harmonious resonance between the two pitches.

Mixtures of perfectly harmonious sound waves tend to reinforce each other and require less amplification to reach the ears of the audience.

Equal Tempered Harmonic Intervals

Chaotic Non-harmonious interference patterns:

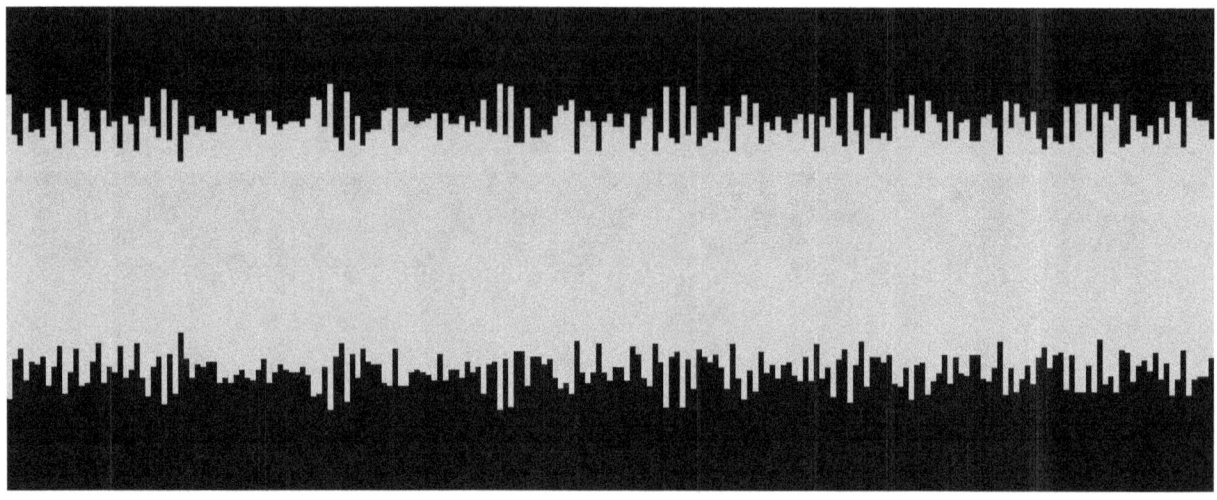

Equal Temperament utilizes harmonic intervals which are based on dividing an octave into 12 parts based on powers of 2. The ratios generated by this system create irrational numbers with endless decimal descriptions. An interval based on these wavelengths can never exactly match up, coincide and reinforce itself harmonically. The shape of these conflicting waveforms creates uneven wave patterns such as the one above.

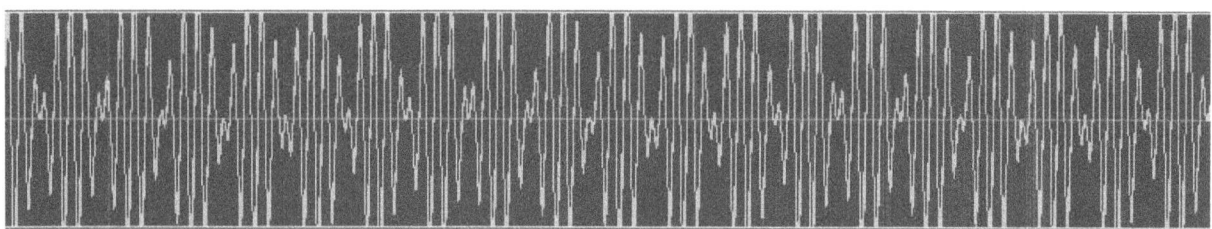

And this chaotic and imperfectly repeating waveform pattern above was created on my Moog synthesizer by combining an equally tempered major 3rd with its tonic.

Mixtures of equal tempered sound waves tend to cancel each other out and require more amplification than do perfectly harmonious sound waves.

"Anyone born after the beginning of the 20th century (in the West) had virtually no awareness of non-equal tempered systems, so they were never in a position to judge what was good and what was bad..." --Duffin 2007

Waveform Illustrations of Various Intervals
Perfectly Harmonious "just" Divisions of an Octave

There are many instances often described with terminology like "music of the spheres" wherein simple mathematical relationships are discovered to underly natural phenomena. Planetary orbits, for example, are not accidentally positioned in their distances from the sun. Mathematicians like Kepler and Einstein have discovered these harmonious relationships. The intervals of Just Intonation produce perfect harmony in music.

> *"Kepler applied his mathematical acumen to the issue of music's ability to represent human emotion; among his conclusions was the proposition that major thirds are inherently masculine and minor thirds feminine. In his view the action of reaching from MI up to FA simulated a male ejaculation. He proclaimed that the minor third is passive; it tends to sink to the ground like a hen preparing to be mounted by a cock." --Isacoff 2001*

> *"We gaze at the cat; gazing back at us we see our mammalian nature long before it was painted over by civilization. ...the pure harmonies of just intonation are like animal guides... When you sing in tune you can go as deeply into existence as you want."*
> *-Mathieu 1997*

> *"Ramos, likely inspired by Arabic texts in his native 15th century Spain, was convinced that certain musical scales had the power to move the bodily humors -- influencing sluggishness, or balancing anger and pride, or moderating sadness and joy. Music works miracles, he asserted, citing the legendary Greek musicians who were able to move wild beasts through the sweetness of their song, to capture the hearts of men, to revive the dead, to bend to mercy the spirits of the underworld, to draw trees from the mountains. For Ramos, the rules defining the relations between musical tones were, in effect, a prescription for soundness of body and mind."*
> *--Isacoff 2001*

Tables available on the internet, such as the "Anatomy of an Octave," show more than 700 Just Notes per octave. Many harmonious intervals could be measured and displayed by waveform as in the following graphics. I will show just a few in the following pages.

Remember that shorter waves create higher pitches.

Interval Wave Patterns
Just 5th

Here is a representation of a wavelength at the frequency of a just 5th above the Tonic. The frequency of the fifth is created by making a wavelength 3/2 as long as that of the tonic. By generating sine waves with a Moog synthesizer I was able to create the picture below.

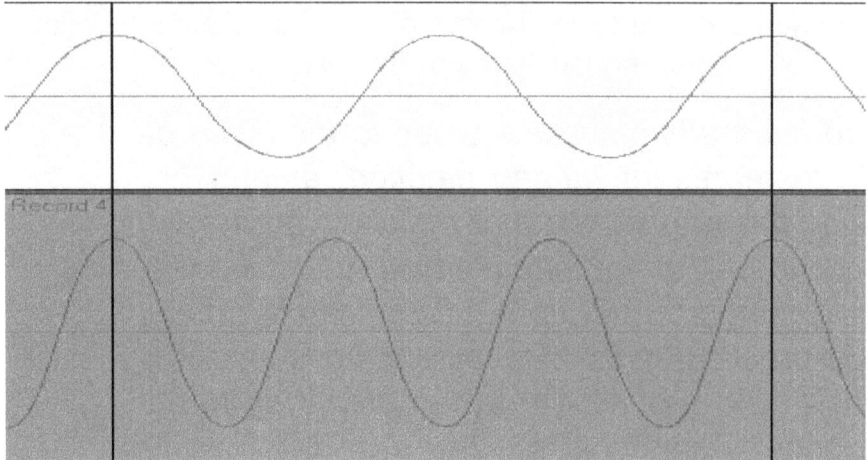

On the top we see the waveform of the tonic and on the bottom we see the waveform of the 5th above the tonic. Three repetitions of the 5th wave and two repetitions of the tonic wave must occur before the peaks of the wave crests line up and exactly coincide again and perfect harmony is created.

So for every 2 oscillations of the tonic pitch we see 3 of the 5th. This relationship can be described by the ratio 3:2.

The tonic note which I used was a D produced at 293.66 Hz (293.66 cycles per second) which is the same D to which equally tempered instruments like pianos are tuned. Since we are arbitrarily defining this D as the tonic we assign 0 cents to its value. The D an octave higher would then be assigned a value of 1200 cents. Of course no matter to what wavelength we assign the definition "tonic", the relationships of all the other notes in the scale associated with this tonic will remain the same. And when we move the *tonic* in just intonation, the values of *all of the other notes in the scale* change along with it.

The just 5th which I used was the A which is found 701.95 cents above the D. This A produces a wavelength of 440.49 Hz.

The following few illustrations of prominant just intervals should make you familiar with the visual forms of these musical realities. Our goal is to refine our abilities to hear pitch and to refine our musicianship. These visual aids are created just to get us started! Remember that equally tempered intervals create wavelengths defined by irrational numbers which never ever create wave peaks which line up with the wave peaks of the tonic. True harmony is therefore not possible in equal temperament. We have reached a very strange place in the evolution of modern Western music which relies so heavily on using these out-of-tune intervals.

Just 4th

Here is a representation of a wavelength at the frequency of a just 4th above the Tonic. The frequency of the fourth is created by making a wavelength 4/3 as long as that of the tonic.

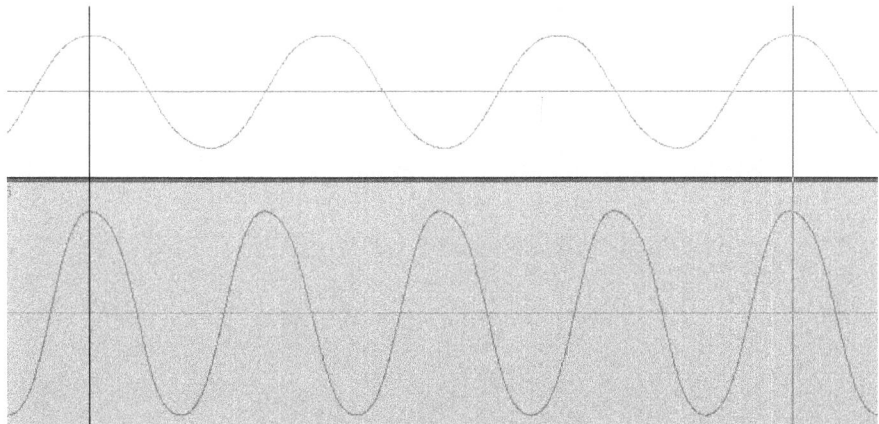

On the top we see the waveform of the tonic and on the bottom we see the waveform of the 4th above the tonic. Four repetiitions of the 4th wave and three repetitions of the tonic wave must occur before the peaks of the wave crests line up and exactly coincide again and perfect harmony is created. This relationship can be described by the ratio 4:3.

The tonic note which I used was the same D produced at 293.66 Hz. The just 4th which I used was the G which is found 498.04 cents above the D. This G produces a wavelength of 391.55 Hz.

Just Major 3rd

Here is a representation of a wavelength at the frequency of a just Major 3rd above the Tonic. The frequency of the Major 3rd is created by making a wavelength 5/4 as long as that of the tonic.

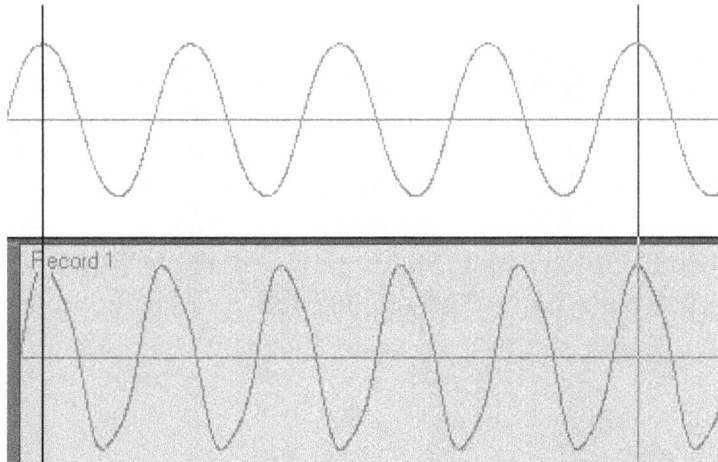

On the top we see the waveform of the tonic and on the bottom we see the waveform of the Major 3rd above the tonic. Five repetiitions of the Major 3rd wave and four repetitions of the tonic wave must occur before the peaks of the wave crests line up and exactly coincide again and perfect harmony is created. This relationship can be described by the ratio 5:4.

The tonic note which I used was the same D produced at 293.66 Hz. The just Major 3rd which I used was the F# which is found 386.31 cents above the D. This F# produces a wavelength of 367.07 Hz.

Just Minor 3rd

Here is a representation of a wavelength at the frequency of a just Minor 3rd above the Tonic. The frequency of the Major 3rd is created by making a wavelength 6/5 as long as that of the tonic.

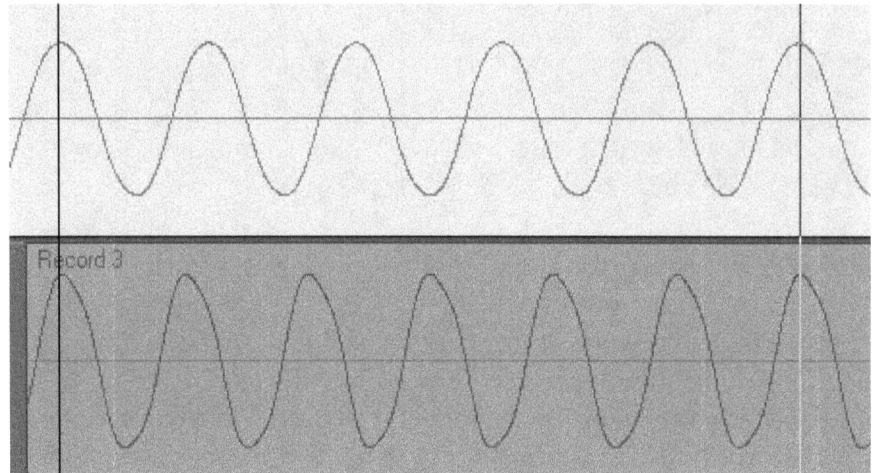

On the top we see the waveform of the tonic and on the bottom we see the waveform of the Minor 3rd above the tonic. Six repetiitions of the Minor 3rd wave and five repetitions of the tonic wave must occur before the peaks of the wave crests line up and exactly coincide again and perfect harmony is created. This relationship can be described by the ratio 6:5.

The tonic note which I used was the same D produced at 293.66 Hz. The just Minor 3rd which I used was the F which is found 315.64 cents above the D. This F produces a wavelength of 352.39 Hz.

Just Major 2nd

Here is a representation of a wavelength at the frequency of a just Major 2nd or "Whole Tone" above the Tonic. The frequency of this Major 2nd is created by making a wavelength 9/8 as long as that of the tonic.

This is not the only pitch which can be called a just "Major 2nd" or "Whole Tone". As you will see from the next few diagrams, there are more than one useable and harmonious Just Major 2nds.

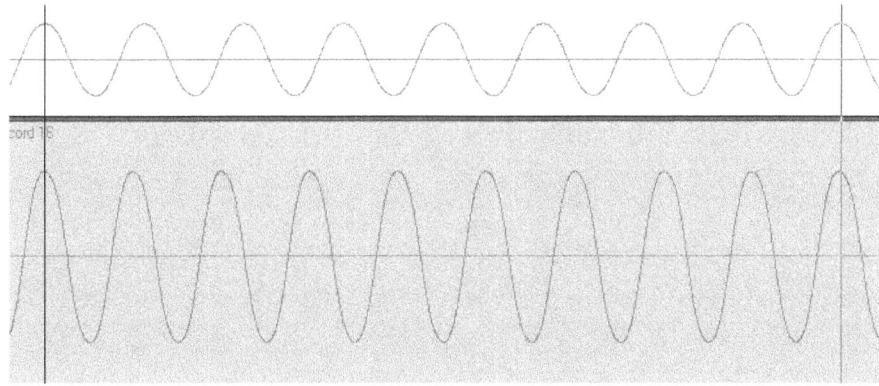

On the top we see the waveform of the tonic and on the bottom we see the waveform of this Major 2nd above the tonic. Nine repetiitions of this Major 2nd wave and eight repetitions of the tonic wave must occur before the peaks of the wave crests line up and exactly coincide again and perfect harmony is created. This relationship can be described by the ratio 9:8.

The tonic note which I used was the same D produced at 293.66 Hz. The Major 2nd which I used was the E which is found 203.91 cents above the D. This E produces a wavelength of 330.37 Hz.

Another Just Major 2nd

Here is a representation of another wavelength which can be called a just "Major 2nd" or "Whole Tone" above the Tonic. The frequency of this Major 2nd is created by making a wavelength 10/9 as long as that of the tonic.

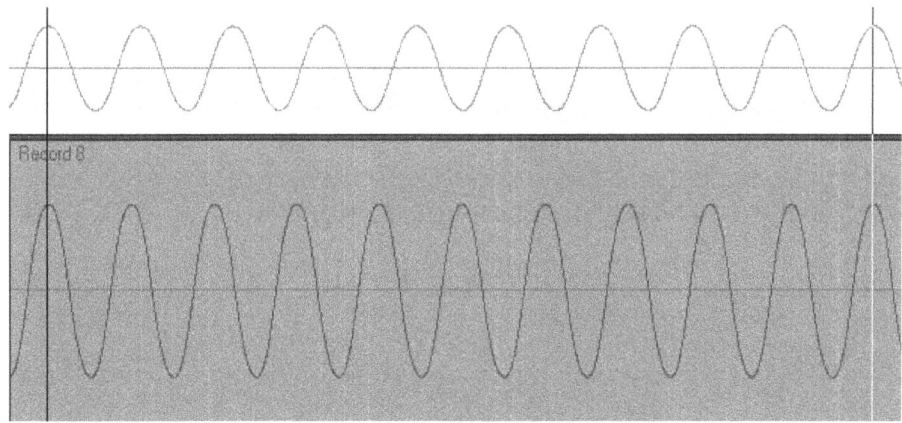

On the top we see the waveform of the tonic and on the bottom we see the waveform of this Major 2nd above the tonic. Ten repetiitions of this Major 2nd wave and nine repetitions of the tonic wave must occur before the peaks of the wave crests line up and exactly coincide again and perfect harmony is created. This relationship can be described by the ratio 10:9.

The tonic note which I used was the same D produced at 293.66 Hz. The Major 2nd which I used for this note is the E which is found 182.40 cents above the D. This E produces a wavelength of 326.29 Hz.

Just Half-flat 2nd

Here is a representation of a wavelength which can be described as a just "Half-flat 2nd" or "Quartertone 2nd" above the Tonic. The frequency of this Half-flat 2nd is created by making a wavelength 11/10 as long as that of the tonic.

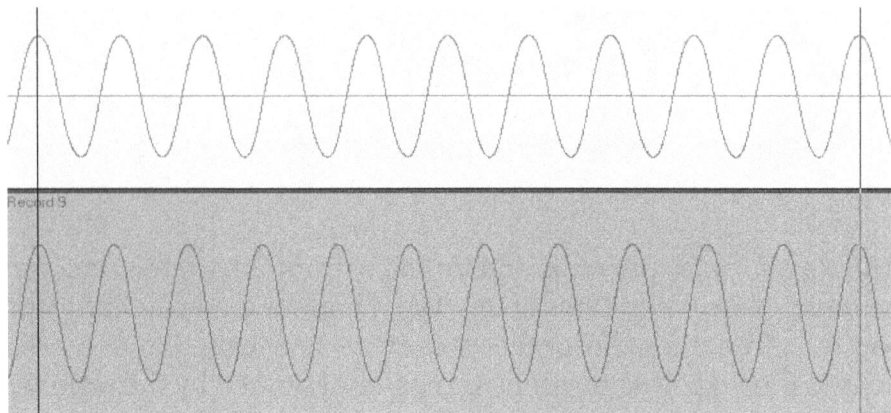

On the top we see the waveform of the tonic and on the bottom we see the waveform of this Half-flat 2nd above the tonic. Eleven repetitions of this Half-flat 2nd wave and ten repetitions of the tonic wave must occur before the peaks of the wave crests line up and exactly coincide again and perfect harmony is created. This relationship can be described by the ratio 11:10.

The tonic note which I used was the same D produced at 293.66 Hz. The Half-flat 2nd which I used for this note is the Half-flat E which is found 165.00 cents above the D. This Half-flat E produces a wavelength of 323.03 Hz.

Another Just Half-flat 2nd

Here is a representation of another wavelength which can also be described as a just "Half-flat 2nd" or "Quartertone 2nd" above the Tonic. The frequency of this Half-flat 2nd is created by making a wavelength 12/11 as long as that of the tonic.

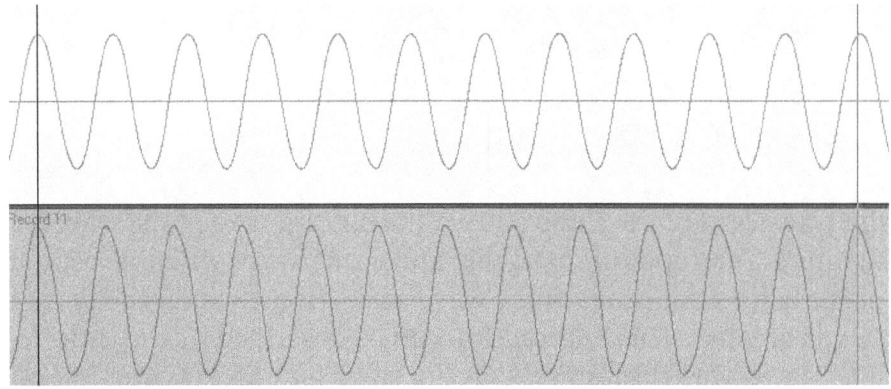

On the top we see the waveform of the tonic and on the bottom we see the waveform of this Half-flat 2nd above the tonic. Twelve repetitions of this Half-flat 2nd wave and eleven repetitions of the tonic wave must occur before the peaks of the wave crests line up and exactly coincide again and perfect harmony is created. This relationship can be described by the ratio 12:11.

The tonic note which I used was the same D produced at 293.66 Hz. The Half-flat 2nd which I used for this note is the Half-flat E which is found 150.64 cents above the D. This Half-flat E produces a wavelength of 320.36 Hz.

Just Major 6th

Here is a representation of an interval further up the scale: a just "Major 6th". The frequency of this Major 6th is created by making a wavelength 5/3 as long as that of the tonic.

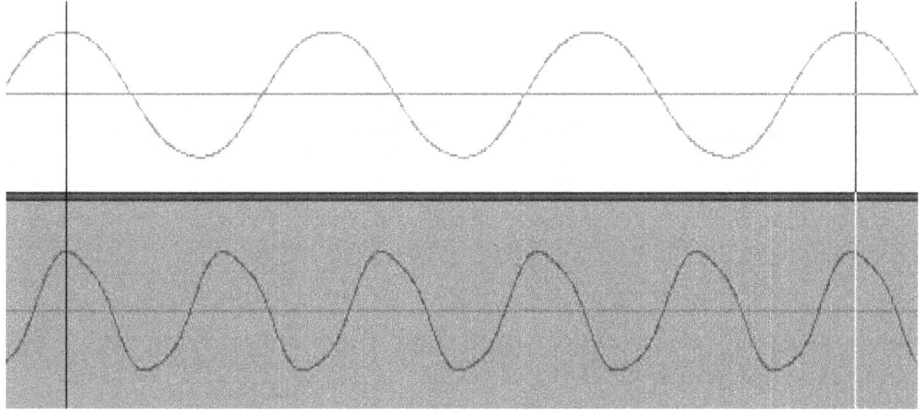

On the top we see the waveform of the tonic and on the bottom we see the waveform of this Major 6th above the tonic. Five repetiitions of this Major 6th wave and three repetitions of the tonic wave must occur before the peaks of the wave crests line up and exactly coincide again and perfect harmony is created. This relationship can be described by the ratio 5:3.

The tonic note which I used was the same D produced at 293.66 Hz. The Major 6th which I used for this note is the B which is found 884.36 cents above the D. This Half-flat B produces a wavelength of 489.43 Hz.

Schematic Waveform Diagrams

The higher note in an interval vibrates more rapidly than the lower note. The simplest interval to understand is the octave. For every one wavelength of the lower note in the interval, the number of wave vibrations in the note one octave higher vibrates two times. This is a ratio of 2:1:

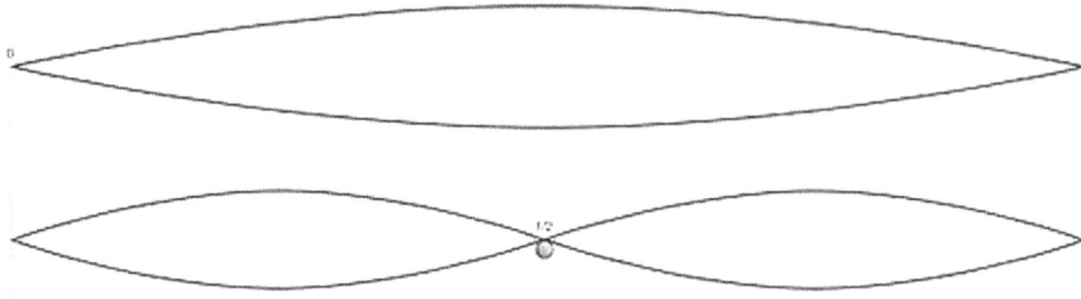

The perfect 5th vibrates exactly 3 times every time the tonic below it from which it is derived vibrates 2 times. This is a ratio of 3:2.

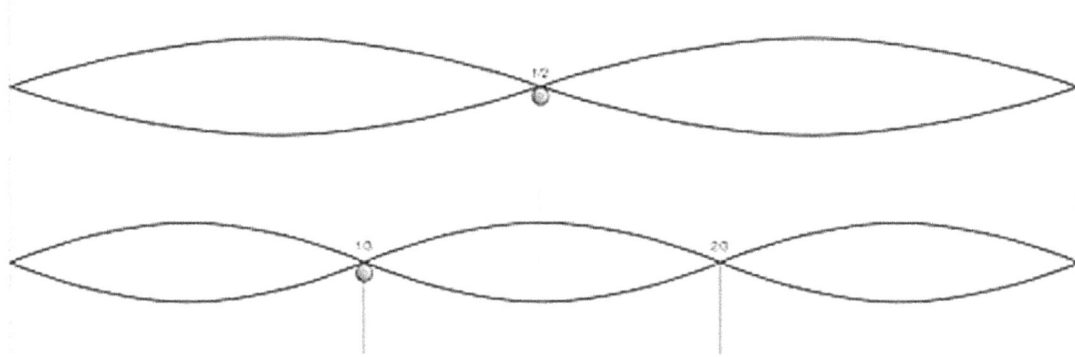

These fractional halves, fourths, fifths, sixths, sevenths, etc, are exact or "just" and the harmonies created when these "justly" intonated wavelengths are played against the droning tonic are in fact perfect! It then only requires that an attentive human ear be listening and this perfection is felt and recognized. This is the physical basis of that magic which we experience at certain profound musical moments.

These most basic justly intonated musical intervals combine and fit together to create perfectly harmonious musical scales.

The fourth, with its ratio of 4:3, plus the fifth, with its ratio of 3:2, added together make an octave. It all works out mathematically: 4/3 x 3/2 = 2/1

The difference between a fourth and a fifth, as an interval, is called a pure whole step, and has a frequency ratio of 9:8. This interval is called a major second.

The frequency ratio 5:4 is called a major third, and 6:5 is a minor third.

A minor sixth, with a ratio of 8:5, together with a major third, make an octave.
A major sixth, with a ratio of 5:3, together with a minor third also make an octave.
A major sixth plus a whole tone is called a major seventh, and has a ratio of 15:8.

The jump or 'difference' between the major third and the fourth is called a half tone or semitone. This is also the 'difference' between the major seventh and the octave.

"Harry Partch loudly disdained what he called the 'harmony armies of mediocrity' growing from equal temperament, and described the piano keyboard as 'twelve black and white bars in front of musical freedom.'" --Isacoff 2001

"During the 17th and 18th centuries, although the concept of equal temperament was known, it was generally not considered musical because it compromised the acoustical purity and beauty of sound. The resulting identical harmonic relationships of each key were considered almost colorless and bland by comparison with the historical just intonation tuning, and other non-equal temperaments such as Mean-Tone and the Werckmeister tunings. However, by the mid-19th century the British piano manufacturer John Broadwood & Sons sent out a manual with all of its pianos worldwide with instructions on how to tune them in equal temperament. The global influence of this piano maker at the height of British imperialism, along with the general trend in Western classical music towards increased harmonic complexity, stretched the limits of tonality to the point where equal temperament became the universally accepted tuning of the Western world. With a new convenient and homogenized system in place it didn't take long before most musicians and institutions forgot almost entirely about everything that came before." --Michael Harrison Website

Frequently Heard Comments

"I have never heard this music before but, now that I have heard it, it feels like the music I have always known!"

"It feels like this is the music which is in my DNA!"

"That's the most beautiful music I have heard in my life!"

Statements like those above are frequently made by Westerners when they are first exposed to Arabic music. What is underlying this magic? Perfect harmony!

"The descriptions of intervals on Attwood's pages include Wolfgang Mozart's handwritten indications of major semitones and minor semitones and it is absolutely clear that the diatonic semitone is large and the chromatic semitone is small...

...Haydn is known to have admired a complicated keyboard. This kind of enthusiasm for an intonation device of such subtle variety - 39 notes to the octave - argues against any inclination toward equal temperament on Hayden's part." --Duffin 2007

"In early 2005 keyboard scholar and performer Bradley Lehman deciphered and published Bach's encoding of the temperament... There is no question that Lehman convincingly solved Bach's puzzle: Bach's temperament is not equal temperament... ...Bach's "Well-Tempered Clavier" ... wasn't even written for equal temperament, but for an irregular temperament that worked in a wide variety of keys. The flavor of the chords was slightly different in each key and the character of each key was thus slightly different." --Duffin 2007

"By the mid 19th century, there were more than 300 piano makers in England alone. In 1868, Paris boasted more than 20,000 piano teachers. Soon, the piano craze spread to other regions of the world -- brought by covered wagons to log cabins of America's western frontier, and by camels to Arabia. As the 20th century began, Americans were buying more than 350,000 pianos a year. And they were all tuned, more or less, in equal temperament." --Isacoff

What Happened to Perfect Harmony in Western Music?

Many people who listen carefully to piano or guitar chords feel frustration and confusion. The system of equal temperment creates music which, no matter in which key you play, is slightly out of tune! The notes actually clash and work to cancel each other out.

> *"For pianos in England, equal temperament did not become a trade usage until 1846. At least eight more years elapsed before equal temperament was generally used for organs, on which its defects are more apparent, although not to such an extent as on the harmonium. In 1851, at the great exhibition, no English organ was tuned in equal temperament, but the only German organ exhibited was so tuned." --Duffin 2007*

It seems that the spread of equal temperament followed the piano and the surge in popularity of personal music-making which followed. Simplifications were welcomed by music teachers who found equal temperament much easier to teach to students who had no desire to master the complexities of multiple tuning systems associated with multiple modes.

With the rise of the popularity of the guitar with its equally-spaced un-moveable frets it became even more attractive for the general public to enter the world of music without having to learn about the fine degrees of tuning which used to be required in earlier times. It is interesting, however, that modern skilled guitar technicians are bending the strings on their instruments and producing perfectly harmonious intervals in this way. They may be entirely unconscious of what they are doing but are drawn to this technique simply because it sounds so good.

Harmony in Arabic Music

It is frequently stated that Arabic music does not utilize harmony since musicians are not always playing more than one note at a time. If this were really true we wouldn't hear the beautiful patterns described in a melody line. Both the listener and the musician are using their listening skills to hold the memories of the sounds of the tonic note at the root of each maqam, or musical scale, in their "mind's ears." Arab musicians also commonly provide on-going decorated musical phrases around and including the tonic so that harmonic intervals continuously are highlighted. So in reality Arabic music is always filled with harmony and the intervals are very precisely generated and very precisely perceived.

> *"Harmony is the way things are together. When a tone is harmonically related to a tonic (whether or not that tonic is sounding in the air), we vibrate sympathetically with that harmony." ---Mathieu 1997 p 115*

> *"In London I listened to the natural intonation of singers who had learned to sing without any instrumental accompaniment at all, and are accustomed to follow their ear alone. This was the Society of Tonic Sol-faists, who are spread in great numbers over the large cities of England. There were 150,000 in 1862. By 1884 it was estimated that this system for teaching had become the most popular system in England and Scotland and had reached some four million students. Their vocal music is not written in ordinary musical notation. When the tonic is changed in modulations, the notation is also changed. The new tonic is now called Do. Since the intervals of the natural scale are transferred to each new tonic as it arises in the course of modulation, all keys are performed without tempering them. Every year the London schools of Sol-faists are accustomed to give a concert of 2 to 3000 children's voices, which, I have been assured by persons who understand music, makes the best impression on the audience by the harmoniousness and exactness of its execution. The Tonic Sol-faists, then, sing by natural, and not by tempered intervals."* --Helmholtz 1885

Careful analysis of Arabic maqamat reveals a system wherein the possibility of performing perfectly in-tune music still exists. It is said that the most pure and deep source for training in maqamat is that of the "readers" (singers) of the Qur'an and that of the muezzin, those who chant the Islamic call to prayer. During the many months of my residences in Egypt, Syria, Jordan, Lebanon, Morocco and Iraq, I have been exposed, at least five times a day, to the varieties of Islamic call to prayer which are broadcast from the minarets of the mosques. I have discovered that these voices are chanting in intervals which are frequently so perfectly in tune that the harmonies which ring through my being seem almost like magic. I now realize that part of the secret of this magic is the natural inclination for singers who are *not* accompanied by equally-tempered instruments to fall into just intonation.

> *"...the Arabian theorist Al-Farabi (d. c. 950) incorporated Ptolemy's hierarchical order of homophonic, symphonic, and emmelic intervals into his own writings, and interpreted the concept of graduated consonance to include 5-limit "major third" and the 5-limit "minor third." Ibn Sina (980-1037) and Safi Al-Din (d. 1294) also classified ratios 5/4 and 6/5 as bona fide consonances. However, European theorists did not begin to accept the former ratio as a consonance until the 15th century, not the latter ratio until the 16th century."* --Forster 2010

Quartertones

When I first began my study of maqamat I found that the Arab musicians who represented the tradition in its more antique forms tended to emphasize that the real intervals within maqamat required a little adjustment from their "quarter-tone" positions when quarter-tones are defined in terms of equal temperament. *Now it seems to me that these adjustments have turned out to be nothing more nor less than positioning of harmonic intervals into justly intonated positions.* Remember that when it comes to just intonation, we are not studying a culturally preferred set of scales: we are entering the magic world of literal physical musical perfection! We are talking about the musical equivalents of the mathematics of the golden ratio and Fibonacci sequences!

> *"Mathieu says that just intonation is like the pure child that lives inside every equal-tempered adult. We are actually built to resonate with the pure musical proportions. Human beings don't have to know about just intonation to understand it, he says. We already ARE it." --Isacoff 2001*

Mikha'il Mishaqa, a self-taught medical doctor from Lebanon who settled in Damascus in 1846, knowledgeable in mathematics, music, politics, literature, and religious studies, has been credited with a description of a theoretical 24-note equal-tempered Arabic scale. But his own experiments, as recounted in his Essay on the Art of Music for the Emir Shihab, revealed that while the Arabs divided the octave into twenty-four equal quartertones in theory, Arabic music did not correspond to a twenty-four equal quartertone scale in practice.

He found that only by sectioning the strings of his tunbur (a fretted long-necked stringed instrument) into sixty-eight notes per octave could he actually perform tunes which satisfied Arab audiences.

At The Congress of Arab Music, held in Cairo in 1932, we see once again that the intervals which sound correct to traditional Arab musicians do not really correspond to the 24-note "quartertone" equally tempered system. Even though European intervals and notation were passionately introduced at this congress as part of a popular movement to "Westernize" oriental music, many musicians at the 1932 congress objected strongly to the new European tuning standards because "the use of instruments with a fixed twelve-semitone scale lacked the appropriate microtonal variation which is unique to the sound of Arabic music." Their use was to be restricted. And two Turkish participants rejected the quartertone system on account of its arbitrary nature and inappropriateness for the accurate measurement of Near Eastern pitch.

The written records from this meeting are filled with comparisons which purport to hold up "new standards of European excellence" and impose these on the music of the indigenous Middle East. Even his Majesty King Fu'ad I, patron of the 1932 conference, expressed his wish that, "Arab music will reach the degree of refinement and perfection that Western music has reached."

What seems to appear in retrospect is that musicians' ear training in the Arab world reflected an ability to discern the fine increments of pitch which we now call "just intonation" and which, as we have seen, are not matched by the intervals in equal temperament.

And Turkish musical theorists have not been satisfied with the 24 note per octave theory and have created a system wherein diatonic whole tones are divided into 9 "komas," an ancient Greek musical term. This yields a fine enough sequence of intervals, with 53 notes per octave, to effectively give theoretical support for the intervals of just intonation. But neither Turkish nor Arab musical theorists, to my knowledge, have formally recognized the potential for interpreting their intervals as "just intervals."

Since it is very difficult to perform music up to speed while mentally and physically tracking such fine intervals as 53 notes per octave, it is reasonable to conclude that Middle-Eastern musicians are actually relying on their natural perception of the beauty of intervals of justly intonated scales.

Early Arabic Music History

Under the Umayyad Caliphate of Damascus (661-750), the Abbasid Caliphate of Baghdad (750-909) and the cities of Andalusian Spain (713-1492), the historical record preserves the names of such revered Arab musicians as Ziryab (died 857 CE), Ibrahim al-Mawsili (died 804 CE), Ishaq al-Mawsili (died 850 CE), and Zalzal (died 791 CE). These musicians and many others formed the foundations of what is now known as The Great Arab Music Tradition. Musical historians such as Al-Farabi (died 950 CE) have preserved detailed musical information from this period now more than one thousand years past. These details include descriptions of 22-note per octave lute frettings as well as alternative fretting systems based on Pythagorean intervals, with 40 notes per octave, which correspond more closely to "just intervals."

The roots of Arabic music from pre-Islamic times are found in Egyptian, Bedouin, Persian and Greek musical traditions, to name a few. And there is a good deal of information available especially concerning Greek musical legacies all the way back to the times of Pythagoras (died 495 BC). Arabic vocabulary came to include large infusions of translated Greek philosophy and science during the 8th through 14th centuries CE when teams of highly educated translators were employed by the ruling Arab families.

The musical system which survives today from these traditions involves knowledge of modes called "maqamat." This music spread extensively throughout the East and has been known in Arab countries as "maqam," in Azerbaijan as "mugam," in Turkey as "makam," in Persia as "dastgah," in India as "paga," in Uzbekistan and Tadjikistan as "makom," or "shashmaqom," in Turkmenistan and Sinkiang province of China (where the Turkish Uygur culture is prominent) as "mukam," in Japan as "gaganu," in Indonesia as "patet," in Kazakhstan as "kuy," in Khirgizistan as "ky," and in Pakistan as "kayyal."

Value of Indigenous Musical Traditions

Any refined and elaborate indigenous musical system from antiquity is likely to be a pathway into just intonation and a kind of harmonic perfection not available in Western music today.

It is so often the case that modern mass-production technologies bring certain advantages but that they also can turn out to have unfortunate side-effects which result in the loss of valuable and natural substance. Modern agriculture has brought us big red unbruisable but obviously out-of-tune tomatoes with no flavor and no nutritional value! And modern medicine has brought us many powerful drugs which can target certain maladies but simultaneously de-tune our holistic well-being!

I am excited to try and explain this musical pathway back into a realm wherein music can regain all of its inherent magic.

> *"It is astounding how thoroughly the resonances of just intonation have been submerged. Entire African villages sing nightlong rituals beautifully in tune, but Americans cannot sing "Happy Birthday" in tune in a restaurant."* -Mathieu 1997

Musicians who delve into Arabic, Chinese, Indian, Greek, Turkish, Byzantine, Javanese, Balinese, Bulgarian, Japanese, Malay, Berber, Mongolian music styles will find that just intervals provide the basic building blocks. Sometimes they appear in pentatonic scales and sometimes in scales built of major thirds. Even when musicians attempt to create equally-tempered scales of say 12 or 9 or 7 notes the harmonic undercurrents of just intervals are likely to appear.

For a few examples from Chinese, Indian, Greek, Turkish and Byzantine traditions see the appendix.

Overtone Analysis and Just Intonation

In the study of music and harmony it has been understood since the time of Pythagoras that the notes used in a common musical scale can be generated in perfectly harmonious "just" form by creating multiples of the interval called a 5th. More recent theoreticians have added the intervals created by stacking multiples of major 3rds, equivalent to dividing an octave into three equal parts. It is very common to see charts like the two below which lay out sequences of 5ths on the mildly sloping lines and sequences of major 3rds on the more steeply sloping lines. We could also be using this method for describing just intervals and their pitches.

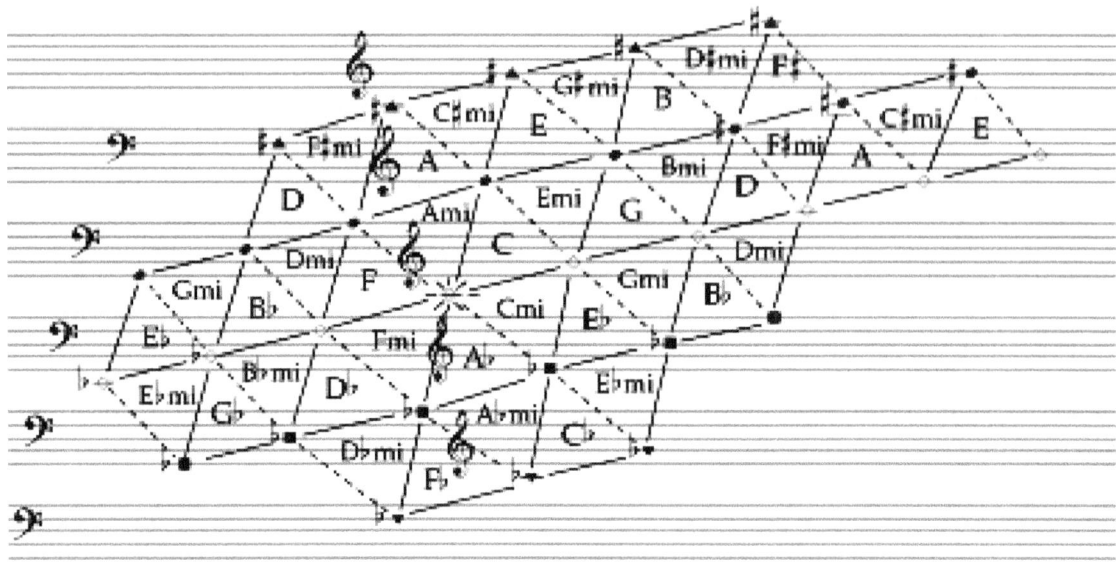

Diagram from Matheiu 1997

Daniélou's Harmonic Division in 5-limit, symmetrized

Diagram from Chris Mohr Notes

This is a marvelous way to understand the series of overtone harmonics generated by a vibrating string, human voice, air column or drum head.

Many stringed instrument tuning traditions incorporate the use of these intervals for tuning. Mandolin and violin tunings can be precisely accomplished by carefully listening to the harmony of plucked adjacent strings which are tuned a 5th apart.

However, since the generated notes represented in the charts on the previous page appear in remotely high or low pitches many octaves away from each other this tuning system can be impractical. This system does not lead to the immediate creation of the just notes as they appear next to each other inside a single octave. For anyone who plays an instrument capable of generating two or more notes at once, understanding harmony in terms of just ratios (or fractions) seems to me to be a more useful approach.

Instruments which do not have bowed strings are less likely to invite overtone analysis and more likely to invite just interval analysis. The oud, for example, with its large resonant body, holds the echos of a plucked note with considerable sustain. This invites the ear to become fascinated with intervals which become easily audible.

> *"Claiming that our ears would get used to altered musical proportions (in equal temperament) was the equivalent of saying that tasteless food will seem savory if it is eaten often enough."*
> *--Isacoff 2001*

> *"The universal adoption of ET in the early 20th century contributed to the widening use of vibrato, as performers sensed that it masked some of the unpleasantness of the thirds."*
> *--Duffin 2007*

> *"I am of the opinion that 24-tone equal temperament constitutes little more than a formulaic imposition to inappropriately simplify the profound complexities of Arabian music."*
> *--Forster 2010*

Arabic Maqamat and Just Intonation

Students of Arabic music hear repeated comments from their teachers which imply that "quartertones" are not really definable as half-steps of ET half-steps. It is commonly taught, for example, that the E half-flat which is the 3rd note of maqam Rast is not the same pitch as the E half-flat which is the 2nd note of maqam Bayati. Arab violinist Sami Shumays says that he can find eleven different E half-flats embedded in various maqamat.

It is also commonly taught that the so-called 1 1/2 step interval in maqam hijaz needs to be narrowed: the 2nd needs to be sharpened and the 3rd needs to be flattened. The resulting interval does not match the ET interval.

What eventually has become clear is that these traditionally taught "fine points" regarding correct intonation in Arabic music generally align with the truly harmonious intervals of just intonation.

> *"Indeed, nothing can exceed the musical effect of well-harmonized part music perfectly executed in just intonation by practiced voices. For the complete harmoniousness of such music it is indispensable and necessary that the several musical intervals should be justly intoned, and our present singers unfortunately seldom learn to take just intervals, because they are accustomed from the first to sing to the accompaniment of instruments which are tuned in equal temperament, and hence with imperfect consonances. It is only such singers as have a delicate musical feeling of their own who find out the correct result, which is no longer taught them... ...After singing some pieces without accompaniment and hence in the just intonation to which the singers had been trained, and with the most delightful effect of harmony, they sang a piece with the piano accompaniment. Of course the piano itself was inaudible among the mass of sound produced by 60 voices. But it had the effect of perverting their intonation, and the whole charm of the singing was at once destroyed."*
> *--Helmholtz 1885*

What are included in this book are tables which actually show the just intervals available for musicians to play and how they seem to fit perfectly into the tradition of maqamat when these "fine points" are taken into account. Once this is understood, everything suddenly becomes simple and makes sense. Musicians playing instruments which are not locked into ET intervals have a wonderful range of truly harmonious intervals which will please almost every Arab ear and bring a welcome relief to discerning Western audiences whose ears are being treated perhaps for the first time to perfect harmony!

The tables in this book which show justly intonated options for musicians playing Arabic maqam music are not to be thought of as necessary for the advanced player. They are simply illustrations of the multitude possibilities available to a musician or singer who has honed his or her listening and playing pitch sensitivites to a finer degree. Once we get the point illustrated by the tables we can forget them again and trust our ears and make music!

> *"Finally, the traditional intonational practice is eloquently exhibited in the vocal performance. Through its exceptionally pliable nature the voice is capable of producing the finer 'urab that evoke ecstasy. Rendered most effectively by the trained vocalist, such microtonally inflections are particularly observable within the purely vocal genres, for instance Sufi hymns that are performed without any instruments. Embracing a similar level of intonational finesse is the unaccompanied vocal solo, the supreme example of which is Qur'anic chanting, particularly the more elaborate mujawwad style as rendered by the masterful reciters." --Racy 2003*

Tawfiq al-Sabbagh, musician from Syria, wrote a book in 1950 about the necessity of performing Arabic music in exactly the right pitches if one hopes to create deeply ecstatic states. (Translatiions are found in AJ Racy's "Making Music in the Arab World: The Culture and Artistry of Tarab"). As you will see as you progress through the study of the primary maqamat, al-Sabbagh's comments about which notes to flatten or sharpen from their 24-tone ET positions make perfect sense in terms of just intonation.

> *"The musical context has enormous significance concerning our perception of intervals. How long the interval is sustained and how it has been approached in the two voices are two obvious determinants. Michael Harrison and Mathieu would contend that what makes just intonation powerful is the fact that we are somehow hard-wired for these musical ratios -- that they resonate with our very nature." --Isacoff 2001*

Note Naming Traditions

Here is a brief summary of varying terminology used to describe notes and intervals (summarized from Mathieu p 100):

1) Letter names and Solfege names: A, B, C, D, E, F, G, and Do, Re, Mi, Fa, Sol, La, Si. Only seven of these letters or syllables are commonly used (even in the Sargam system from India) so they are not sufficient for describing the vast numbers of just notes in an octave.

2) Degree names: tonic, dominant, etc. There is a lot of inconsistency in the use of these labels and again, there are too few to use in descriptions of just intervals.

3) Intervalic names and their modifiers: major second, minor second, major, augmented, diminished... Again, there are not enough of these labels and although they can serve to describe the 12 ET notes in an octave, they can't begin to cover just intonation.

4) Ratios (Fractions): This is the only way to precisely describe the interval between two notes. It becomes necessary to prefer ratios with lower denominators as more likely to be the most clearly harmonious and the most commonly used in indigenous music, but that is a relative, not an absolute, statement.

"People who read music, especially keyboard players, are conditioned to suppose that music consists of a series of points in space, and that to make a melody we proceed from point to point. In the sounds produced by keyboards, keyed woodwinds, fretboards and valved brass, the fixed-pitch model engendered by our notation is carried forward into a culture of Connect-the-Dots music.... Most of the rest of the world's music neither proceeds from nor is communicated by notation... it passes aurally from musician to musician, parent to child, mouth to mouth, heart to heart. The tones of such music are not so much dots as they are shapes in and of themselves, impatiently alive and wiggling."
-Mathieu 1997

For a list of Arabic music note names see Tables A and B. Several of these basic note names, like Iraq, Sikah and Awj, refer to "quartertone" notes which are not found in equal temperament.

Present day Arab musicians also use Do Re Mi Fa Sol La Si, which are note labels which come from European "Solfege." The term, again borrowed from Europe, for "flat" is "bemol." The term for "sharp" is "diese," pronounced and herein spelled "diaz." "Nuss diaz" means "half-sharp." And the term for "half-flat" is "nuss bemol" or "reboton."

Frequently hybrid terms like "Si Sikah," meaning "B half-flat" are employed to designate specifically "quartertone" notes, but this use may be confusing since "sikah" is a specific Arab note name which refers to "E half-flat."

Arab musicians may also know the Western note names C D E F G A B but they are more familiar with the solfege labels.

Some historians actually ascribe the root of Solfege to Arab tradition: It has been argued that the solfège syllables (do, re, mi, fa, sol, la, ti) may have been derived from the syllables of the Arabic solmization system درر مفصّلات Durar Mufaṣṣalāt ("Separated Pearls") (dāl, rā', mīm, fā', ṣād, lām, tā') during the Islamic contributions to Medieval Europe.

Table showing similarity between musical notes and the Arabic alphabet.

Arabic letters	م mīm	ف fā'	ص ṣād	ل lām	س sīn	د dāl	ر rā'
Musical Notes	mi	fa	sol	la	si	do	re

Since the advent of the 20th century, Western musicians from Europe and America have come to exclusively use equal temperament. They are usually not even aware that even into the times of great European classical composers such as Mozart, Bach and Chopin, the distinctions between "major and minor semitones" (4-koma vs 5-koma half-steps) were still employed and keyboards were frequently in "mean tunings" rather than equal temperament. So it was most natural for these Western musicians (and the Arab musicians who undertook to teach Arabic music to Westerners) to divide ET half-steps in half and create ET "quarter-tones." At first glance it seemed as if these intervals provided greater resolution and could adequately describe the intervals found in Arabic music.

So in the world of maqams it has become common for certain notes to be called "quartertones." They have degrees of flatness or sharpness which are halfway between the equal-tempered notes.

Middle Easterners who've grown up with maqam-based music don't really need to think of particular notes as being "half-flat" or "half-sharp." That's an invention for those of us who are anchored in equal-tempered systems.

The names of the basic notes in Arabic (see Table A) make it clear that for them the E half-flat and B half-flat are more fundamental than the nearby equal-tempered notes Eb, E, Bb and B which sound so familiar to Westerners.

Sometimes in the teachings of maqams, "ascending scales" are shown with sharper pitches than "descending scales." There are no hard and fast rules around this, although for a musician playing only in his home town of Aleppo or Damascus or Baghdad some very precise maqam definitions do survive. The point is that, in composition or in improvisation, we are free to sharpen or flatten notes in maqams in an ornamental or decorative sense and that is done all the time.

Of course these maqams are most easily played on fretless instruments like the oud, or on a violin or a cello... or on open-holed flutes such as they have in the Middle East (the nay or kawal). If you're working on a keyboard you will have to program pitch adjustments. And if you're working on keyed wind instruments like clarinet, for example, the bending of the notes can be accomplished by using different key arrangements and by using the strength of the embouchure on the reed. Of course, the human voice is an ultimately flexible instrument. However, if you've grown up in the West, then your natural tendency will be to land on the equal-tempered notes and you'll find that it's difficult and that it takes some training to learn to sing notes which fall "in between" equal-tempered notes.

The most commonly used quartertone notes are the E half-flat and the B half-flat... and sometimes the A half-flat and the F half-sharp.

> *"The composer Lou Harrison refers to the equal tempered intervals as 'fake' and worse."* --Isacoff 2001

Like anywhere else in the world, simpler folk tunes which come from village regions are usually done in one maqam with few changes in the structure of the scales, but the more complex compositions from the larger cities (Like Cairo and Istanbul) and from traditional musical hot-spots (like Aleppo, Syria) include varieties of complex maneuvers from one maqam to another. And it's the job of a Middle Eastern musician, when it's his turn to do an improvisation, or "taqasim," to see if he can artfully show the transitions from one maqam to another and then modulate back to the original maqam. Taqasims usually open with certain trademark decorations (shakhsiyyah) which serve to identify the home-base maqam. Traditional hallmark melodies (dulabs) can also serve this pupose of identifying a maqam at the beginning of a song. From there the musician works (al amal) the transitions and modulations in ways that reflect both a knowledge of tradition and personal innovation until the taqasim is brought to a close back in the home-base maqam with traditional ending phrases (qaflat). The Arab or Turkish audience oohs and aahs at appropriate moments when the traditional and the individual qualities are intermixed.

> *"Just intervals are really natural for uncorrupted ears; the deviations of tempered intonation are really perceptible and unpleasant to uncorrupted ears; and correct singing by natural intervals is much easier than singing in tempered intonation... ...I think that many of our best musical performances owe their beauty to an unconscious introduction of the natural system, and that we should oftener enjoy their charms if that system were taught pedagogically, and made the foundation of all instruction in music, in place of the tempered intonation which endeavors to prevent the human voice and bowed instruments from developing their full harmoniousness, for the sake of not interfering with the convenience of performers on the piano and the organ."*
> --Helmholtz 1885

Classification of Maqamat

There are 7 basic groups of maqams. One group is taught with D, or Re, as a tonic, or base beginning note, and another group is taught with C, or Do, as the tonic. There are also groups of maqams based on Bb, E half-flat and on F.

Each maqam in this book is described by naming the notes with traditional Western names (A through G) and Solfege names (Do through Si). The step intervals between these named notes are also indicated by fractions such as 1/4, 1/2, 3/4, 1, 1 1/4, and 1 1/2. These are based on the 24-Equal-Tempered Steps per Octave system commonly used as a starting point.

The most basic maqams are also described with their most common justly intonated notes highlighted in Tables. This information is provided so that musicians can gain an intellectual understanding of perfect harmony. Once understood, it becomes easier to sharpen listening and performance skills to bring this knowledge to life and refine it until it becomes natural and intuitive.

Transposing maqams to different keys yields additional groups of scales based on other tonics and is commonly done to help enable both traditional and artful modulations from one maqam to another. These transpositions frequently involve moving the tonic of one of the 4 basic groups up or down a fourth or a fifth, which is an interval of 4 or 5 notes.

Of course transpositions are also commonly made to match the range of a particular singer's voice. The entire system of maqamat can be moved to any pitch by skilled musicians.

There are maqamat which begin on a D and move up through the next octave and a half without ever including a higher D. This is rare but it does happen and this illustrates the complexity of the tradition. Where maqams go when they get up into higher octaves is sometimes defined but there is enough variety from one teaching to another to make that subject controversial. Some of the books listed in the bibliography go into greater detail on this subject.

Similarly, where maqams go below their tonics, especially the leading tones immediately below the tonic can depend on a variety of structures in an individual song. It is not uncommon for a repetitive bass sequence involving G, A, B half-flat, C, D to underly D-based maqamat which don't even include a B half-flat or other quartertones.

Arabic music is highly decorated with little musical comments and frills, some designed to be obvious while others are played almost subliminally, like "the wink of an eye" (ghammaz). Ghammaz is the term used to define the second most important note in a maqam. These decorations, combined with the capacity of an Arab singer to sing complex long phrases without ever needing to take a breath, lead into a dazzling array of emotional territories. Many of these emotions are not easily found in Western musical traditions. By listening and living in Arab-speaking countries, these emotional worlds can be brought to life. And whichever musical instrument you play, an endless series of delightful discoveries awaits those who enter the world of Arab maqam music.

Arabic notes begin on G. When it comes to tuning an instrument for Arabic music it helps to tune just intervals with G as the tonic. See Table C on page 149 for the Most Useful Fifty-Eight Just Notes in One Octave --Tonic on G

If we move to other tonics in Arabic music, usually we move to other related tonics which are positioned either one or two 5ths above or below the G.
From G: up by 5ths we find: D, A, E
From G: down by 5ths we find: C, F, Bb
The just notes in the scales of these tonics will be similar in pitch to the just notes tuned to the G tonic because of this close relationship.

Remember: the simpler the ratio of an interval, the more "in tune" it will sound. The repeating troughs and crests of the two wave-lengths in the interval will line up more often and not cancel each other out.
They will reinforce each other and the sound will sustain. This is the basis for true harmony or "just intonation."

> *" ...each maqam is part of a fabric that includes all the maqamat (or at least a large number of neighboring maqamat). To know any one maqam fully, a student must know all the places to which one can modulate. This stands in marked contrast to Indian music, where the ragas are understood to exist independently."*
> *--Marcus quoted by Forster 2010*

> *Ibn Sina (980-1037) says:*
> *"It behooves that the musician should tune the time of the false dawn with Rahawi, the true dawn with Husain, sunrise with Rast, forenoon with Busalik, midday with Zankula, noon with Ushshaq, between prayers with Hijaz, afternoon with Iraq, sunset with Isfahan, nightfall with Nawa, evening prayer with Buzurq, and time of sleep with Mukhalif."*
> *--Ibn Sina quoted by Farmer quoted by Forster 2010*

Practical Tools

How can we tell if we are generating the musical pitches we are aiming for, both with our voices and with our instruments? Since we are working with fine tuning it is not so easy, especially in the beginning. We have to take into consideration that Westerners come from a musical culture which no longer requires musicians to be able to discern micro-tonal intervals. Westerners rely on their keyboards and their frets to define "in-tune-ness" for them and generally don't need to listen really carefully.

But here is a device which you probably already have if you are a string player: An electronic tuner.

Whoever designed this inexpensive little model was already aware that equal-tempered intervals may not satisfy everyone and put two little triangles to the right and left of the center zero point which marks ET in-tune-ness.

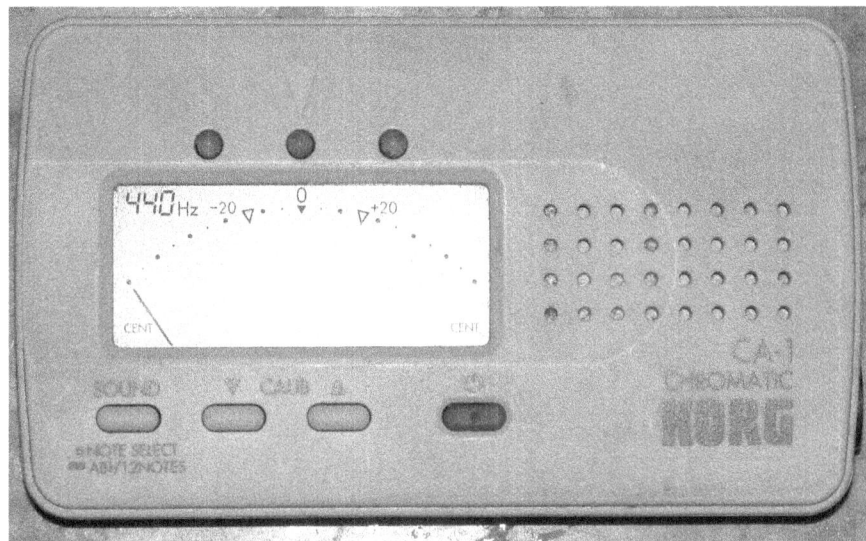

The little triangle to the left of the center defines a correct justly intonated major 3rd.
The little triangle to the right of the center defines a correct justly intonated minor 3rd.

You can learn to sing finely tuned intervals with this device: just sing away and watch the needle.

Of course you can do the same with any instrument. Oh what the ancient musicians might have given to have had one of these!

Pretty soon you will find yourself easily hearing and creating pitch changes of 10 cents or less. Five cent changes are fairly easy to hear but controlling your voice or fingered intonations on an oud or nay or violin get rather difficult. But practice makes perfect and pretty soon a real enjoyment comes as you start to perceive notes which actually sound exactly right. The downside is that you will begin to notice all the slight imperfections which you make and will have to deal with the fact that you have now set a much higher standard for your musicianship.

If you are playing a tuneable stringed instrument like oud or violin you will have additional choices to make. Since your tunings involve 4ths and 5ths you will be able to still use the ET versions of open-string notes like A, D, G and C without being more than about 2 cents away from perfect just intonation in certain keys. I suggest beginning with the just intervals in the key of G. Then you will find that Arabic music is easy to play in perfect tune in C and D because these tonics are defined as either 4ths or 5ths of the G tonic. And using tonics which are 4ths or 5ths of C and D, like F and A make it easy to stay in tune in those keys too. I find that when I have open B or E strings they sound great in most of these related keys if tuned about 15 cents flat. After all, the B is the major 3rd of G and the E is the major 3rd of C.

The Essential Building Blocks of Maqamat: Ajnas

Although there are dozens and dozens of maqamat, they are composed of a much smaller number of building blocks. These building blocks are 3 or 4 or 5 note sequences called "ajnas."

Studying Arabic music has a very satisfying progression. At first it seems complicated to have so many scales to learn and then choose from. However, once you have learned the most common ones and looked at the ajnas from which they are composed you will suddenly see a much simpler picture. When you become aware of these building blocks you suddenly find that your musical improvisations are quite easy to compose. If you create a taqasim (improvisation) jins by jins you will find this not only very easy, but by learning how to substitute one jins for another within the structures of certain maqamat you will find a vast world of musical eloquence suddenly opening wide.

So I am going to present these 15 building blocks right at the beginning.

Presented on D Tonic:
  Jins Hijaz
  Jins Kurd
  Jins Bayat
  Jins Saba
  Jins Saba Zamazama

Presented on C Tonic:
  Jins Rast
  Jins Nahawand
  Jins Nawa Athar
  Jins Athar Kurd
  Jins Sazkar
  Jins Zawil -- Rare

Presented on Bb Tonic:
  Jins Ajem

Presented on E half-flat Tonic:
  Jins Sikah
  Jins Mustaar -- Rare except in Iraq

Presented on B half-flat Tonic:
   Awj Ara -- Rare

As we then go through the maqamat I will present the ajnas which form the building blocks by using brackets and descriptions.

Each jins inside a maqam creates a potential "subdominant" note which can become starting and ending points for a musician who is showing and elaborating a maqam during an improvisation. The most important subdominant note inside a maqam is called the "ghammaz."

Notes on Terminology & Abbreviations Used in the following Tables

The Arabic plural of the word "maqam" is "maqamat." By adopting the word into the English language we create the plural word "maqams." Both plural forms are used interchangeably in this book.

The Arabic plural of the word "jins" is "ajnas." These are the three, four or five-note sequences called "tetrachords" which form the building blocks of the maqamat.

Spelling in English, using the Roman alphabet, is only a rough approximation of actual Arabic spelling. You will find names of maqamat and other Arabic musical terms spelled in varieties of ways. There is no "correct" way to spell Arabic terms in English.

Approximate Interval: Closest Western music named interval. This is not really necessary but these labels can be used to help us understand which intervals are being considered or defined.

Sm: Small

Lg: Large

Approximate Note Names: Quartertone note names are not really very precise.

hf : half-flat (this term is often loosely used to refer to any pitch which is not ET even if the pitch is quite close to the 12-note ET note which may actually place it a long way from being truly half-flat)

hs: half-sharp (this term is often loosely used to refer to any pitch which is not ET even if the pitch is quite close to the 12-note ET note which may actually place it a long way from being truly half-sharp)

Ratio of Interval: This is exact. The smaller the second number in the ratio, the more often the wavelengths of the two notes will coincide and re-inforce the harmony. Unlike ET intervals, which are all expressed as powers of the square root of 2, these Just intervals sound wonderful.

Just Cents: There are 100 cents in every ET half-step. As you can see, the number of cents in just intervals is precisely determined by the ratios. They are exact and will yield true harmony.

ET: Equal Tempered

12-note ET Scale: You can see how clumsy this system is for performing truly in-tune music. You can see how out-of-tune many of these intervals are compared to the truly harmonic just intervals.

24-note ET Scale: Quartertones divide the half-steps into quarter-steps and achieve a greater degree of refinement regarding possible pitch productions. But these intervals don't give us true harmony either.

Just Hz: These are the exact frequencies of the sequence of notes described by the Ratios of the Intervals.

24-note ET Hz: These are the exact frequencies produced by an ET quartertone system. Since musical instruments are commonly tuned in such a way that some of their basic notes correspond to these frequencies, as a matter of practicality we need to see how far away the Just Hz pitches are from the ET pitches. These frequencies reflect standard half-step pitches built from standard ET Tonics used in ET tunings where A = 440

Tonic: Beginning note of scale.

Just Hz of Tonic: The pitch of the standard ET note is generally used to provide a starting point.

Grey Rows: Intervals selected for a particular maqam

Just Intonation on Various Tonics: Some readily available harmonious intervals for the musician to choose from. These are just some of the harmonious options available, not a complete list.

> *"Over the centuries the purity of these natural musical proportions was gradually compromised to facilitate chord changes and modulation between various key relationships. This culminated in a tuning, called equal temperament, that has been the standard for the modern piano for over a hundred years. This contemporary tuning divides the octave into 12 equal half steps, like dividing the face of a clock into twelve hours. The result is a musical democracy in which all tones are created equal, in place of the natural hierarchy based on the fundamental principles of harmony. However, the downside of this compromised system is that now every interval except the octave is slightly out of tune with its pure state of resonance." --Michael Harrison Website*

Jins Hijaz on D

Approximate Interval	Approx. Note Names	Ratio of Interval	Exact Just Cents	Exact Just Hz	Nearest 12-note ET Cents	Nearest 24-note ET Cents	Nearest 24-note ET Hz
ET Tonic on D	D - D	1:1	0.00	293.66	0	0	293.66
	D - D hs	25:24	70.67	305.90	100	50	302.26
	D - D#	19/18	93.60	309.97	100	100	311.13
ET Minor 2nd	D - D# or Eb	2 to the 1/12th			100		311.13
Just Minor 2nd	D - Eb	16:15	111.73	313.24	100	100	311.13
	D - E hf	13:12	138.57	318.13	100	150	320.24
	D - E hf	12:11	150.64	320.36	200	150	320.24
	D - E hf	11:10	165.00	323.03	200	150	320.24
Just Major 2nd Sm	D - E	10:9	182.40	326.29	200	200	329.63
ET Major 2nd	D - E	2 to the 1/6th			200		329.63
Just Major 2nd Lg	D - E	9:8	203.91	330.37	200	200	329.63
	D - E hs	8:7	231.17	335.61	200	250	339.28
	D - E hs	7:6	266.87	342.60	200	250	339.28
ET Minor 3rd	D - F	2 to the 1/4th			300		349.23
Just Minor 3rd	D - F	6:5	315.64	352.39	300	300	349.23
Just Major 3rd	D - F#	5:4	386.31	367.07	400	350	359.45
ET Major 3rd	D - F#	2 to the 1/3rd			400		369.99
	D - Gb	9:7	435.08	377.56	400	450	380.83
Just 4th	D - G	4:3	498.04	391.55	500	500	392.00

Jins Kurd on D

Approximate Interval	Approx Note Names	Ratio of Interval	Exact Just Cents	Exact Just Hz	Nearest 12-note ET Cents	Nearest 24-note ET Cents	Nearest 24-note ET Hz
ET Tonic on D	D - D	1:1	0.00	293.66	0	0	293.66
	D - D hs	25:24	70.67	305.90	100	50	302.26
	D - D#	19:18	93.60	309.97	100	100	311.13
ET Minor 2nd	D - D# or Eb	2 to the 1/12th			100		311.13
Just Minor 2nd	D - Eb	16:15	111.73	313.24	100	100	311.13
	D - E hf	13:12	138.57	318.13	100	150	320.24
	D - E hf	12:11	150.64	320.36	200	150	320.24
	D - E hf	11:10	165.00	323.03	200	150	320.24
Just Major 2nd Sm	D - E	10:9	182.40	326.29	200	200	329.63
ET Major 2nd	D - E	2 to the 1/6th			200		329.63
Just Major 2nd Lg	D - E	9:8	203.91	330.37	200	200	329.63
	D - E hs	8:7	231.17	335.61	200	250	339.28
	D - E hs	7:6	266.87	342.60	200	250	339.28
ET Minor 3rd	D - F	2 to the 1/4th			300		349.23
Just Minor 3rd	D - F	6:5	315.64	352.39	300	300	349.23
Just Major 3rd	D - F#	5:4	386.31	367.07	400	350	359.45
ET Major 3rd	D - F#	2 to the 1/3rd			400		369.99
	D - Gb	9:7	435.08	377.56	400	450	380.83
Just 4th	D - G	4:3	498.04	391.55	500	500	392.00

Jins Bayat on D

Approximate Interval	Approx. Note Names	Ratio of Interval	Exact Just Cents	Exact Just Hz	Nearest 12-note ET Cents	Nearest 24-note ET Cents	Nearest 24-note ET Hz
ET Tonic on D	D - D	1:1	0.00	293.66	0	0	293.66
	D - D hs	25:24	70.67	305.90	100	50	302.26
	D - D#	19/18	93.60	309.97	100	100	311.13
ET Minor 2nd	D - D# or Eb	2 to the 1/12th			100		311.13
Just Minor 2nd	D - Eb	16:15	111.73	313.24	100	100	311.13
	D - E hf	13:12	138.57	318.13	100	150	320.24
	D - E hf	12:11	150.64	320.36	200	150	320.24
	D - E hf	35:32	155.14	321.19	200	150	320.24
	D - E hf	11:10	165.00	323.03	200	150	320.24
	D - E hf	21:19	173.27	324.57	200	150	320.24
Just Major 2nd Sm	D - E	10:9	182.40	326.29	200	200	329.63
ET Major 2nd	D - E	2 to the 1/6th			200		329.63
Just Major 2nd Lg	D - E	9:8	203.91	330.37	200	200	329.63
	D - E hs	8:7	231.17	335.61	200	250	339.28
	D - E hs	7/6	266.87	342.60	200	250	339.28
ET Minor 3rd	D - F	2 to the 1/4th			300		349.23
Just Minor 3rd	D - F	6:5	315.64	352.39	300	300	349.23
Just Major 3rd	D - F#	5:4	386.31	367.07	400	350	359.45
ET Major 3rd	D - F#	2 to the 1/3rd			400		369.99
	D - Gb	9:7	435.08	377.56	400	450	380.83
Just 4th	D - G	4:3	498.04	391.55	500	500	392.00

Jins Saba on D

Approximate Interval	Approx Note Names	Ratio of Interval	Exact Just Cents	Exact Just Hz	Nearest 12-note ET Cents	Nearest 24-note ET Cents	Nearest 24-note ET Hz
ET Tonic on D	D - D	1:1	0.00	293.66	0	0	293.66
	D - D hs	25:24	70.67	305.90	100	50	302.26
	D - D#	19/18	93.60	309.97	100	100	311.13
ET Minor 2nd	D - D# or Eb	2 to the 1/12th			100		311.13
Just Minor 2nd	D - Eb	16:15	111.73	313.24	100	100	311.13
	D - E hf	13:12	138.57	318.13	100	150	320.24
	D - E hf	12:11	150.64	320.36	200	150	320.24
	D - E hf	11:10	165.00	323.03	200	150	320.24
Just Major 2nd Sm	D - E	10:9	182.40	326.29	200	200	329.63
ET Major 2nd	D - E	2 to the 1/6th			200		329.63
Just Major 2nd Lg	D - E	9:8	203.91	330.37	200	200	329.63
	D - E hs	8:7	231.17	335.61	200	250	339.28
	D - E hs	7/6	266.87	342.60	200	250	339.28
ET Minor 3rd	D - F	2 to the 1/4th			300		349.23
Just Minor 3rd	D - F	6:5	315.64	352.39	300	300	349.23
Just Major 3rd	D - F#	5:4	386.31	367.07	400	350	359.45

Jins Saba Zamazama on D

Approximate Interval	Approx. Note Names	Ratio of Interval	Exact Just Cents	Exact Just Hz	Nearest 12-note ET Cents	Nearest 24-note ET Cents	Nearest 24-note ET Hz
ET Tonic on D	D - D	1:1	0.00	293.66	0	0	293.66
	D - D hs	25:24	70.67	305.90	100	50	302.26
	D - D#	19/18	93.60	309.97	100	100	311.13
ET Minor 2nd	D - D# or Eb	2 to the 1/12th			100		311.13
Just Minor 2nd	D - Eb	16:15	111.73	313.24	100	100	311.13
	D - E hf	13:12	138.57	318.13	100	150	320.24
	D - E hf	12:11	150.64	320.36	200	150	320.24
	D - E hf	11:10	165.00	323.03	200	150	320.24
Just Major 2nd Sm	D - E	10:9	182.40	326.29	200	200	329.63
ET Major 2nd	D - E	2 to the 1/6th			200		329.63
Just Major 2nd Lg	D - E	9:8	203.91	330.37	200	200	329.63
	D - E hs	8:7	231.17	335.61	200	250	339.28
	D - E hs	7:6	266.87	342.60	200	250	339.28
ET Minor 3rd	D - F	2 to the 1/4th			300		349.23
Just Minor 3rd	D - F	6:5	315.64	352.39	300	300	349.23
Just Major 3rd	D - F#	5:4	386.31	367.07	400	350	359.45

Jins Rast on C

Approximate Interval	Approx. Note Names	Ratio of Interval	Exact Just Cents	Exact Just Hz	Nearest 12-note ET Cents	Nearest 24-note ET Cents	Nearest 24-note ET Hz
ET Tonic on C	C - C	1:1	0.00	261.63	0	0	261.63
	C - C hs	25:24	70.67	272.53	100	50	269.30
	C - C#	19:18	93.60	276.16	100	100	277.18
ET Minor 2nd	C - C# or Db	2 to the 1/12th			100		277.18
Just Minor 2nd	C - Db	16:15	111.73	279.07	100	100	277.18
	C - D hf	13:12	138.57	283.43	100	150	285.31
	C - D hf	12:11	150.64	285.42	200	150	285.31
	C - D hf	11:10	165.00	287.79	200	150	285.31
Just Major 2nd Sm	C - D	10:9	182.40	290.70	200	200	293.66
ET Major 2nd	C - D	2 to the 1/6th			200		293.66
Just Major 2nd Lg	C - D	9:8	203.91	294.33	200	200	293.66
	C - D hs	8:7	231.17	299.01	200	250	302.27
	C - D hs	7:6	266.87	305.23	200	250	302.27
ET Minor 3rd	C - Eb	2 to the 1/4th			300		311.13
Just Minor 3rd	C - Eb	6:5	315.64	313.95	300	300	311.13
	C - E hf	11:9	347.40	319.77	300	350	320.25
ET Qrtrtone	C - E hf	2 to the 1/4ths	350.00		300	350	320.25
	C - E hf	16/13	359.47	322.01	400	350	320.25
	C - E hf	21/17	365.82	323.19	400	350	320.25
Just Major 3rd	C - E hf	5:4	386.31	327.03	400	350	329.63
ET Major 3rd	C - E	2 to the 1/3rd			400		329.63
	C - E	81/64	407.82	331.13	400	400	329.63
	C - E	19:15	409.24	331.40	400	400	329.63
	C - E	14/11	417.51	332.98	400	400	329.63
	C - Fb	9:7	435.08	336.38	400	450	339.29
Just 4th	C - F	4:3	498.04	348.83	500	500	349.23

Jins Nahawand on C

Approximate Interval	Approx. Note Names	Ratio of Interval	Exact Just Cents	Exact Just Hz	Nearest 12-note ET Cents	Nearest 24-note ET Cents	Nearest 24-note ET Hz
ET Tonic on C	C - C	1:1	0.00	261.63	0	0	261.63
	C - C hs	25:24	70.67	272.53	100	50	269.30
	C - C#	19/18	93.60	276.16	100	100	277.18
ET Minor 2nd	C - C# or Db	2 to the 1/12th			100		277.18
Just Minor 2nd	C - Db	16:15	111.73	279.07	100	100	277.18
	C - D hf	13:12	138.57	283.43	100	150	285.31
	C - D hf	12:11	150.64	285.42	200	150	285.31
	C - D hf	11:10	165.00	287.79	200	150	285.31
Just Major 2nd Sm	C - D	10:9	182.40	290.70	200	200	293.66
ET Major 2nd	C - D	2 to the 1/6th			200		293.66
Just Major 2nd Lg	C - D	9:8	203.91	294.33			
	C - D hs	8:7	231.17	299.01	200	250	302.27
	C - D hs	7/6	266.87	305.23	200	250	302.27
ET Minor 3rd	C - Eb	2 to the 1/4th			300	300	311.13
Just Minor 3rd	C - Eb	6:5	315.64	313.95			
	C - E hf	11:9	347.40	319.77	300	350	320.25
ET Qrtrtone	C - E hf	2 to the 1/4ths	350.00		300	350	320.25
Just Major 3rd	C - E hf	5:4	386.31	327.03	400	350	329.63
ET Major 3rd	C - E	2 to the 1/3rd			400		329.63
	C - Fb	9:7	435.08	336.38	400	450	339.29
Just 4th	C - F	4:3	498.04	348.83	500	500	349.23

Jins Nawa Athar on C

Approximate Interval	Approx. Note Names	Ratio of Interval	Exact Just Cents	Exact Just Hz	Nearest 12-note ET Cents	Nearest 24-note ET Cents	Nearest 24-note ET Hz
ET Tonic on C	C - C	1:1	0.00	261.63	0	0	261.63
	C - C hs	25:24	70.67	272.53	100	50	269.30
	C - C#	19:18	93.60	276.16	100	100	277.18
ET Minor 2nd	C - C# or Db	2 to the 1/12th			100		277.18
Just Minor 2nd	C - Db	16:15	111.73	279.07	100	100	277.18
	C - D hf	13:12	138.57	283.43	100	150	285.31
	C - D hf	12:11	150.64	285.42	200	150	285.31
	C - D hf	11:10	165.00	287.79	200	150	285.31
Just Major 2nd Sm	C - D	10:9	182.40	290.70	200	200	293.66
ET Major 2nd	C - D	2 to the 1/6th			200		293.66
Just Major 2nd Lg	C - D	9:8	203.91	294.33	200	200	293.66
	C - D hs	8:7	231.17	299.01	200	250	302.27
	C - D hs	7:6	266.87	305.23	200	250	302.27
ET Minor 3rd	C - Eb	2 to the 1/4th			300		311.13
Just Minor 3rd	C - Eb	6:5	315.64	313.95	300	300	311.13
	C - E hf	11:9	347.40	319.77	300	350	320.25
ET Qrtrtone	C - E hf	2 to the 1/4ths	350.00		300	350	320.25
Just Major 3rd	C - E hf	5:4	386.31	327.03	400	350	329.63
ET Major 3rd	C - E	2 to the 1/3rd			400		329.63
	C - Fb	9:7	435.08	336.38	400	450	339.29
Just 4th	C - F	4:3	498.04	348.83	500	500	349.23
ET 4th	C - F	2 to the 5/12ths			500		349.23
	C - F#	11:8	551.32	359.74	600	550	359.47
Just Tritone	C - Gb	7:5	582.51	366.28	600	600	369.99
	C - Gb	10:7	617.49	373.76	600	600	369.99
ET 5th	C - G	2 to the 7/12ths			700		392.00
Just 5th	C - G	3:2	701.95	392.46	700	700	392.00

Jins Athar Kurd on C

Approximate Interval	Approx. Note Names	Ratio of Interval	Exact Just Cents	Exact Just Hz	Nearest 12-note ET Cents	Nearest 24-note ET Cents	Nearest 24-note ET Hz
ET Tonic on C	C - C	1:1	0.00	261.63	0	0	261.63
	C - C hs	25:24	70.67	272.53	100	50	269.30
	C - C#	19/18	93.60	276.16	100	100	277.18
ET Minor 2nd	C - C# or Db	2 to the 1/12th			100		277.18
Just Minor 2nd	C - Db	16:15	111.73	279.07	100	100	277.18
	C - D hf	13:12	138.57	283.43	100	150	285.31
	C - D hf	12:11	150.64	285.42	200	150	285.31
	C - D hf	11:10	165.00	287.79	200	150	285.31
Just Major 2nd Sm	C - D	10:9	182.40	290.70	200	200	293.66
ET Major 2nd	C - D	2 to the 1/6th			200		293.66
Just Major 2nd Lg	C - D	9:8	203.91	294.33	200	200	293.66
	C - D hs	8:7	231.17	299.01	200	250	302.27
	C - D hs	7:6	266.87	305.23	200	250	302.27
ET Minor 3rd	C - Eb	2 to the 1/4th			300		311.13
Just Minor 3rd	C - Eb	6:5	315.64	313.95	300	300	311.13
	C - E hf	11:9	347.40	319.77	300	350	320.25
ET Qrtrtone	C - E hf	2 to the 1/4ths	350.00		300	350	320.25
Just Major 3rd	C - E hf	5:4	386.31	327.03	400	350	329.63
ET Major 3rd	C - E	2 to the 1/3rd			400		329.63
	C - Fb	9:7	435.08	336.38	400	450	339.29
Just 4th	C - F	4:3	498.04	348.83	500	500	349.23
ET 4th	C - F	2 to the 5/12ths			500		349.23
	C - F#	11:8	551.32	359.74	600	550	359.47
Just Tritone	C - Gb	7:5	582.51	366.28	600	600	369.99
	C - Gb	10:7	617.49	373.76	600	600	369.99
ET 5th	C - G	2 to the 7/12ths			700		392.00
Just 5th	C - G	3:2	701.95	392.46	700	700	392.00

Jins Ajam on Bb

Approximate Interval	Approx Note Names	Ratio of Interval	Exact Just Cents	Exact Just Hz	Nearest 12-note ET Cents	Nearest 24-note ET Cents	Nearest 24-note ET Hz
ET Tonic	Bb - Bb	1:1	0.00	233.08	0	0	233.08
Sm Minor 2nd	Bb - B hf	25:24	70.67	242.79	100	50	239.91
Sm Minor 2nd	Bb - B hf	19:18	93.60	246.03	100	100	246.94
ET Minor 2nd	Bb - B				100		246.94
Minor 2nd	Bb - B hs	16:15	111.73	248.62	100	100	246.94
Lg Minor 2nd	Bb - B hs	13:12	138.57	252.50	100	150	254.18
Lg Minor 2nd	Bb - B hs	12:11	150.64	254.27	200	150	254.18
Sm Major 2nd	Bb - C hf	11:10	165.00	256.39	200	150	254.18
Sm Major 2nd	Bb - C	10:9	182.40	258.98	200	200	261.62
Major 2nd	Bb - C	9:8	203.91	262.21	200	200	261.62
Lg Major 2nd	Bb - C hs	8:7	231.17	266.38	200	250	269.29
Lg Major 2nd	Bb - C hs	7/6	266.87	271.93	200	250	269.29
ET Minor 3rd	Bb - C#				300		277.18
Just Minor 3rd	Bb - C#	6:5	315.64	279.70	300	300	277.18
Just Major 3rd	Bb - D	5:4	386.31	291.35	400	350	285.30
ET Major 3rd	Bb - D				400		293.66
Lg Major 3rd	Bb - D hs	9:7	435.08	299.67	400	450	302.27
Just 4th	Bb - Eb	4:3	498.04	310.77	500	500	311.12
Sm Tritone	Bb - E hf	11:8	551.32	320.49	600	550	320.24
Tritone	Bb - E hf	7:5	582.51	326.31	600	600	329.62
Lg Tritone	Bb - E	10:7	617.49	332.97	600	600	329.62
ET 5th	Bb - F				700	700	349.23
Just 5th	Bb - F	3:2	701.95	349.62	700	700	349.23

Jins Sikah on E half-flat

Approximate Interval	Approx. Note Names	Ratio of Interval	Exact Just Cents	Exact Just Hz	Nearest 12-note ET Cents	Nearest 24-note ET Cents	Nearest 24-note ET Hz
Tonic	E hf - E hf	1:1	0.00	326.67	0	0	329.63
Sm Minor 2nd	E hf - F hf	25:24	70.67	340.28	100	50	339.29
Sm Minor 2nd	E hf - F	19:18	93.60	344.82	100	100	349.23
ET Minor 2nd					100		349.23
Minor 2nd	E hf - F	16:15	111.73	348.45	100	100	349.23
Lg Minor 2nd	E hf - F	13:12	138.57	353.89	100	150	359.46
Lg Minor 2nd	E hf - F#	12:11	150.64	356.37	200	150	359.46
Sm Major 2nd	E hf - F#	11:10	165.00	359.33	200	150	359.46
Sm Major 2nd	E hf - Gb	10:9	182.40	362.97	200	200	370.00
Major 2nd	E hf - Gb	9:8	203.91	367.50	200	200	370.00
Lg Major 2nd	E hf - G hf	8:7	231.17	373.34	200	250	380.84
Lg Major 2nd	E hf - G hf	7:6	266.87	381.11	200	250	380.84
ET Minor 3rd					300		392.00
Minor 3rd	E hf - G	6:5	315.64	392.00	300	300	392.00

Indigenous Middle Eastern Modes

Since there are large numbers of "in tune" just intervals to choose from it is not possible to dictate exactly which ones should be employed to create perfectly in-tune traditional Arabic music. And we also want to acknowledge that musicians will bend notes into non-harmonious positions in order to create "blue" notes which can exert extra emotional power.

But nevertheless, the intervals highlighted with light grey color on this and subsequent tables may well be the ones most often employed by traditional musicians seeking to create maximum musical magic.

D-Based Maqams
Hijaz Family

Associated Moods:
The Hijazi region of Saudi Arabia is desert. This maqam is associated with the lonely treks of the camel caravans and with fascination and enchantment with the East and its beauty. Very commonly used in popular dance and folk music as well as in religious music and the call to prayer. Has been called simple, pretty, pastoral.

Hijaz

Closely Related Maqamat: Hijaz Humayun, Ajami, al-Isba'ayn (Tunisia), al-Zayyidan (Algeria), Hijaz al-kabir (Morocco), al-Mathnawi (Iraq).

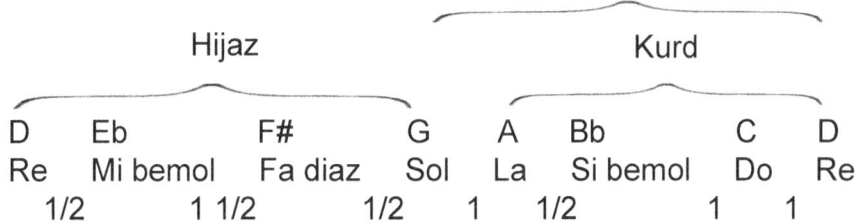

D	Eb	F#	G	A	Bb	C	D
Re	Mi bemol	Fa diaz	Sol	La	Si bemol	Do	Re
1/2		1 1/2	1/2	1	1/2	1	1

Possible Descriptions: Hijaz tetrachord on bottom; nahawand pentachord on 4th; kurd tetrachord on 5th.

It is common practice in the West where keyboards and fretboards are dominant, to play the equal-tempered versions of these notes. There is another more highly tuned option, however, as we shall see on the next page with Hijaz Gharib!

Hijaz Gharib

D	Eb+	F#-	G	A	Bb	C	D
Re	Mi bemol	Fa diaz	Sol	La	Si bemol	Do	Re
1/2+	1 1/2-	1/2+	1	1/2	1	1	

Possible Descriptions: Hijaz tetrachord on bottom; kurd tetrachord on 5th; nahawand pentachord on 4th.

"Gharib" means "old." So this is the "old" version of hijaz. According to most Arab musicians, before the equal-tempered 1 1/2 step interval became common, musicians tended to play this interval a little bit differently by slightly raising the Eb (Eb+) and slightly lowering the F# (F#-). To Arab ears it still sounds better to play the "old" interval.

This is a perfect example of a theme running throughout the Arab maqam tradition: the intervals which sound correct to traditional Arab musicians do not really correspond to the 24-note "quartertone" equally tempered system.

It makes perfect sense to interpret these "traditionally correct sounding intervals" as reflecting the naturally perfect harmonies of just intonation. As you will see, the traditional prescription for playing these intervals correctly corresponds quite nicely with employing justly-intonated intervals!

The chart on the next page offers a number of just intervals which sensitive musicians can gravitate toward, as long as they are playing microtonal instruments or using their voices. I have included the Equally Tempered intervals in the table also so that we can see where they are.

Related Audio Tracks on Harmonic Secrets CD1:

Track 2. Hijaz Gharib in D
Track 3. Hijaz Gharib Melody in D -- Rhythm: 8/8 Tsiftitelli
Track 4. Hijaz Taqasim in D by Jihad
Track 5. Hijaz Vocal Taqasim in G by Saadoun
Track 6. Hijaz Dulab in G by Saadoun

Maqam Hijaz Gharib on D

Approximate Interval	Approx. Note Names	Ratio of Interval	Exact Just Cents	Exact Just Hz	Nearest 12-note ET Cents	Nearest 24-note ET Cents	Nearest 24-note ET Hz
ET Tonic on D	D - D	1:1	0.00	293.66	0	0	293.66
	D - D hs	25:24	70.67	305.90	100	50	302.26
	D - D#	19:18	93.60	309.97	100	100	311.13
ET Minor 2nd	D - D# or Eb	2 to the 1/12th			100		311.13
Just Minor 2nd	D - Eb	16:15	111.73	313.24	100	100	311.13
	D - E hf	13:12	138.57	318.13	100	150	320.24
	D - E hf	12:11	150.64	320.36	200	150	320.24
	D - E hf	11:10	165.00	323.03	200	150	320.24
Just Major 2nd Sm	D - E	10:9	182.40	326.29	200	200	329.63
ET Major 2nd	D - E	2 to the 1/6th			200		329.63
Just Major 2nd Lg	D - E	9:8	203.91	330.37	200	200	329.63
	D - E hs	8:7	231.17	335.61	200	250	339.28
	D - E hs	7:6	266.87	342.60	200	250	339.28
ET Minor 3rd	D - F	2 to the 1/4th			300		349.23
Just Minor 3rd	D - F	6:5	315.64	352.39	300	300	349.23
Just Major 3rd	D - F#	5:4	386.31	367.07	400	350	359.45
ET Major 3rd	D - F#	2 to the 1/3rd			400		369.99
	D - Gb	9:7	435.08	377.56	400	450	380.83
Just 4th	D - G	4:3	498.04	391.55	500	500	392.00
ET 4th	D - G	2 to the 5/12th			500		392.00
	D - G#	11:8	551.32	403.78	600	550	403.48
Just Tritone	D - Ab	7:5	582.51	411.12	600	600	415.30
	D - Ab	10:7	617.49	419.51	600	600	415.30
ET 5th	D - A	2 to the 7/12ths			700		440.00
Just 5th	D - A	3:2	701.95	440.49	700	700	440.00
	D - A#	11:7	782.49	461.47	800	750	452.89
ET Minor 6th	D - A# or Bb	2 to the 2/3rds			800		466.16
Just Minor 6th	D - Bb	8:5	813.69	469.86	800	800	466.16
	D - B hf	13:8	840.53	477.20	800	850	479.82
Just Major 6th	D - B hf	5:3	884.36	489.43	900	900	493.88
ET Major 6th	D - B	2 to the 3/4ths			900		493.88
	D - B	12:7	933.13	503.42	900	950	508.35
	D - B	7:4	968.83	513.91	1000	950	508.35
Just Minor7th Sm	D - C	16:9	996.09	522.06	1000	1000	523.25
ET Minor 7th	D - C	2 to the 5/6ths			1000		523.25
Just Minor 7th Lg	D - C	9:5	1017.60	528.59	1000	1000	523.25
	D - C	11:6	1049.36	538.38	1000	1050	538.57
	D - C hs	13:7	1071.70	545.37	1100	1050	538.57
Just Major 7th	D - C hs	15:8	1088.27	550.61	1100	1050	538.57
ET Major 7th	D - C#	2 to the 11/12ths			1100		554.37
	D - C#	17:9	1101.04	554.69	1100	1100	554.37
	D - C#	19:10	1111.20	557.95	1100	1100	554.37
	D - C#	125:64	1158.94	573.55	1100	1150	570.60
ET Octave	D - D	2:1	1200.00	587.32	1200	1200	587.33

Bracket groupings: Hijaz (upper), Kurd and Nahawand (lower).

The highlighted note choices in the table are suggested just intervals which should not only sound perfect but are quite likely to be the intervals which sound best to the trained indigenous Middle Easterners' ears.

But as you can see, those are not the only possible choices.

As your facility with your instrument grows and as your listening skills grow, you can make it a habit to "fish" for perfect sounding intervals and include them in your songs and improvisations. It is of course quite likely that you will be treading the same musical paths which others before you have traveled over hundreds, even thousands, of years of music-making.

Words like "tarab" and "saltanah" which come out of the Arabic language point to the achievablility of certain ecstatic states which result from the skilled application of certain musical formulas. Knowing about the existence of these perfectly harmonic intervals can give you confidence to build your own skills for producing truly magical musical moments.

According to AJ Racy, Tawfiq al-Sabbagh refers to at least 2 different sharpened degrees for the Hijaz Eb. (We can choose from the notes defined by the 16:15, 13:12, 12:11 or the 11:10 intervals).

He also refers to the flattening of the F#. (We can choose from the 16:13 or 11:9 intervals as well as from the 5:4).

And he gives a hint from the tradition: touching briefly on a certain Ab can be powerful and ecstatic. (We could try either the just tritone at 7:5 or the nearby 10:7 note.)

Hijaz Awji

Closely Related Maqamat: Hijaz, Hijaz Masri, Araba (old name)

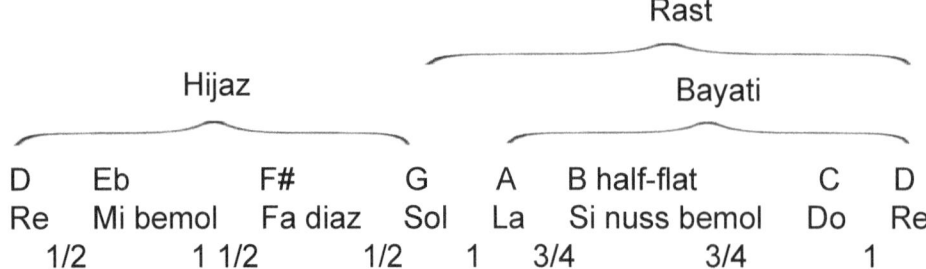

Possible Descriptions: Hijaz tetrachord on bottom; rast pentachord on 4th; bayyati tetrachord on 5th.

Many songs are played in this maqam. Older sources make it clear that this was the basic form of the maqam "hijaz" until a few decades ago when it began to become common to assume a Bb instead of a B half-flat. But now musicians may simply state that the song moves from "Hijaz on Re" to "Rast on Sol" at some point during the song without actually knowing the name "hijaz awji."

 **Related Audio Tracks on Harmonic Secrets CD1:**

Track 7.   Hijaz Awji in D
Track 8.   Hijaz Awji Melody in D -- Rhythm: 8/8 Tsiftitelli

Maqam Hijaz Awji on D

Note:
Distance from the tonic to the just minor 2nd is defined by the 16:15 ratio which contains 111.73 cents.

Distance from the just major 3rd to the just 4th is also defined by the same exact 16:15 ratio which contains 111.73 cents.

Approximate Interval	Approx. Note Names	Ratio of Interval	Exact Just Cents	Exact Just Hz	Nearest 12-note ET Cents	Nearest 24-note ET Cents	Nearest 24-note ET Hz
ET Tonic on D	D - D	1:1	0.00	293.66	0	0	293.66
	D - D hs	25:24	70.67	305.90	100	50	302.26
	D - D#	19:18	93.60	309.97	100	100	311.13
ET Minor 2nd	D - D# or Eb	2 to the 1/12th			100		311.13
Just Minor 2nd	D - Eb	16:15	111.73	313.24	100	100	311.13
	D - E hf	13:12	138.57	318.13	100	150	320.24
	D - E hf	12:11	150.64	320.36	200	150	320.24
	D - E hf	11:10	165.00	323.03	200	150	320.24
Just Major 2nd Sm	D - E	10:9	182.40	326.29	200	200	329.63
ET Major 2nd	D - E	2 to the 1/6th			200		329.63
Just Major 2nd Lg	D - E	9:8	203.91	330.37	200	200	329.63
	D - E hs	8:7	231.17	335.61	200	250	339.28
	D - E hs	7:6	266.87	342.60	200	250	339.28
ET Minor 3rd	D - F	2 to the 1/4th			300		349.23
Just Minor 3rd	D - F	6:5	315.64	352.39	300	300	349.23
Just Major 3rd	D - F#	5:4	386.31	367.07	400	350	359.45
ET Major 3rd	D - F#	2 to the 1/3rd			400		369.99
	D - Gb	9:7	435.08	377.56	400	450	380.83
Just 4th	D - G	4:3	498.04	391.55	500	500	392.00
ET 4th	D - G	2 to the 5/12th			500		392.00
	D - G#	11:8	551.32	403.78	600	550	403.48
Just Tritone	D - Ab	7:5	582.51	411.12	600	600	415.30
	D - Ab	10:7	617.49	419.51	600	600	415.30
ET 5th	D - A	2 to the 7/12ths			700		440.00
Just 5th	D - A	3:2	701.95	440.49	700	700	440.00
	D - A#	11:7	782.49	461.47	800	750	452.89
ET Minor 6th	D - A# or Bb	2 to the 2/3rds			800		466.16
Just Minor 6th	D - Bb	8:5	813.69	469.86	800	800	466.16
	D - B hf	13:8	840.53	477.20	800	850	479.82
Just Major 6th	D - B hf	5:3	884.36	489.43	900	900	493.88
ET Major 6th	D - B	2 to the 3/4ths			900		493.88
	D - B	12:7	933.13	503.42	900	950	508.35
	D - B	7:4	968.83	513.91	1000	950	508.35
Just Minor 7th Sm	D - C	16:9	996.09	522.06	1000	1000	523.25
ET Minor 7th	D - C	2 to the 5/6ths			1000		523.25
Just Minor 7th Lg	D - C	9:5	1017.60	528.59	1000	1000	523.25
	D - C	11:6	1049.36	538.38	1000	1050	538.57
	D - C hs	13:7	1071.70	545.37	1100	1050	538.57
Just Major 7th	D - C#	15:8	1088.27	550.61	1100	1050	538.57
ET Major 7th	D - C#	2 to the 11/12ths			1100		554.37
	D - C#	17:9	1101.04	554.69	1100	1100	554.37
	D - C#	19:10	1111.20	557.95	1100	1100	554.37
	D - C#	125:64	1158.94	573.55	1100	1150	570.60
ET Octave	D - D	2:1	1200.00	587.32	1200	1200	587.33

Brackets (right side): 16:15 ratio (tonic to just minor 2nd); 16:15 ratio (just major 3rd to just 4th).

Brackets (left side): Hijaz, Rast, Bayati.

Shehnaz

Closely Related Maqamat: Sikah Baladi, Zirgule Hijaz, (Turkey)

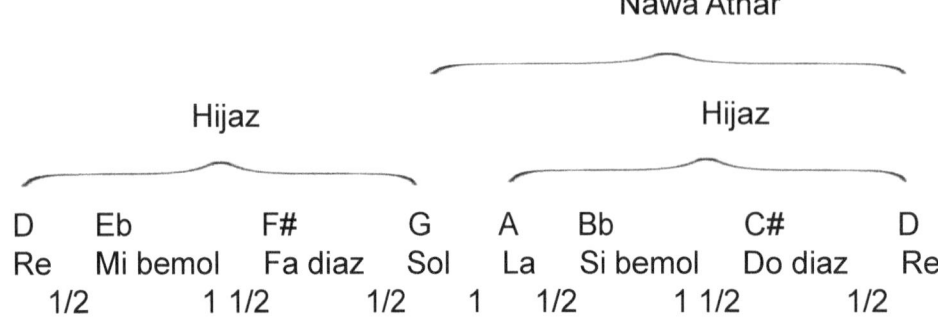

D	Eb	F#	G	A	Bb	C#	D
Re	Mi bemol	Fa diaz	Sol	La	Si bemol	Do diaz	Re
1/2	1 1/2	1/2	1	1/2	1 1/2	1/2	

Possible Descriptions: Hijaz tetrachord on bottom; hijaz tetrachord on 5th; nawa athar pentachord on 4th.

When the intervals in the two hijaz ajnas are changed so that they are in just intonation as described in the chart on the opposite page, this maqam can also then be called sikah baladi.

Related Audio Tracks on Harmonic Secrets CD1:

Track 9. Shehnaz in D
Track 10. Shehnaz Melody in D -- Rhythm: 4/4 Maqsum

Maqam Shehnaz on D

Hijaz

Nawa Athar

Hijaz

Approximate Interval	Approx. Note Names	Ratio of Interval	Exact Just Cents	Exact Just Hz	Nearest 12-note ET Cents	Nearest 24-note ET Cents	Nearest 24-note ET Hz
ET Tonic on D	D - D	1:1	0.00	293.66	0	0	293.66
	D - D hs	25:24	70.67	305.90	100	50	302.26
	D - D#	19/18	93.60	309.97	100	100	311.13
ET Minor 2nd	D - D# or Eb	2 to the 1/12th			100		311.13
Just Minor 2nd	D - Eb	16:15	111.73	313.24	100	100	311.13
	D -E hf	13:12	138.57	318.13	100	150	320.24
	D -E hf	12:11	150.64	320.36	200	150	320.24
	D - E hf	11:10	165.00	323.03	200	150	320.24
Just Major 2nd Sm	D - E	10:9	182.40	326.29	200	200	329.63
ET Major 2nd	D - E	2 to the 1/6th			200		329.63
Just Major 2nd Lg	D - E	9:8	203.91	330.37	200	200	329.63
	D - E hs	8:7	231.17	335.61	200	250	339.28
	D - E hs	7/6	266.87	342.60	200	250	339.28
ET Minor 3rd	D - F	2 to the 1/4th			300		349.23
Just Minor 3rd	D - F	6:5	315.64	352.39	300	300	349.23
Just Major 3rd	D - F#	5:4	386.31	367.07	400	350	359.45
ET Major 3rd	D - F#	2 to the 1/3rd			400		369.99
	D - Gb	9:7	435.08	377.56	400	450	380.83
Just 4th	D - G	4:3	498.04	391.55	500	500	392.00
ET 4th	D - G	2 to the 5/12th			500		392.00
	D - G#	11:8	551.32	403.78	600	550	403.48
Just Tritone	D - Ab	7:5	582.51	411.12	600	600	415.30
	D - Ab	10:7	617.49	419.51	600	600	415.30
ET 5th	D - A	2 to the 7/12ths			700		440.00
Just 5th	D - A	3:2	701.95	440.49	700	700	440.00
	D - A#	11:7	782.49	461.47	800	750	452.89
ET Minor 6th	D - A# or Bb	2 to the 2/3rds			800		466.16
Just Minor 6th	D - Bb	8:5	813.69	469.86	800	800	466.16
	D - B hf	13:8	840.53	477.20	800	850	479.82
Just Major 6th	D - B hf	5:3	884.36	489.43	900	900	493.88
ET Major 6th	D - B	2 to the 3/4ths			900		493.88
	D - B	12:7	933.13	503.42	900	950	508.35
	D - B	7:4	968.83	513.91	1000	950	508.35
Just Minor7th Sm	D - C	16:9	996.09	522.06	1000	1000	523.25
ET Minor 7th	D - C	2 to the 5/6ths			1000		523.25
Just Minor 7th Lg	D - C	9:5	1017.60	528.59	1000	1000	523.25
	D - C	11:6	1049.36	538.38	1000	1050	538.57
	D - C hs	13:7	1071.70	545.37	1100	1050	538.57
Just Major 7th	D - C#	15:8	1088.27	550.61	1100	1050	538.57
ET Major 7th	D - C#	2 to the 11/12ths			1100		554.37
	D - C#	17:9	1101.04	554.69	1100	1100	554.37
	D - C#	19:10	1111.20	557.95	1100	1100	554.37
	D - C#	125:64	1158.94	573.55	1100	1150	570.60
ET Octave	D - D	2:1	1200.00	587.32	1200	1200	587.33

Note the amazing symmetry in this maqam.

The interval between the octave and the major 7th is a precise inversion of the just minor 2nd.

And the interval between the octave and the just minor 6th is a precise inversion of the just mayor 3rd.

And of course the interval between the octave and the 5th is a precise inversion of the just 4th.

Look and see:

The minor 2nd just interval: 111.73

The interval between the octave and the just major 7th:
1200 - 1088.27 = 111.73
Same!

The major 3rd just interval: 386.31

The interval between the octave and the just minor 6th:
1200 - 813.69 = 386.31
Same!

The just 4th interval: 498.04

The interval between the octave and the just 5th:
1200 - 701.95 = 498.05
Same!

This maqam is like a hall of mirrors!

D-Based Maqams
Kurd Family

Associated Moods:
The Kurdish people live in present day southern Turkey, Northern Iraq and western Iran. Possibly this maqam is associated with them. Indeed, songs from southern Turkey are frequently in this maqam. But since "kurd" is also the name of the note Eb in Arabic music, it is also quite likely that this explains the name of the maqam. The mood varies from gently romantic, sweet and pleasant, to more powerfully exciting and dance oriented, to association with extreme longing in love songs.

Kurd

Closely Related: Phrygian Mode

```
                      Nahawand
              ┌─────────────────────┐
       Kurd                 Kurd
    ┌─────────┐         ┌─────────┐
D     Eb    F    G    A    Bb    C    D
Re  Mi bemol Fa  Sol  La Si bemol Do   Re
   1/2    1    1    1  1/2    1    1
```

Possible Descriptions: Kurd tetrachord on bottom; nahawand pentachord on 4th; kurd tetrachord on 5th.

Ghammaz on 4th.

Related Audio Tracks on Harmonic Secrets CD1:

Track 11. Kurd in D
Track 12. Kurd Melody in D -- Rhythm: 10/8 Jurjina
Track 13. Kurd Taqasim in D by Jihad

We see that most likely the minor 2nd and the minor 3rd will sound really good if they are audibly sharper than their ET counterparts.

But the minor 6th offers some interesting options: we could play the sharper version which is shown highlighted, or we could play the flatter version which corresponds to the 11:7 ratio. This puts the Bb closer to the A than ET versions would have it. It sometimes sounds very cozy that way: a magical intimacy between the 5th and the 6th. Try it.

Maqam Kurd on D

Approximate Interval	Approx. Note Names	Ratio of Interval	Exact Just Cents	Exact Just Hz	Nearest 12-note ET Cents	Nearest 24-note ET Cents	Nearest 24-note ET Hz
ET Tonic on D	D - D	1:1	0.00	293.66	0	0	293.66
	D - D hs	25:24	70.67	305.90	100	50	302.26
	D - D#	19:18	93.60	309.97	100	100	311.13
ET Minor 2nd	D - D# or Eb	2 to the 1/12th			100		311.13
Just Minor 2nd	D - Eb	16:15	111.73	313.24	100	100	311.13
	D - E hf	13:12	138.57	318.13	100	150	320.24
	D - E hf	12:11	150.64	320.36	200	150	320.24
	D - E hf	11:10	165.00	323.03	200	150	320.24
Just Major 2nd Sm	D - E	10:9	182.40	326.29	200	200	329.63
ET Major 2nd	D - E	2 to the 1/6th			200		329.63
Just Major 2nd Lg	D - E	9:8	203.91	330.37	200	200	329.63
	D - E hs	8:7	231.17	335.61	200	250	339.28
	D - E hs	7:6	266.87	342.60	200	250	339.28
ET Minor 3rd	D - F	2 to the 1/4th			300		349.23
Just Minor 3rd	D - F	6:5	315.64	352.39	300	300	349.23
Just Major 3rd	D - F#	5:4	386.31	367.07	400	350	359.45
ET Major 3rd	D - F#	2 to the 1/3rd			400		369.99
	D - Gb	9:7	435.08	377.56	400	450	380.83
Just 4th	D - G	4:3	498.04	391.55	500	500	392.00
ET 4th	D - G	2 to the 5/12th			500		392.00
	D - G#	11:8	551.32	403.78	600	550	403.48
Just Tritone	D - Ab	7:5	582.51	411.12	600	600	415.30
	D - Ab	10:7	617.49	419.51	600	600	415.30
ET 5th	D - A	2 to the 7/12ths			700		440.00
Just 5th	D - A	3:2	701.95	440.49	700	700	440.00
	D - A#	11:7	782.49	461.47	800	750	452.89
ET Minor 6th	D - A# or Bb	2 to the 2/3rds			800		466.16
Just Minor 6th	D - Bb	8:5	813.69	469.86	800	800	466.16
	D - B hf	13:8	840.53	477.20	800	850	479.82
Just Major 6th	D - B hf	5:3	884.36	489.43	900	900	493.88
ET Major 6th	D - B	2 to the 3/4ths			900		493.88
	D - B	12:7	933.13	503.42	900	950	508.35
	D - B	7:4	968.83	513.91	1000	950	508.35
Just Minor 7th Sm	D - C	16:9	996.09	522.06	1000	1000	523.25
ET Minor 7th	D - C	2 to the 5/6ths			1000		523.25
Just Minor 7th Lg	D - C	9:5	1017.60	528.59	1000	1000	523.25
	D - C	11:6	1049.36	538.38	1000	1050	538.57
	D - C hs	13:7	1071.70	545.37	1100	1050	538.57
Just Major 7th	D - C hs	15:8	1088.27	550.61	1100	1050	538.57
ET Major 7th	D - C#	2 to the 11/12ths			1100		554.37
	D - C#	17:9	1101.04	554.69	1100	1100	554.37
	D - C#	19:10	1111.20	557.95	1100	1100	554.37
	D - C#	125:64	1158.94	573.55	1100	1150	570.60
ET Octave	D - D	2:1	1200.00	587.32	1200	1200	587.33

Bracket groupings: Kurd spans from Tonic through approx Just Major 3rd region; Nahawand spans from around Just Minor 3rd through Just Minor 7th; Kurd spans from around Just 5th through ET Octave.

"The maqam Rast, for instance, evokes a feeling of pride, power, soundness of mind, and masculinity. The maqam Bayati, on the other hand, expresses vitality, joy, and femininity, while the maqam Sikah is associated with feelings of love, and the maqam Saba evokes sadness and pain. Finally, the maqam Hijaz conjures up the distant desert."
--Touma 1996

"Today, rather than referring to a specific historical tuning, just intonation represents an almost infinite variety of tunings which are based upon the principles of whole number ratios. In contrast to most tempered tunings, harmonies in just intonation ring with clarity and stability, and when certain complex ratios are used, the music shimmers with exotic resonance. Given that there are an infinite number of whole number ratios, one can only imagine how many new musical possibilities are waiting to be explored."
--Michael Harrison Website

D-Based Maqams
Bayyati Family

Associated Moods:
Romantic, very popular maqam in both Arabic and Turkish worlds. The chanting of the Quran begins and ends in Bayati. Folk singing from southern Turkey, as well as the ashik, or Turkish sufi music, is frequently in this maqam. Common in wedding songs. Husayni, Shuri and Saba are all closely related maqams.
Members of the Turkoman Bayat tribe in Northern Iraq sometimes lay claim to this maqam. But it has been mentioned in Arab music history for at least the last thousand years.

Related Audio Tracks on Harmonic Secrets CD1:

Track 14. Bayati in D
Track 15. Bayati Melody in D -- Rhythm: 8/8 Dabke
Track 16. Bayati Taqasim in D by Adif
Track 17. Bayati Taqasim in D by Jihad
Track 18. Bayati Taqasim in D by Saadoun
Track 19. Bayati Dulab in D by Adif

Related Audio Tracks on Harmonic Secrets CD1:

Track 20. Husayni in D
Track 21. Husayni Melody in D -- Rhythm: 8/8 Wahda

Related Audio Tracks on Harmonic Secrets CD1:

Track 22. Saba in D
Track 23. Saba Melody in D -- Rhythm: 4/4 Sufi
Track 24. Saba Taqasim in D by Jihad
Track 25. Saba Taqasim in D by Adif

Bayati

Closely Related Maqamat: Ushaq (Turkey), Bayati Sultani, Ardibar, Isfahan

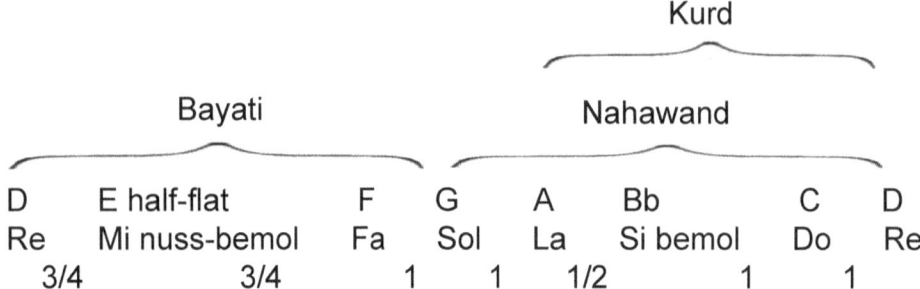

Possible Descriptions: Bayyati tetrachord on bottom; Kurd tetrachord on 5th; Nahawand pentachord on 4th.

Traditionally it is taught that the E half-flat in Bayyati is very slightly lower than the E half-flat in Rast and Sikah. When we look at the Just Intonation charts for Bayati and for Rast we see that the most obvious harmonious choice for the E half-flat in Bayati generates the pitch 323.03 Hz while the most likely pitch for the E half-flat in Rast generates the pitch 327.03 Hz which is audibly sharper. (See the chart accompanying the description of maqam Rast.)

But this is not the end of the story. Look at the chart on the opposite page. There are other harmonious choices for the E half-flat in Bayati which generate the following pitches: 318.13 Hz, 320.36 Hz, 321.19 Hz, 324.57 Hz and 326.29 Hz.
Habib Hassan Touma mentions three of these possibilities and the other two are obvious.
And there is a harmonious option for the E half-flat in Rast which generates a pitch of 319.77 Hz.

Isn't it wonderful that a musician has so many harmonious choices!

Tawfiq al-Sabbagh also suggests that for maximum ecstatic effect the F should be slightly sharp and the G slightly flat. He acknowledges the difficulty of adjusting the 4th on instruments which use G as an open string. But notice that the just minor 3rd, the F is indeed 15 cents sharper than the ET position while the just G is slightly flatter than its ET position!

The Ghammaz in maqam Bayati falls on G where the Nahawand jins begins. It is common for musicians to emphasize this G very strongly almost immediately upon opening a Bayati taqasim.

Maqam Bayati on D

Magic of the ghammaz in Maqam Bayati:

The 4th derives its special magic in a scale partly from the fact that its pitch is never found in the overtone series *above* a particular tonic.

It is the other way around: the tonic is defineable as *the 5th above the note which is an octave below the 4th above the tonic.* It is a mystery why this note which resounds a 4th above a tonic carries such power!

In Western music when this note is heard it is taken as a signal that the chord has changed. If we were playing in C and we hear an F, the whole band makes the F into a temporary tonic and the only interval emphasized which includes the C is the 5th which creates the C above the F.

But in Arabic and Balkan music the magic of the 4th is greatly honored. The tonic is held while the 4th resounds over it and the whole world, upon hearing this, knows that it's party time!

Mathieu calls this 4th note a "mother tone!" It gives birth to the tonic!

Approximate Interval	Approx Note Names	Ratio of Interval	Exact Just Cents	Exact Just Hz	Nearest 12-note ET Cents	Nearest 24-note ET Cents	Nearest 24-note ET Hz
ET Tonic on D	D - D	1:1	0.00	293.66	0	0	293.66
	D - D hs	25:24	70.67	305.90	100	50	302.26
	D - D#	19:18	93.60	309.97	100	100	311.13
ET Minor 2nd	D - D# or Eb	2 to the 1/12th			100		311.13
Just Minor 2nd	D - Eb	16:15	111.73	313.24	100	100	311.13
	D - E hf	13:12	138.57	318.13	100	150	320.24
	D - E hf	12:11	150.64	320.36	200	150	320.24
	D - E hf	35:32	155.14	321.19	200	150	320.24
	D - E hf	11:10	165.00	323.03	200	150	320.24
	D - E hf	21:19	173.27	324.57	200	150	320.24
Just Major 2nd Sm	D - E	10:9	182.40	326.29	200	200	329.63
ET Major 2nd	D - E	2 to the 1/6th			200		329.63
Just Major 2nd Lg	D - E	9:8	203.91	330.37	200	200	329.63
	D - E hs	8:7	231.17	335.61	200	250	339.28
	D - E hs	7:6	266.87	342.60	200	250	339.28
ET Minor 3rd	D - F	2 to the 1/4th			300		349.23
Just Minor 3rd	D - F	6:5	315.64	352.39	300	300	349.23
Just Major 3rd	D - F#	5:4	386.31	367.07	400	350	359.45
ET Major 3rd	D - F#	2 to the 1/3rd			400		369.99
	D - Gb	9:7	435.08	377.56	400	450	380.83
Just 4th	D - G	4:3	498.04	391.55	500	500	392.00
ET 4th	D - G	2 to the 5/12th			500		392.00
	D - G#	11:8	551.32	403.78	600	550	403.48
Just Tritone	D - Ab	7:5	582.51	411.12	600	600	415.30
	D - Ab	10:7	617.49	419.51	600	600	415.30
ET 5th	D - A	2 to the 7/12ths			700		440.00
Just 5th	D - A	3:2	701.95	440.49	700	700	440.00
	D - A#	11:7	782.49	461.47	800	750	452.89
ET Minor 6th	D - A# or Bb	2 to the 2/3rds			800		466.16
Just Minor 6th	D - Bb	8:5	813.69	469.86	800	800	466.16
	D - B hf	13:8	840.53	477.20	800	850	479.82
Just Major 6th	D - B hf	5:3	884.36	489.43	900	900	493.88
ET Major 6th	D - B	2 to the 3/4ths			900		493.88
	D - B	12:7	933.13	503.42	900	950	508.35
	D - B	7:4	968.83	513.91	1000	950	508.35
Just Minor 7th Sm	D - C	16:9	996.09	522.06	1000	1000	523.25
ET Minor 7th	D - C	2 to the 5/6ths			1000		523.25
Just Minor 7th Lg	D - C	9:5	1017.60	528.59	1000	1000	523.25
	D - C	11:6	1049.36	538.38	1000	1050	538.57
	D - C hs	13:7	1071.70	545.37	1100	1050	538.57
Just Major 7th	D - C hs	15:8	1088.27	550.61	1100	1050	538.57
ET Major 7th	D - C#	2 to the 11/12ths			1100		554.37
	D - C#	17:9	1101.04	554.69	1100	1100	554.37
	D - C#	19:10	1111.20	557.95	1100	1100	554.37
	D - C#	125:64	1158.94	573.55	1100	1150	570.60
ET Octave	D - D	2:1	1200.00	587.32	1200	1200	587.33

Bayati

Nahawand

Kurd

Husayni

Closely Related Maqamat: Tahir, Hawzi, Nawa, Kutshuk, Sultani Iraq, Gulizar, Kardan

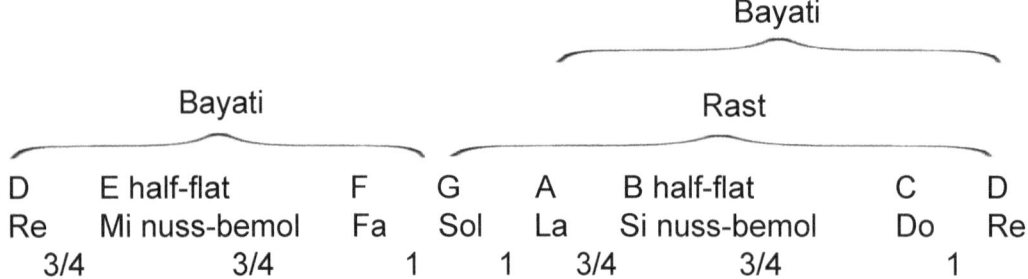

| | Bayati | | | | Rast | | | |
						Bayati		
D	E half-flat		F	G	A	B half-flat	C	D
Re	Mi nuss-bemol		Fa	Sol	La	Si nuss-bemol	Do	Re
	3/4	3/4		1	1	3/4	3/4	1

Possible Descriptions: Bayyati tetrachord on bottom; bayyati tetrachord on 5th; rast pentachord on 4th. Ghammaz on A.

This maqam is very basic. Like maqam Rast, it includes only original Arab-world notes and intervals.

The Arabic scale (see Tables at end of book) begins and ends on G. It is possible to see this scale as a very basic tuning which underlies almost all maqamat. The two charts on the opposite page show two different ways of calculating just intervals for this very basic maqam called husayni. For one chart we do the obvious thing: we begin our calculations from the tonic note D. For the other we begin on the low G in which case the D is actually calculated as a 5th rather than as a tonic.

As you can see, the pitches of every note in maqam huseyni are very close to each other no matter which way the calculations are done. The E half-flats differ by a couple of Hz but all the other notes are virtually identical. This tells us something about the translateability of tonics which are a 5th apart and about the long-term influence of the note G in Arabic music.

As you shall see when we look at maqamat based on B-half-flat (like Rahat el Arwah, Iraq and Farahnak) the power of this underlying G appears again. Awareness of this power of the G tonic can help us make choices as we tune our instruments which lead to powerfully harmonious results.

Maqam Huseyni on D

Approximate Interval	Approx Note Names	Ratio of Interval	Exact Just Cents	Exact Just Hz	Nearest 12-note ET Cents	Nearest 24-note ET Cents	Nearest 24-note ET Hz
ET Tonic on D	D - D	1:1	0.00	293.66	0	0	293.66
	D - D hs	25:24	70.67	305.90	100	50	302.26
	D - D#	19/18	93.60	309.97	100	100	311.13
ET Minor 2nd	D - D# or Eb	2 to the 1/12th			100		311.13
Just Minor 2nd	D - Eb	16:15	111.73	313.24	100	100	311.13
	D - E hf	13:12	138.57	318.13	100	150	320.24
	D - E hf	12:11	150.64	320.36	200	150	320.24
	D - E hf	11:10	165.00	323.03	200	150	320.24
Just Major 2nd Sm	D - E	10:9	182.40	326.29	200	200	329.63
ET Major 2nd	D - E	2 to the 1/6th			200		329.63
Just Major 2nd Lg	D - E	9:8	203.91	330.37	200	200	329.63
	D - E hs	8:7	231.17	335.61	200	250	339.28
	D - E hs	7:6	266.87	342.60	200	250	339.28
ET Minor 3rd	D - F	2 to the 1/4th			300		349.23
Just Minor 3rd	D - F	6:5	315.64	352.39	300	300	349.23
Just Major 3rd	D - F#	5:4	386.31	367.07	400	350	359.45
ET Major 3rd	D - F#	2 to the 1/3rd			400		369.99
	D - Gb	9:7	435.08	377.56	400	450	380.83
Just 4th	D - G	4:3	498.04	391.55	500	500	392.00
ET 4th	D - G	2 to the 5/12th			500		392.00
	D - G#	11:8	551.32	403.78	600	550	403.48
Just Tritone	D - Ab	7:5	582.51	411.12	600	600	415.30
	D - Ab	10:7	617.49	419.51	600	600	415.30
ET 5th	D - A	2 to the 7/12ths			700		440.00
Just 5th	D - A	3:2	701.95	440.49	700	700	440.00
	D - A#	11:7	782.49	461.47	800	750	452.89
ET Minor 6th	D - A# or Bb	2 to the 2/3rds			800		466.16
Just Minor 6th	D - Bb	8:5	813.69	469.86	800	800	466.16
	D - B hf	13:8	840.53	477.20	800	850	479.82
Just Major 6th	D - B hf	5:3	884.36	489.43	900	900	493.88
ET Major 6th	D - B	2 to the 3/4ths			900		493.88
	D - B	12:7	933.13	503.42	900	950	508.35
	D - B	7:4	968.83	513.91	1000	950	508.35
Just Minor7th Sm	D - C	16:9	996.09	522.06	1000	1000	523.25
ET Minor 7th	D - C	2 to the 5/6ths			1000		523.25
Just Minor 7th Lg	D - C	9:5	1017.60	528.59	1000	1000	523.25
	D - C hs	11:6	1049.36	538.38	1000	1050	538.57
	D - C hs	13:7	1071.70	545.37	1100	1050	538.57
Just Major 7th	D - C hs	15:8	1088.27	550.61	1100	1050	538.57
ET Major 7th	D - C#	2 to the 11/12ths			1100		554.37
	D - C#	17:9	1101.04	554.69	1100	1100	554.37
	D - C#	19:10	1111.20	557.95	1100	1100	554.37
	D - C#	125:64	1158.94	573.55	1100	1150	570.60
ET Octave	D - D	2:1	1200.00	587.32	1200	1200	587.33

Maqam Huseyni on D with hidden Tonic on G

Approximate Interval	Approx Note Names	Ratio of Interval	Exact Just Cents	Exact Just Hz	Nearest 12-note ET Cents	Nearest 24-note ET Cents	Nearest 24-note ET Hz
ET Tonic on G becomes 4th	G - G	1:1	0.00	196.00	0	0	196.00
Just Major 2nd Lg becomes 5th	G - A	9:8	203.91	220.50	200	200	220.00
Just Major 3rd becomes 6th	G - B hf	5:4	386.31	245.00	400	350	239.91
Just 4th becomes 7th	G - C	4:3	498.04	261.33	500	500	261.63
ET 5th becomes Tonic	G - D	2 to the 7/12ths			700	700	293.66
Just 5th	G - D	3:2	701.95	294.00	700	700	293.66
	G - D#	11:7	782.49	308.00	800	750	302.27
ET Minor 6th	G - D# or Eb	2 to the 2/3rds			800		311.13
Just Minor 6th	G - Eb	8:5	813.69	313.60	800	800	311.13
	G - E hf	13:8	840.53	318.50	800	850	320.25
Just Major 6th becomes 2nd	G - E hf	5:3	884.36	326.67	900	900	329.63
ET Major 6th	G - E	2 to the 3/4ths			900		329.63
	G - E#	7:4	968.83	343.00	1000	950	339.29
ET Minor 7th	G - F	2 to the 5/6ths			1000		349.23
Just Minor 7th Lg becomes Minor 3rd	G - F	9:5	1017.60	352.80	1000	1000	349.23
	G - F hs	11:6	1049.36	359.33	1000	1050	359.47
	G - F hs	13:7	1071.70	364.00	1100	1050	359.47
Just Major 7th	G - F#	15:8	1088.27	367.50	1100	1050	359.47
ET Major 7th	G - F#	2 to the 11/12ths			1100		369.99
	G - F#	17:9	1101.04	370.22	1100	1100	369.99
	G - F#	19:10	1111.20	372.40	1100	1100	369.99
	G - Gb	125:64	1158.94	382.81	1100	1150	380.84
ET Octave becomes 4th	G - G	2:1	1200.00	392.00	1200	1200	392.00
	G - G hs	25:24	1270.67	408.33	1300	1250	403.49
	G - G#	19:18	1293.60	413.78	1300	1300	415.31
ET Minor 2nd	G - G# or Ab	2 to the 1/12th			1300		415.31
Just Minor 2nd	G - Ab	16:15	1311.73	418.13	1300	1300	415.31
Just Major 2nd Sm	G - A	10:9	1382.40	435.55	1400	1400	440.00
ET Major 2nd	G - A	2 to the 1/6th	1400.00				440.00
Just Major 2nd Lg Becomes 5th	G - A	9:8	1403.91	440.00	1400	1400	440.00
	G - A hs	8:7	1431.17	448.00	1400	1450	452.90
	G - A hs	7:6	1466.87	457.33	1400	1450	452.90
ET Minor 3rd	G - Bb	2 to the 1/4th			1500		466.17
Just Minor 3rd	G - Bb	6:5	1515.64	470.40	1500	1500	466.17
	G - Bhf	11:9	1547.40	479.11	1500	1550	479.83
ET Qrtrtone	G - B hf	2 to the 1/4ths			1600	1550	479.83
Just Major 3rd Becomes 6th	G - B hf	5:4	1586.31	490.00	1600	1550	479.83
	G - B	9:7	1635.08	504.00	1600	1650	508.36
Just 4th becomes 7th	G - C	4:3	1698.04	522.67	1700	1700	523.26
ET 4th	G - C	2 to the 5/12th			1700	1700	523.26
Just Tritone	G - C#	7:5	1782.51	411.12	1800	1800	554.37
ET 5th becomes Tonic	G - D	2 to the 7/12ths			1900	1900	587.34
Just 5th	G - G	3:2	1901.95		1900	1900	587.34

Saba

Associated Moods:
Very powerfully mystical mood. Very different from Western scales. Used extensively in Sufi music. Sad, moving, sincere, tender. Common in folk music about unrequited love.

Closely Related Maqamat: Isfanak, Dugah, Sipahr, Naziniyaz

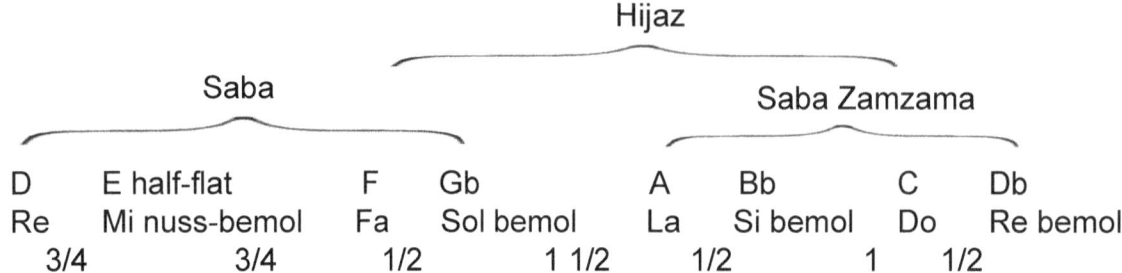

Possible Descriptions: Bayyati trichord on bottom; Saba tetrachord on bottom; Hijaz tetrachord on 3rd; Shehnaz maqam on 3rd; Saba Zamzama tetrachord on 5th.

Ghammaz on F. Staying in maqam shehnaz on F for extended periods is common before resolving back down through the saba jins to the D.

The notes above Db are E, F, Gb. (The E half-flat doesn't necessarily repeat in the high part of the maqam.)

Can be used as an ornamentation inside bayyati. Brief modulation to ajem ushayran common.

Since this scale has both a minor 3rd and a major 3rd it become possible to create a very unique mood with this maqam. Musicians find ways to play the F and the Gb in highly repetitive ways to emphasize the magic which they can produce together.

Since the minor and major 3rds in just intonation are very close together (only 70 cents apart) the interval between them becomes something very beautiful when played accurately, sometimes fading back and forth from one to the other with a small but continuous pitch shift which, although small, carries a huge amount of emotional power!

Tawfiq al-Sabbagh also suggests that for maximum ecstatic effect the F should be slightly sharp. The just minor 3rd, like the F in bayyati, is indeed 15 cents sharper than the ET position. He also suggests that an ecstatic variant for the F# can be found in a slightly sharper location. We could try the note generated by the 9:7 interval.

Maqam Saba on D

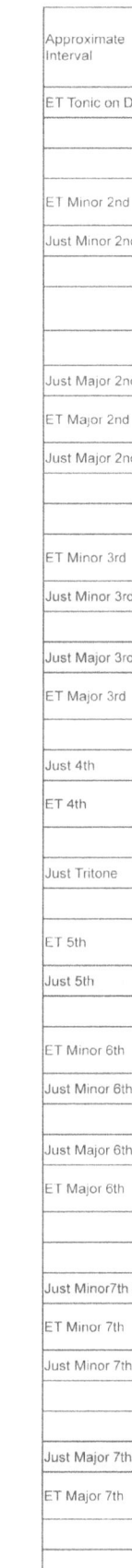

Approximate Interval	Approx Note Names	Ratio of Interval	Exact Just Cents	Exact Just Hz	Nearest 12-note ET Cents	Nearest 24-note ET Cents	Nearest 24-note ET Hz
ET Tonic on D	D - D	1:1	0.00	293.66	0	0	293.66
	D - D hs	25:24	70.67	305.90	100	50	302.26
	D - D#	19:18	93.60	309.97	100	100	311.13
ET Minor 2nd	D - D# or Eb	2 to the 1/12th			100		311.13
Just Minor 2nd	D - Eb	16:15	111.73	313.24	100	100	311.13
	D - E hf	13:12	138.57	318.13	100	150	320.24
	D - E hf	12:11	150.64	320.36	200	150	320.24
	D - E hf	11:10	165.00	323.03	200	150	320.24
Just Major 2nd Sm	D - E	10:9	182.40	326.29	200	200	329.63
ET Major 2nd	D - E	2 to the 1/6th			200		329.63
Just Major 2nd Lg	D - E	9:8	203.91	330.37	200	200	329.63
	D - E hs	8:7	231.17	335.61	200	250	339.28
	D - E hs	7:6	266.87	342.60	200	250	339.28
ET Minor 3rd	D - F	2 to the 1/4th			300		349.23
Just Minor 3rd	D - F	6:5	315.64	352.39	300	300	349.23
	D - F	11:9	347.41	358.92	300	350	359.45
Just Major 3rd	D - F#	5:4	386.31	367.07	400	350	359.45
ET Major 3rd	D - F#	2 to the 1/3rd			400		369.99
	D - Gb	9:7	435.08	377.56	400	450	380.83
Just 4th	D - G	4:3	498.04	391.55	500	500	392.00
ET 4th	D - G	2 to the 5/12th			500		392.00
	D - G#	11:8	551.32	403.78	600	550	403.48
Just Tritone	D - Ab	7:5	582.51	411.12	600	600	415.30
	D - Ab	10:7	617.49	419.51	600	600	415.30
ET 5th	D - A	2 to the 7/12ths			700		440.00
Just 5th	D - A	3:2	701.95	440.49	700	700	440.00
	D - A#	11:7	782.49	461.47	800	750	452.89
ET Minor 6th	D - A# or Bb	2 to the 2/3rds			800		466.16
Just Minor 6th	D - Bb	8:5	813.69	469.86	800	800	466.16
	D - B hf	13:8	840.53	477.20	800	850	479.82
Just Major 6th	D - B hf	5:3	884.36	489.43	900	900	493.88
ET Major 6th	D - B	2 to the 3/4ths			900		493.88
	D - B	12:7	933.13	503.42	900	950	508.35
	D - B	7:4	968.83	513.91	1000	950	508.35
Just Minor 7th Sm	D - C	16:9	996.09	522.06	1000	1000	523.25
ET Minor 7th	D - C	2 to the 5/6ths			1000		523.25
Just Minor 7th Lg	D - C	9:5	1017.60	528.59	1000	1000	523.25
	D - C	11:6	1049.36	538.38	1000	1050	538.57
	D - C hs	13:7	1071.70	545.37	1100	1050	538.57
Just Major 7th	D - C#	15:8	1088.27	550.61	1100	1050	538.57
ET Major 7th	D - C#	2 to the 11/12ths			1100		554.37
	D - C#	17:9	1101.04	554.69	1100	1100	554.37
	D - C#	19:10	1111.20	557.95	1100	1100	554.37
	D - C#	125:64	1158.94	573.55	1100	1150	570.60
ET Octave	D - D	2:1	1200.00	587.32	1200	1200	587.33

"Since, in just intonation, the destination is a discrete absolute, the singer can continuously contrast the fleeting adventures of the journey with the certainty of the outcome. This lends even 'simple' melodies a dramatic, emotionally redolent context that becomes the through line of the music, the plot of the story. As Pandit Pran Nath used to say, 'the music is between the notes.'"
-Mathieu 1997

"Just intonation is the basis for the music of ancient Greece, as well as other cultures, including those of India, Persia, China, and Japan. Just intonation is also vital to the 'a cappella' music of the West, from Gregorian chant and renaissance polyphony, to 'barbershop' harmonies."
--Michael Harrison Website

C-Based Maqams
Nahawand Family

Associated Moods: Nahawand is a straightforward and sweet maqam. It has two forms which correspond to the Natural Minor and the Harmonic Minor in Western music. Common in love songs. Delicate, sweet, tender, sentimental, sad.

Western music, especially from Greece, uses minor 3rd harmony extensively to achieve a deep soulful feeling. When just intervals are used these harmonies become exquisite and extremely magical to Western ears. Arab musicians play these harmonic intervals very occasionally but generally prefer ornamentation with decorative sequences of notes designed to paint the same intervals but with more motion in the music.

Related Audio Tracks on Harmonic Secrets CD1:

Track 26. Nahawand in C
Track 27. Nahawand Melody in C -- Rhythm: 3/4 Waltz
Track 28. Nahawand Taqasim in C by Adif
Track 29. Nahawand Taqasim in C by Jihad
Track 30. Nahawand Dulab in C by Adif
Track 31. Nahawand Vocal Taqasim in G by Saadoun

Nahawand

Closely Related Maqamat and Modes: Nihavent (Turkey), Buselik (Turkey), Natural Minor, Harmonic Minor, Aeolian Mode, Rahawi or Sahili (Algeria), Muhayar Sikah (Tunisia), Isfahan (Persia)

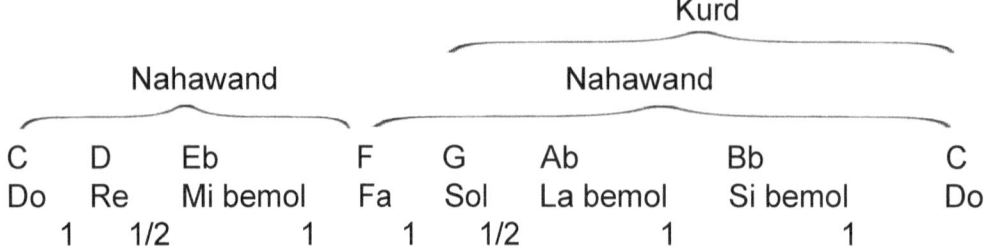

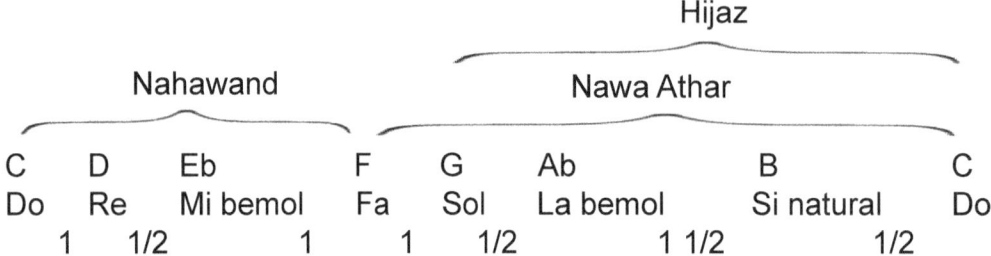

There are two variants of Nahawand which differ only by the position of the 7th. We will call them Nahawand 1 and Nahawand 2.

Possible Descriptions of Nahawand 1: Nahawand tetrachord on bottom; Nahawand pentachord on 4th; Kurd tetrachord on 5th.

Possible Descriptions of Nahawand 2: Nahawand tetrachord on bottom; Nawa Athar pentachord on 4th; Hijaz tetrachord on 5th.

The minor 3rd is harmonious in its "just" position which is a bit sharper than the ET Eb.

Maqam Nahawand 1 on C

Approximate Interval	Approx Note Names	Ratio of Interval	Exact Just Cents	Exact Just Hz	Nearest 12-note ET Cents	Nearest 24-note ET Cents	Nearest 24-note ET Hz
ET Tonic on C	C - C	1:1	0.00	261.63	0	0	261.63
	C - C hs	25:24	70.67	272.53	100	50	269.30
	C - C#	19/18	93.60	276.16	100	100	277.18
ET Minor 2nd	C - C# or Db	2 to the 1/12th			100		277.18
Just Minor 2nd	C - Db	16:15	111.73	279.07	100	100	277.18
	C - D hf	13:12	138.57	283.43	100	150	285.31
	C - D hf	12:11	150.64	285.42	200	150	285.31
	C - D hf	11:10	165.00	287.79	200	150	285.31
Just Major 2nd Sm	C - D	10:9	182.40	290.70	200	200	293.66
ET Major 2nd	C - D	2 to the 1/6th			200		293.66
Just Major 2nd Lg	C - D	9:8	203.91	294.33			
	C - D hs	8:7	231.17	299.01	200	250	302.27
	C - D hs	7:6	266.87	305.23	200	250	302.27
ET Minor 3rd	C - Eb	2 to the 1/4th			300	300	311.13
Just Minor 3rd	C - Eb	6:5	315.64	313.95			
	C - E hf	11:9	347.40	319.77	300	350	320.25
ET Qrtrtone	C - E hf	2 to the 1/4ths	350.00		300	350	320.25
Just Major 3rd	C - E hf	5:4	386.31	327.03	400	350	329.63
ET Major 3rd	C - E	2 to the 1/3rd			400		329.63
	C - Fb	9:7	435.08	336.38	400	450	339.29
Just 4th	C - F	4:3	498.04	348.83	500	500	349.23
ET 4th	C - F	2 to the 5/12ths			500		349.23
	C - F#	11:8	551.32	359.74	600	550	359.47
Just Tritone	C - Gb	7:5	582.51	366.28	600	600	369.99
	C - Gb	10:7	617.49	373.76	600	600	369.99
ET 5th	C - G	2 to the 7/12ths			700		392.00
Just 5th	C - G	3:2	701.95	392.46	700	700	392.00
	C - G#	11:7	782.49	411.13	800	750	403.49
ET Minor 6th	C - Ab	2 to the 2/3rds			800		415.30
Just Minor 6th	C - Ab	8:5	813.69	418.61	800		
	C - A hf	13:8	840.53	425.15	800	850	427.48
Just Major 6th	C - A	5:3	884.36	436.06	900	900	440
ET Major 6th	C - A	2 to the 3/4ths			900		440.00
	C - A#	12:7	933.13	448.51	900	950	452.90
	C - A#	7:4	968.83	457.85	1000	950	452.90
Just Minor 7th Sm	C - Bb	16:9	996.09	465.12	1000	1000	466.16
ET Minor 7th	C - Bb	2 to the 5/6ths			1000		466.16
Just Minor 7th Lg	C - Bb	9:5	1017.60	470.94	1000	1000	466.16
	C - B hf	11:6	1049.36	479.65	1000	1050	479.83
	C - B hf	13:7	1071.70	485.88	1100	1050	479.83
Just Major 7th	C - B	15:8	1088.27	490.57	1100	1050	479.83
ET Major 7th	C - B	2 to the 11/12ths			1100		493.88
	C - B	17:9	1101.04	494.19	1100	1100	493.88
	C - B	19:10	1111.20	497.10	1100	1100	493.88
	C - B#	125:64	1158.94	510.98	1100	1150	508.36
ET Octave	C - C	2:1	1200.00	523.26	1200	1200	523.25

Nahawand

Maqam Nahawand 2 on C

Approximate Interval	Approx Note Names	Ratio of Interval	Exact Just Cents	Exact Just Hz	Nearest 12-note ET Cents	Nearest 24-note ET Cents	Nearest 24-note ET Hz
ET Tonic on C	C - C	1:1	0.00	261.63	0	0	261.63
	C - C hs	25:24	70.67	272.53	100	50	269.30
	C - C#	19/18	93.60	276.16	100	100	277.18
ET Minor 2nd	C - C# or Db	2 to the 1/12th			100		277.18
Just Minor 2nd	C - Db	16:15	111.73	279.07	100	100	277.18
	C - D hf	13:12	138.57	283.43	100	150	285.31
	C - D hf	12:11	150.64	285.42	200	150	285.31
	C - D hf	11:10	165.00	287.79	200	150	285.31
Just Major 2nd Sm	C - D	10:9	182.40	290.70	200	200	293.66
ET Major 2nd	C - D	2 to the 1/6th			200		293.66
Just Major 2nd Lg	C - D	9:8	203.91	294.33	200	200	293.66
	C - D hs	8:7	231.17	299.01	200	250	302.27
	C - D hs	7:6	266.87	305.23	200	250	302.27
ET Minor 3rd	C - Eb	2 to the 1/4th			300	300	311.13
Just Minor 3rd	C - Eb	6:5	315.64	313.95	300	300	311.13
	C - E hf	11:9	347.40	319.77	300	350	320.25
ET Qrtrtone	C - E hf	2 to the 1/4ths	350.00		300	350	320.25
Just Major 3rd	C - E hf	5:4	386.31	327.03	400	350	329.63
ET Major 3rd	C - E	2 to the 1/3rd			400		329.63
	C - Fb	9:7	435.08	336.38	400	450	339.29
Just 4th	C - F	4:3	498.04	348.83	500	500	349.23
ET 4th	C - F	2 to the 5/12ths			500		349.23
	C - F#	11:8	551.32	359.74	600	550	359.47
Just Tritone	C - Gb	7:5	582.51	366.28	600	600	369.99
	C - Gb	10:7	617.49	373.76	600	600	369.99
ET 5th	C - G	2 to the 7/12ths			700		392.00
Just 5th	C - G	3:2	701.95	392.46	700	700	392.00
	C - G#	11:7	782.49	411.13	800	750	403.49
ET Minor 6th	C - Ab	2 to the 2/3rds			800		415.30
Just Minor 6th	C - Ab	8:5	813.69	418.61	800	800	415.30
	C - A hf	13:8	840.53	425.15	800	850	427.48
Just Major 6th	C - A	5:3	884.36	436.06	900	900	440.00
ET Major 6th	C - A	2 to the 3/4ths			900		440.00
	C - A#	12:7	933.13	448.51	900	950	452.90
	C - A#	7:4	968.83	457.85	1000	950	452.90
Just Minor 7th Sm	C - Bb	16:9	996.09	465.12	1000	1000	466.16
ET Minor 7th	C - Bb	2 to the 5/6ths			1000		466.16
Just Minor 7th Lg	C - Bb	9:5	1017.60	470.94	1000	1000	466.16
	C - B hf	11:6	1049.36	479.65	1000	1050	479.83
	C - B hf	13:7	1071.70	485.88	1100	1050	479.83
Just Major 7th	C - B	15:8	1088.27	490.57	1100	1050	479.83
ET Major 7th	C - B	2 to the 11/12ths			1100		493.88
	C - B	17:9	1101.04	494.19	1100	1100	493.88
	C - B	19:10	1111.20	497.10	1100	1100	493.88
	C - B#	125:64	1158.94	510.98	1100	1150	508.36
ET Octave	C - C	2:1	1200.00	523.26	1200	1200	523.25

Nahawand

Hijaz

"In cultures where in-tune singing is primary, the singing voice is essentially straight, with vibrato used deliberately for ornamental and evocative purposes. The situation in the West is quite different... ...a vibrato so wide...that the center of pitch easily becomes unfocused... refinement of pitch is rare. Once you know you are in tune, once you feel that, then you can use vibrato intentionally as a beautiful conscious refinement."
-Mathieu 1997

"This was readily noticed in the sound of the equal tempered major thirds: lustrous and calm in their pure form, they were now slightly rough and somewhat bland."
--Isacoff 2001

C-Based Maqams
Rast Family

Associated Moods: Common in religious music, call to prayer. Romantic and positive, cheerful, stately and elegant. Classical. Beautiful landscapes, morning or daytime energy. Joy, liveliness, gravity, dignity, enthusiasm, courage, exhaltedness, austere joy, unflinching zeal, strength, vigor, burning passion.

Maqam Rast contains only notes originating from the ancient basic Arab scale. It is often considered to be the most fundamental Arab maqam with all others deriving therefrom. This may be even more truly the case when Rast is transposed to G and may be named "Yakah." It appears that when G is used as the tonic for a justly intonated major scale, we automatically generate most of the notes found in most maqamat. The ajnas which compose the various maqamat can largely be found within the justly intonated G major scale. Of course different artists from different parts of the Arab world have differing favored pitches and are seldom aware of the concept of just intonation so there is no absolute rule. The practice of using 24-note Equal Temperament has had a very large influence which pulls artists away from the justly intonated intervals. But people with refined listening skills will inevitably be attracted to the perfect harmonies of the just intervals and agree that these pitches are the correct ones for the Arabic scales.

Maqams Suznak, Suzdilar, Nerz Rast, Rast Beshayer, Dalanshin and Zawil are all commonly employed during modulations within Rast.

"The major third is where equal temperament fails the harmonic purity test... This interval is the invisible elephant in our musical system today. Nobody notices how awful the major thirds are. Nobody comments. Nobody even recognizes that the elephant exists. Living with this elephant is assumed to be so much better than the unknown alternatives that it's a nonissue. Asked about it, some people even claim to prefer the elephant; they have grown to like the elephantine thirds. I'm here to shake those people out of their cozy state of denial. It's the acoustics, baby: ya gotta feel the vibrations."
--Duffin 2007

Rast

Closely Related Maqamat: Buzurg, Shawqidil

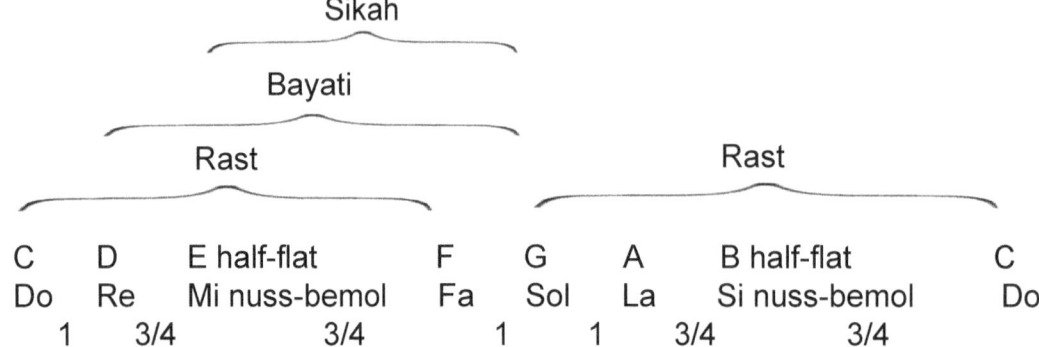

C	D	E half-flat	F	G	A	B half-flat	C
Do	Re	Mi nuss-bemol	Fa	Sol	La	Si nuss-bemol	Do
1	3/4	3/4	1	1	3/4	3/4	

Possible Descriptions: Rast pentachord on bottom; Rast tetrachord on 5th; Bayyati tetrachord on the 2nd; Husayni maqam on the 2nd; Sikah trichord on the 3rd; Sikah maqam on the 3rd.

This maqam is very basic. Like maqam Husayni, it includes only original Arab-world notes and intervals. The E half-flat in Rast is very slightly sharper than the E half-flat in Bayyati, as we would expect from studying the just intervals.

 **Related Audio Tracks on Harmonic Secrets CD2:**

Track 1. **Rast in C**
Track 2. **Rast Melody in C -- Rhythm: 2/4 Ayub**
Track 3. **Rast Taqasim in C by Jihad**
Track 4. **Rast Taqasim in C by Adif**
Track 5. **Rast Taqasim in C by Saadoun**
Track 6. **Rast Dulab in C by Adif**

Maqam Rast on C

Arab musicians usually claim that the E half-flat in Rast is sharper than the E half-flat in Bayati. This makes it clear that they are not really following the 24-note ET system although that system is used for teaching beginners.

The E half-flat defined by the 5:4 ratio is frequently what they are describing.

Of course the E half-flat defined by the 16:13 or the 11:9 ratio is also a harmonious interval for anyone looking to play an audibly flatter note which is also close to the ET quartertone position.

Instruments like the oud, the violin and the buzuq have open strings commonly tuned to notes like D and G. Less attention is customarily paid to variable pitch possibilities of these notes as they end up being fixed. I have created the tables in this book in a manner which reflects this reality.

The obvious just 6th in maqam Rast is 15 cents flatter than the ET equivalent.
The just choices for the 7th are plentiful. I picked the 11:6 interval to highlight but I could have chosen the 13:7 or the 15:8 interval.
When musicians have 2 or 3 equally appealing choices it is difficult to establish teaching standards. This is probably why we don't hear as many comments attempting to describe the exact pitch of the Rast 7th.

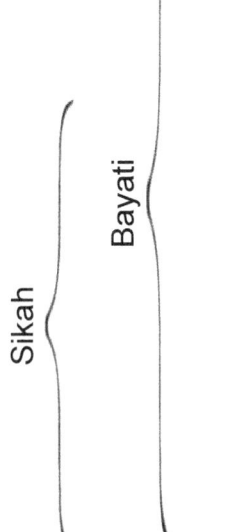

Approximate Interval	Approx Note Names	Ratio of Interval	Exact Just Cents	Exact Just Hz	Nearest 12-note ET Cents	Nearest 24-note ET Cents	Nearest 24-note ET Hz
ET Tonic on C	C - C	1:1	0.00	261.63	0	0	261.63
	C - C hs	25:24	70.67	272.53	100	50	269.30
	C - C#	19:18	93.60	276.16	100	100	277.18
ET Minor 2nd	C - C# or Db	2 to the 1/12th			100		277.18
Just Minor 2nd	C - Db	16:15	111.73	279.07	100	100	277.18
	C - D hf	13:12	138.57	283.43	100	150	285.31
	C - D hf	12:11	150.64	285.42	200	150	285.31
	C - D hf	11:10	165.00	287.79	200	150	285.31
Just Major 2nd Sm	C - D	10:9	182.40	290.70	200	200	293.66
ET Major 2nd	C - D	2 to the 1/6th			200		293.66
Just Major 2nd Lg	C - D	9:8	203.91	294.33	200	200	293.66
	C - D hs	8:7	231.17	299.01	200	250	302.27
	C - D hs	7:6	266.87	305.23	200	250	302.27
ET Minor 3rd	C - Eb	2 to the 1/4th			300		311.13
Just Minor 3rd	C - Eb	6:5	315.64	313.95	300	300	311.13
	C - E hf	11:9	347.40	319.77	300	350	320.25
ET Qrtrtone	C - E hf	2 to the 1/4ths	350.00		300	350	320.25
	C - E hf	16:13	359.47	322.01	400	350	320.25
	C - E hf	21:17	365.82	323.19	400	350	320.25
Just Major 3rd	C - E hf	5:4	386.31	327.03	400	350	329.63
ET Major 3rd	C - E	2 to the 1/3rd			400		329.63
	C - E	81/64	407.82	331.13	400	400	329.63
	C - E	19:15	409.24	331.40	400	400	329.63
	C - E	14:11	417.51	332.98	400	400	329.63
	C - Fb	9:7	435.08	336.38	400	450	339.29
Just 4th	C - F	4:3	498.04	348.83	500	500	349.23
ET 4th	C - F	2 to the 5/12ths			500		349.23
	C - F#	11:8	551.32	359.74	600	550	359.47
Just Tritone	C - Gb	7:5	582.51	366.28	600	600	369.99
	C - Gb	10:7	617.49	373.76	600	600	369.99
ET 5th	C - G	2 to the 7/12ths			700		392.00
Just 5th	C - G	3:2	701.95	392.46	700	700	392.00
	C - G#	11:7	782.49	411.13	800	750	403.49
ET Minor 6th	C - Ab	2 to the 2/3rds			800		415.30
Just Minor 6th	C - Ab	8:5	813.69	418.61	800	800	415.30
	C - A hf	13:8	840.53	425.15	800	850	427.48
Just Major 6th	C - A	5:3	884.36	436.06	900	900	440.00
ET Major 6th	C - A	2 to the 3/4ths			900		440.00
	C - A#	12:7	933.13	448.51	900	950	452.90
	C - A#	7:4	968.83	457.85	1000	950	452.90
Just Minor 7th Sm	C - Bb	16:9	996.09	465.12	1000	1000	466.16
ET Minor 7th	C - Bb	2 to the 5/6ths			1000		466.16
Just Minor 7th Lg	C - Bb	9:5	1017.60	470.94	1000	1000	466.16
	C - B hf	11:6	1049.36	479.65	1000	1050	479.83
	C - B hf	13:7	1071.70	485.88	1100	1050	479.83
Just Major 7th	C - B	15:8	1088.27	490.57	1100	1050	479.83
ET Major 7th	C - B	2 to the 11/12ths			1100		493.88
	C - B	17:9	1101.04	494.19	1100	1100	493.88
	C - B	19:10	1111.20	497.10	1100	1100	493.88
	C - B#	125:64	1158.94	510.98	1100	1150	508.36
ET Octave	C - C	2:1	1200.00	523.26	1200	1200	523.25

Suznak

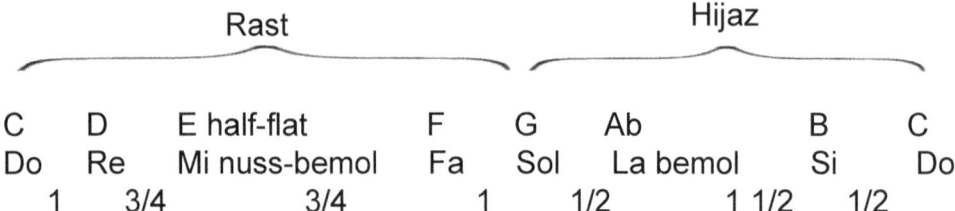

C	D	E half-flat	F	G	Ab	B	C
Do	Re	Mi nuss-bemol	Fa	Sol	La bemol	Si	Do
1	3/4	3/4	1	1/2	1 1/2	1/2	

Possible Descriptions: Rast pentachord on bottom; Hijaz tetrachord on 5th; Bayati tetrachord on the 2nd; Shuri Maqam on the 2nd; Sikah trichord on the 3rd; Huzam maqam on the 3rd, Nawa Athar pentachord on the 4th.
Very frequently used as ornament in Rast.

Associated Moods: Longing, desire, agony, burning, sorrow, grief.

"No matter how masterful they are as musicians, many performers today don't hear how the ET major third is because it's what they're used to (conditioning) and because they've never heard an acoustically pure major third (ignorance). They're convinced that the ET major third must be the proper sound because it's what modern -- and therefore obviously more enlightened -- theorists have devised (delusion), and they wouldn't want to change because it would be too much trouble (convenience). Mostly they don't want to think about it (oblivion). As inconvenient as it may be, it's time for modern musicians to think about this and, where appropriate, make some changes."
--Duffin 2007

Related Audio Tracks on Harmonic Secrets CD2:

Track 7.   Suznak in C
Track 8.   Suznak Melody in C -- Rhythm: 8/8 Wahda

Maqam Suznak on C

Approximate Interval	Approx Note Names	Ratio of Interval	Exact Just Cents	Exact Just Hz	Nearest 12-note ET Cents	Nearest 24-note ET Cents	Nearest 24-note ET Hz
ET Tonic on C	C - C	1:1	0.00	261.63	0	0	261.63
	C - C hs	25:24	70.67	272.53	100	50	269.30
	C - C#	19/18	93.60	276.16	100	100	277.18
ET Minor 2nd	C - C# or Db	2 to the 1/12th			100		277.18
Just Minor 2nd	C - Db	16:15	111.73	279.07	100	100	277.18
	C - D hf	13:12	138.57	283.43	100	150	285.31
	C - D hf	12:11	150.64	285.42	200	150	285.31
	C - D hf	11:10	165.00	287.79	200	150	285.31
Just Major 2nd Sm	C - D	10:9	182.40	290.70	200	200	293.66
ET Major 2nd	C - D	2 to the 1/6th			200		293.66
Just Major 2nd Lg	C - D	9:8	203.91	294.33	200	200	293.66
	C - D hs	8:7	231.17	299.01	200	250	302.27
	C - D hs	7/6	266.87	305.23	200	250	302.27
ET Minor 3rd	C - Eb	2 to the 1/4th			300		311.13
Just Minor 3rd	C - Eb	6:5	315.64	313.95	300	300	311.13
	C - E hf	11:9	347.40	319.77	300	350	320.25
ET Qrtrtone	C - E hf	2 to the 1/4ths	350.00		300	350	320.25
	C - E hf	16/13	359.47	322.01	400	350	320.25
	C - E hf	21/17	365.82	323.19	400	350	320.25
Just Major 3rd	C - E hf	5:4	386.31	327.03	400	350	329.63
ET Major 3rd	C - E	2 to the 1/3rd			400		329.63
	C - E	24/19	404.44	330.48	400	400	329.63
	C - E	19:15	409.24	331.40	400	400	329.63
	C - E	14/11	417.51	332.98	400	400	329.63
	C - Fb	9:7	435.08	336.38	400	450	339.29
Just 4th	C - F	4:3	498.04	348.83	500	500	349.23
ET 4th	C - F	2 to the 5/12ths			500		349.23
	C - F#	11:8	551.32	359.74	600	550	359.47
Just Tritone	C - Gb	7:5	582.51	366.28	600	600	369.99
	C - Gb	10:7	617.49	373.76	600	600	369.99
ET 5th	C - G	2 to the 7/12ths			700		392.00
Just 5th	C - G	3:2	701.95	392.46	700	700	392.00
	C - G#	11:7	782.49	411.13	800	750	403.49
ET Minor 6th	C - Ab	2 to the 2/3rds			800		415.30
Just Minor 6th	C - Ab	8:5	813.69	418.61	800	800	415.30
	C - A hf	13:8	840.53	425.15	800	850	427.48
Just Major 6th	C - A	5:3	884.36	436.06	900	900	440.00
ET Major 6th	C - A	2 to the 3/4ths			900		440.00
	C - A#	12:7	933.13	448.51	900	950	452.90
	C - A#	7:4	968.83	457.85	1000	950	452.90
Just Minor 7th Sm	C - Bb	16:9	996.09	465.12	1000	1000	466.16
ET Minor 7th	C - Bb	2 to the 5/6ths			1000		466.16
Just Minor 7th Lg	C - Bb	9:5	1017.60	470.94	1000	1000	466.16
	C - B hf	11:6	1049.36	479.65	1000	1050	479.83
	C - B hf	13:7	1071.70	485.88	1100	1050	479.83
Just Major 7th	C - B	15:8	1088.27	490.57	1100	1050	479.83
ET Major 7th	C - B	2 to the 11/12ths			1100		493.88
	C - B	17:9	1101.04	494.19	1100	1100	493.88
	C - B	19:10	1111.20	497.10	1100	1100	493.88
	C - B#	125:64	1158.94	510.98	1100	1150	508.36
ET Octave	C - C	2:1	1200.00	523.26	1200	1200	523.25

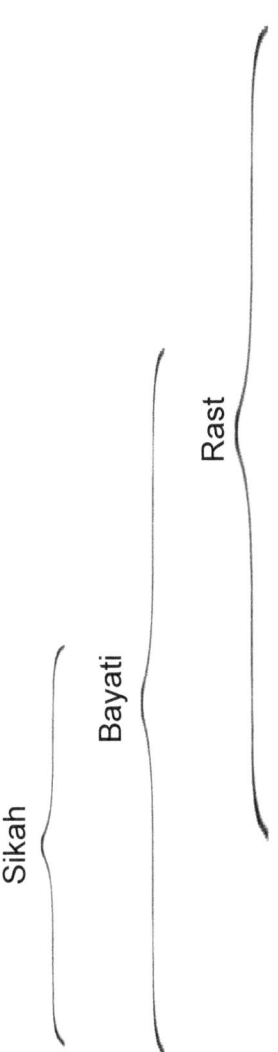

Suznak is to Rast what Nahawand 2 is to Nahawand 1.
(Both Suznak and Nahawand 2 have jins hijaz on the 5th.)

C-Based Maqams
Nawa Athar Family

Associated Moods: Enchantment, delicate, amorous affection.

Nawa Athar

Closely Related Maqamat: Hayan, Nevaser (Turkey)

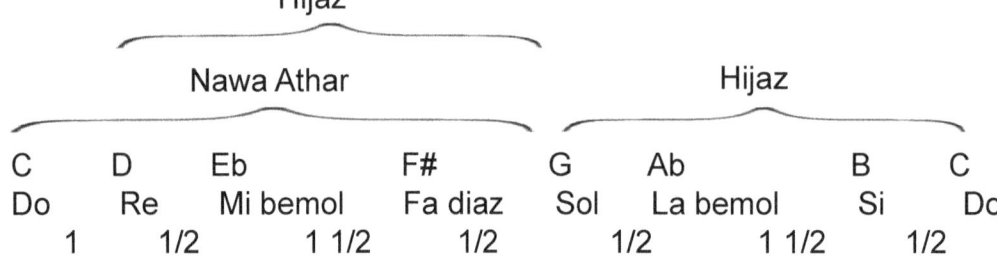

Possible Descriptions: Nawa Athar pentachord on bottom; Hijaz tetrachord on 2nd; Hijaz tetrachord on the 5th.
Ghammaz is G and it is vocally and instrumentally elegant to create musical ornaments showing off the two half-step intervals above and below the G.

Related Audio Tracks on Harmonic Secrets CD2:

Track 9. Nawa Athar in C
Track 10. Nawa Athar Melody in C -- Rhythm: 5/4

Maqam Nawa Athar on C

Approximate Interval	Approx Note Names	Ratio of Interval	Exact Just Cents	Exact Just Hz	Nearest 12-note ET Cents	Nearest 24-note ET Cents	Nearest 24-note ET Hz
ET Tonic on C	C - C	1:1	0.00	261.63	0	0	261.63
	C - C hs	25:24	70.67	272.53	100	50	269.30
	C - C#	19/18	93.60	276.16	100	100	277.18
ET Minor 2nd	C - C# or Db	2 to the 1/12th			100		277.18
Just Minor 2nd	C - Db	16:15	111.73	279.07	100	100	277.18
	C - D hf	13:12	138.57	283.43	100	150	285.31
	C - D hf	12:11	150.64	285.42	200	150	285.31
	C - D hf	11:10	165.00	287.79	200	150	285.31
Just Major 2nd Sm	C - D	10:9	182.40	290.70	200	200	293.66
ET Major 2nd	C - D	2 to the 1/6th			200		293.66
Just Major 2nd Lg	C - D	9:8	203.91	294.33	200	200	293.66
	C - D hs	8:7	231.17	299.01	200	250	302.27
	C - D hs	7:6	266.87	305.23	200	250	302.27
ET Minor 3rd	C - Eb	2 to the 1/4th			300		311.13
Just Minor 3rd	C - Eb	6:5	315.64	313.95	300	300	311.13
	C - E hf	11:9	347.40	319.77	300	350	320.25
ET Qrtrtone	C - E hf	2 to the 1/4ths	350.00		300	350	320.25
Just Major 3rd	C - E hf	5:4	386.31	327.03	400	350	329.63
ET Major 3rd	C - E	2 to the 1/3rd			400		329.63
	C - Fb	9:7	435.08	336.38	400	450	339.29
Just 4th	C - F	4:3	498.04	348.83	500	500	349.23
ET 4th	C - F	2 to the 5/12ths			500		349.23
	C - F#	11:8	551.32	359.74	600	550	359.47
Just Tritone	C - Gb	7:5	582.51	366.28	600	600	369.99
	C - Gb	10:7	617.49	373.76	600	600	369.99
ET 5th	C - G	2 to the 7/12ths			700		392.00
Just 5th	C - G	3:2	701.95	392.46	700	700	392.00
	C - G#	11:7	782.49	411.13	800	750	403.49
ET Minor 6th	C - Ab	2 to the 2/3rds			800		415.30
Just Minor 6th	C - Ab	8:5	813.69	418.61	800	800	415.30
	C - A hf	13:8	840.53	425.15	800	850	427.48
Just Major 6th	C - A	5:3	884.36	436.06	900	900	440.00
ET Major 6th	C - A	2 to the 3/4ths			900		440.00
	C - A#	12:7	933.13	448.51	900	950	452.90
	C - A#	7:4	968.83	457.85	1000	950	452.90
Just Minor 7th Sm	C - Bb	16:9	996.09	465.12	1000	1000	466.16
ET Minor 7th	C - Bb	2 to the 5/6ths			1000		466.16
Just Minor 7th Lg	C - Bb	9:5	1017.60	470.94	1000	1000	466.16
	C - B hf	11:6	1049.36	479.65	1000	1050	479.83
	C - B hf	13:7	1071.70	485.88	1100	1050	479.83
Just Major 7th	C - B	15:8	1088.27	490.57	1100	1050	479.83
ET Major 7th	C - B	2 to the 11/12ths			1100		493.88
	C - B	17:9	1101.04	494.19	1100	1100	493.88
	C - B	19:10	1111.20	497.10	1100	1100	493.88
	C - B#	125:64	1158.94	510.98	1100	1150	508.36
ET Octave	C - C	2:1	1200.00	523.26	1200	1200	523.25

Bracket groupings: Nawa Athar spans the upper portion; Hijaz brackets appear on both the upper (C to E hf region) and lower (G to B region) sections.

Athar Kurd

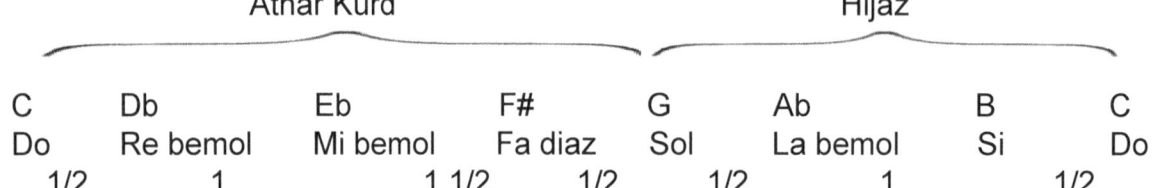

C	Db	Eb	F#	G	Ab	B	C
Do	Re bemol	Mi bemol	Fa diaz	Sol	La bemol	Si	Do
1/2	1	1 1/2	1/2	1/2	1	1/2	

Possible Descriptions: Athar Kurd pentachord on bottom; Hijaz tetrachord on 5th.

"In the 16th century, as a cartography rage swept over Europe, meantone temperaments proliferated like maps of musical neighborhoods."
--Isacoff 2001

Related Audio Tracks on Harmonic Secrets CD2:

Track 11. Athar Kurd in C
Track 12. Athar Kurd Melody in C -- Rhythm: 8/8 Tsiftitelli

Maqam Athar Kurd on C

Approximate Interval	Approx. Note Names	Ratio of Interval	Exact Just Cents	Exact Just Hz	Nearest 12-note ET Cents	Nearest 24-note ET Cents	Nearest 24-note ET Hz
ET Tonic on C	C - C	1:1	0.00	261.63	0	0	261.63
	C - C hs	25:24	70.67	272.53	100	50	269.30
	C - C#	19/18	93.60	276.16	100	100	277.18
ET Minor 2nd	C - C# or Db	2 to the 1/12th			100		277.18
Just Minor 2nd	C - Db	16:15	111.73	279.07	100	100	277.18
	C - D hf	13:12	138.57	283.43	100	150	285.31
	C - D hf	12:11	150.64	285.42	200	150	285.31
	C - D hf	11:10	165.00	287.79	200	150	285.31
Just Major 2nd Sm	C - D	10:9	182.40	290.70	200	200	293.66
ET Major 2nd	C - D	2 to the 1/6th			200		293.66
Just Major 2nd Lg	C - D	9:8	203.91	294.33	200	200	293.66
	C - D hs	8:7	231.17	299.01	200	250	302.27
	C - D hs	7:6	266.87	305.23	200	250	302.27
ET Minor 3rd	C - Eb	2 to the 1/4th			300		311.13
Just Minor 3rd	C - Eb	6:5	315.64	313.95	300	300	311.13
	C - E hf	11:9	347.40	319.77	300	350	320.25
ET Qrtrtone	C - E hf	2 to the 1/4ths	350.00		300	350	320.25
Just Major 3rd	C - E hf	5:4	386.31	327.03	400	350	329.63
ET Major 3rd	C - E	2 to the 1/3rd			400		329.63
	C - Fb	9:7	435.08	336.38	400	450	339.29
Just 4th	C - F	4:3	498.04	348.83	500	500	349.23
ET 4th	C - F	2 to the 5/12ths			500		349.23
	C - F#	11:8	551.32	359.74	600	550	359.47
Just Tritone	C - Gb	7:5	582.51	366.28	600	600	369.99
	C - Gb	10:7	617.49	373.76	600	600	369.99
ET 5th	C - G	2 to the 7/12ths			700		392.00
Just 5th	C - G	3:2	701.95	392.46	700	700	392.00
	C - G#	11:7	782.49	411.13	800	750	403.49
ET Minor 6th	C - Ab	2 to the 2/3rds			800		415.30
Just Minor 6th	C - Ab	8:5	813.69	418.61	800	800	415.30
	C - A hf	13:8	840.53	425.15	800	850	427.48
Just Major 6th	C - A	5:3	884.36	436.06	900	900	440.00
ET Major 6th	C - A	2 to the 3/4ths			900		440.00
	C - A#	12:7	933.13	448.51	900	950	452.90
	C - A#	7:4	968.83	457.85	1000	950	452.90
Just Minor 7th Sm	C - Bb	16:9	996.09	465.12	1000	1000	466.16
ET Minor 7th	C - Bb	2 to the 5/6ths			1000		466.16
Just Minor 7th Lg	C - Bb	9:5	1017.60	470.94	1000	1000	466.16
	C - B hf	11:6	1049.36	479.65	1000	1050	479.83
	C - B hf	13:7	1071.70	485.88	1100	1050	479.83
Just Major 7th	C - B	15:8	1088.27	490.57	1100	1050	479.83
ET Major 7th	C - B	2 to the 11/12ths			1100		493.88
	C - B	17:9	1101.04	494.19	1100	1100	493.88
	C - B	19:10	1111.20	497.10	1100	1100	493.88
	C - B#	125:64	1158.94	510.98	1100	1150	508.36
ET Octave	C - C	2:1	1200.00	523.26	1200	1200	523.25

Athar Kurd: rows from ET Tonic on C through Just 5th

Hijaz: rows from C - G# through ET Octave

C-Based Maqams
Hijaz Kar Family

Hijaz Kar

Closely Related Maqamat: Chargah or Chahargah (Persia)

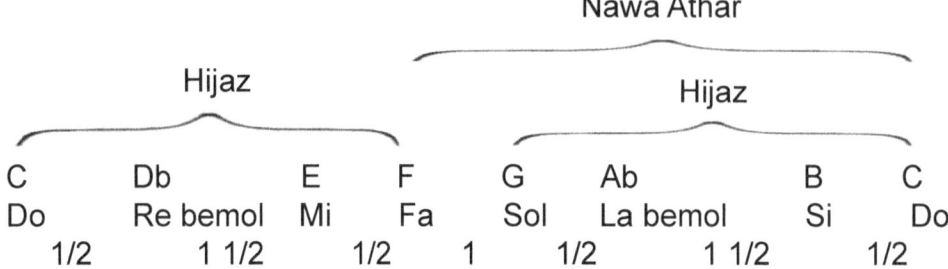

Possible Descriptions: Hijaz pentachord on bottom; Hijaz tetrachord on 5th; Nakriz pentachord on the 4th.

It is also traditional to regard Shehnaz as a transposition of Hijaz Kar rather than Hijaz Kar as a transposition of Shehnaz. Either way the notes remain the same.

The more advanced traditional teachings present distinctions about phrasing within different maqamat although they may employ the same ajnas (tetrachords). Frequently differences are taught which affect ascending runs versus descending patterns. More serious students can consult some of the references mentioned in the bibliography for information about these traditional movement patterns.

Related Audio Tracks on Harmonic Secrets CD2:

Track 13. Hijaz Kar in C
Track 14. Hijaz Kar Melody in C -- Rhythm: 4/4 Maqsum
Track 15. Hijaz Kar Taqasim in C by Jihad
Track 16. Hijaz Kar Taqasim in C by Adif

Maqam Hijaz Kar on C

Approximate Interval	Approx. Note Names	Ratio of Interval	Exact Just Cents	Exact Just Hz	Nearest 12-note ET Cents	Nearest 24-note ET Cents	Nearest 24-note ET Hz
ET Tonic on C	C - C	1:1	0.00	261.63	0	0	261.63
	C - C hs	25:24	70.67	272.53	100	50	269.30
	C - C#	19:18	93.60	276.16	100	100	277.18
ET Minor 2nd	C - C# or Db	2 to the 1/12th			100		277.18
Just Minor 2nd	C - Db	16:15	111.73	279.07	100	100	277.18
	C - D hf	13:12	138.57	283.43	100	150	285.31
	C - D hf	12:11	150.64	285.42	200	150	285.31
	C - D hf	11:10	165.00	287.79	200	150	285.31
Just Major 2nd Sm	C - D	10:9	182.40	290.70	200	200	293.66
ET Major 2nd	C - D	2 to the 1/6th			200		293.66
Just Major 2nd Lg	C - D	9:8	203.91	294.33	200	200	293.66
	C - D hs	8:7	231.17	299.01	200	250	302.27
	C - D hs	7:6	266.87	305.23	200	250	302.27
ET Minor 3rd	C - Eb	2 to the 1/4th			300		311.13
Just Minor 3rd	C - Eb	6:5	315.64	313.95	300	300	311.13
	C - E hf	11:9	347.40	319.77	300	350	320.25
ET Qrtrtone	C - E hf	2 to the 1/4ths	350.00		300	350	320.25
Just Major 3rd	C - E	5:4	386.31	327.03	400	350	329.63
ET Major 3rd	C - E	2 to the 1/3rd			400		329.63
	C - Fb	9:7	435.08	336.38	400	450	339.29
Just 4th	C - F	4:3	498.04	348.83	500	500	349.23
ET 4th	C - F	2 to the 5/12ths			500		349.23
	C - F#	11:8	551.32	359.74	600	550	359.47
Just Tritone	C - Gb	7:5	582.51	366.28	600	600	369.99
	C - Gb	10:7	617.49	373.76	600	600	369.99
ET 5th	C - G	2 to the 7/12ths			700		392.00
Just 5th	C - G	3:2	701.95	392.46	700	700	392.00
	C - G#	11:7	782.49	411.13	800	750	403.49
ET Minor 6th	C - Ab	2 to the 2/3rds			800		415.30
Just Minor 6th	C - Ab	8:5	813.69	418.61	800	800	415.30
	C - A hf	13:8	840.53	425.15	800	850	427.48
Just Major 6th	C - A	5:3	884.36	436.06	900	900	440.00
ET Major 6th	C - A	2 to the 3/4ths			900		440.00
	C - A#	12:7	933.13	448.51	900	950	452.90
	C - A#	7:4	968.83	457.85	1000	950	452.90
Just Minor 7th Sm	C - Bb	16:9	996.09	465.12	1000	1000	466.16
ET Minor 7th	C - Bb	2 to the 5/6ths			1000		466.16
Just Minor 7th Lg	C - Bb	9:5	1017.60	470.94	1000	1000	466.16
	C - B hf	11:6	1049.36	479.65	1000	1050	479.83
	C - B hf	13:7	1071.70	485.88	1100	1050	479.83
Just Major 7th	C - B	15:8	1088.27	490.57	1100	1050	479.83
ET Major 7th	C - B	2 to the 11/12ths			1100		493.88
	C - B	17:9	1101.04	494.19	1100	1100	493.88
	C - B	19:10	1111.20	497.10	1100	1100	493.88
	C - B#	125:64	1158.94	510.98	1100	1150	508.36
ET Octave	C - C	2:1	1200.00	523.26	1200	1200	523.25

Brackets on left (outermost to innermost):
- Nawa Athar (spans from ET Tonic through most of the table to Just 5th area and beyond)
- Hijaz (upper: from ET Tonic through Just Major 3rd / ET Major 3rd area)
- Hijaz (lower: from Just 5th / C-G# through ET Octave area)

Bb-Based Maqams
Ajam Family

Associated Moods: Bright, happy, majesty, pride, loftiness, national anthems, strength, seriousness.

Ajam Ushayran (Bb Major)

Closely Related: Huezawi (Iraqi), Ionian Mode

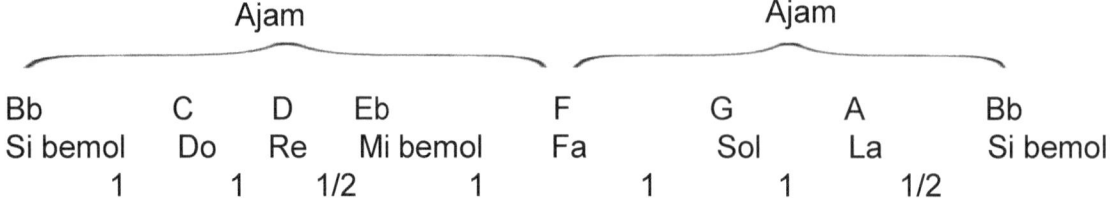

Possible Descriptions: Ajam or "Jaharka" pentachord on bottom; Ajam or "Jaharka" tetrachord on 5th; Farahfaza maqam on 6th; Ajam Ushayran is "relative major" to Farahfaza (G minor scale).

Some say that the 3rd note in Ajam should be slightly flatter than the 3rd in a Western major scale. Justly intonated major thirds are, of course, flattened from their ET positions by about 18 cents.

It is common to show a brief interlude into Ajam during taqasims based in Saba or Bayyati. This is accomplished by first emphasizing the 6th note in one of those maqams which is, of course, Bb, then descending the Ajam scale and re-ascending it back to the Bb. Once this has been shown, the maqam usually returns to Saba or Bayati.

Related Audio Tracks on Harmonic Secrets CD2:

Track 17. Ajam Ushayran in Bb
Track 18. Ajam Ushayran Melody in Bb -- Rhythm: 7/8
Track 19. Ajam Ushayran Vocal Improv in Bb by Saadoun
Track 20. Ajam Taqasim in C by Jihad

Maqam Ajam on Bb

Approximate Interval	Approx. Note Names	Ratio of Interval	Exact Just Cents	Exact Just Hz	Nearest 12-note ET Cents	Nearest 24-note ET Cents	Nearest 24-note ET Hz
ET Tonic	Bb - Bb	1:1	0.00	233.08	0	0	233.08
Sm Minor 2nd	Bb - B hf	25:24	70.67	242.79	100	50	239.91
Sm Minor 2nd	Bb - B hf	19:18	93.60	246.03	100	100	246.94
ET Minor 2nd	Bb - B				100		246.94
Minor 2nd	Bb - B hs	16:15	111.73	248.62	100	100	246.94
Lg Minor 2nd	Bb - B hs	13:12	138.57	252.50	100	150	254.18
Lg Minor 2nd	Bb - B hs	12:11	150.64	254.27	200	150	254.18
Sm Major 2nd	Bb - C hf	11:10	165.00	256.39	200	150	254.18
Sm Major 2nd	Bb - C	10:9	182.40	258.98	200	200	261.62
Major 2nd	Bb - C	9:8	203.91	262.21	200	200	261.62
Lg Major 2nd	Bb - C hs	8:7	231.17	266.38	200	250	269.29
Lg Major 2nd	Bb - C hs	7:6	266.87	271.93	200	250	269.29
ET Minor 3rd	Bb - C#				300		277.18
Just Minor 3rd	Bb - C#	6:5	315.64	279.70	300	300	277.18
Just Major 3rd	Bb - D	5:4	386.31	291.35	400	350	285.30
ET Major 3rd	Bb - D				400		293.66
Lg Major 3rd	Bb - D hs	9:7	435.08	299.67	400	450	302.27
Just 4th	Bb - Eb	4:3	498.04	310.77	500	500	311.12
Sm Tritone	Bb - E hf	11:8	551.32	320.49	600	550	320.24
Tritone	Bb - E hf	7:5	582.51	326.31	600	600	329.62
Lg Tritone	Bb - E	10:7	617.49	332.97	600	600	329.62
ET 5th	Bb - F				700	700	349.23
Just 5th	Bb - F	3:2	701.95	349.62	700	700	349.23
Sm minor 6th	Bb - F hs	11:7	782.49	366.27	800	750	359.46
ET Minor 6th	Bb - F#				800	800	369.99
Minor 6th	Bb - F#	8:5	813.69	372.93	800	800	369.99
Lg Minor 6th	Bb - G hf	13:8	840.53	378.76	800	850	380.83
Major 6th	Bb - G	5:3	884.36	388.47	900	900	391.99
Lg Major 6th	Bb - G hs	12:7	933.13	399.57	900	950	403.48
Sm Minor 7th	Bb - G hs	7:4	968.83	407.89	1000	950	403.48
Sm Minor7th	Bb - Ab	16:9	996.09	414.36	1000	1000	415.30
ET Minor 7th	Bb - Ab				1000	1000	415.30
Minor 7th	Bb - Ab	9:5	1017.60	419.54	1000	1000	415.30
Lg Minor 7th	Bb - A hf	11:6	1049.36	427.31	1000	1050	427.47
Sm Major 7th	Bb - A hf	13:7	1071.70	432.86	1100	1050	427.47
Sm Major 7th	Bb - A hf	15:8	1088.27	437.03	1100	1050	427.47
Major 7th	Bb - A	17:9	1101.04	440.26	1100	1100	440.00
Lg Major 7th	Bb - A hs	19:10	1111.20	442.85	1100	1100	440.00
Lg Major 7th	Bb - A hs	125:64	1158.94	455.23	1100	1150	452.89
ET Octave	Bb - Bb	2:1	1200.00	466.16	1200	1200	466.16

Ajam (upper and lower brackets)

Maqam Ajam Ushayran on Bb as Transposition of Maqam Kurd on D

Approximate Interval	Approx. Note Names	Ratio of Interval	Exact Just Cents	Exact Just Hz	Nearest 12-note ET Cents	Nearest 24-note ET Cents	Nearest 24-note ET Hz
ET D Silent Tonic becomes Major 3rd	D - D	1:1	0.00	146.83	0	0	146.83
Just Minor 6th becomes Tonic	D - Bb	8:5	813.69	234.93	800	800	233.08
Just Major 6th	D - B hf	5:3	884.36	244.72	900	900	246.94
ET Major 6th	D - B	2 to the 3/4ths			900		246.94
Just Minor 7th Sm becomes Major 2nd	D - C	16:9	996.09	261.03	1000	1000	261.62
ET Minor 7th	D - C	2 to the 5/6ths			1000		261.62
Just Minor 7th Lg	D - C	9:5	1017.60	264.29	1000	1000	261.62
Just Major 7th	D - C hs	15:8	1088.27	275.31	1100	1050	269.29
ET Major 7th	D - C#	2 to the 11/12ths			1100		277.18
ET D becomes Major 3rd	D - D	2:1	1200.00	293.66	1200	1200	293.66
	D - D hs	25:24	1270.67	305.90	1300	1250	302.26
	D - D#	19:18	1293.60	309.97	1300	1300	311.13
ET Minor 2nd	D - D# or Eb	2 to the 1/12th			1300		311.13
Just Minor 2nd becomes 4th	D - Eb	16:15	1311.73	313.24	1300	1300	311.13
Just Major 2nd Sm	D - E	10:9	1382.40	326.29	1400	1400	329.63
ET Major 2nd	D - E	2 to the 1/6th			1400		329.63
Just Major 2nd Lg	D - E	9:8	1403.91	330.37	1400	1400	329.63
ET Minor 3rd	D - F	2 to the 1/4th			1500		349.23
Just Minor 3rd becomes 5th	D - F	6:5	1515.64	352.39	1500	1500	349.23
Just Major 3rd	D - F#	5:4	1586.31	367.07	1600	1550	359.45
ET Major 3rd	D - F#	2 to the 1/3rd			1600		369.99
Just 4th becomes Major 6th	D - G	4:3	1698.04	391.55	1700	1700	392.00
ET 4th	D - G	2 to the 5/12th			1700		392.00
	D - G#	11:8	1751.32	403.78	1800	1750	403.48
Just Tritone	D - Ab	7:5	1782.51	411.12	1800	1800	415.30
	D - Ab	10:7	1817.49	419.51	1800	1800	415.30
ET 5th	D - A	2 to the 7/12ths			1900		440.00
Just 5th become Major 7th	D - A	3:2	1901.95	440.49	1900	1900	440.00
	D - A#	11:7	1982.49	461.47	2000	1950	452.89
ET Minor 6th	D - A# or Bb	2 to the 2/3rds			2000		466.16
Just Minor 6th becomes Tonic	D - Bb	8:5	2013.69	469.86	2000	2000	466.16

Although the modulation from Bayati or Saba into Ajam on Bb is traditional, it is maqam Kurd which actually shares identical notes with Ajam.

On the previous page we see the Just Intervals for maqam Ajam calculated from the ET Bb tonic.

However it is interesting to compare these intervals with the Justly Intonated notes in maqam Kurd calculated from the ET D tonic. Studying the chart at the left enables us to see that the actual pitches of the notes as measured in Hz end up being very similar, never more than about 3 Hz away from each other.

This reflects the underlying relationship of D as a Major 3rd above Bb (with slight adjustments required due to the use of the ET Bb and ET D as tonics.)

Actual Just Pitches for Maqam Ajam on Bb compared to Actual Just Pitches for Maqam Ajam as transposition from D Kurd

Approximate Interval	Approx. Note Names	Exact Just Hz From Bb Tonic	Exact Just Hz From D Tonic
Tonic	Bb - Bb	233.08	234.93
Major 2nd	Bb - C	262.21	261.03
Just Major 3rd	Bb - D	291.35	293.66
Just 4th	Bb - Eb	310.77	313.24
Just 5th	Bb - F	349.62	352.39
Major 6th	Bb - G	388.47	391.55
Major 7th	Bb - A	440.26	440.49
Octave	Bb - Bb	466.16	469.85

E half-flat-Based Maqams
Sikah Family

Associated Moods: Sacred, mystical. Common in folk melodies.

The word Sikah means "third position" which refers to the fact that the E half-flat is the 3rd note above the tonic in Rast, the most basic of all Arab maqamat.

"'Db is higher than C# and Ab is higher than G#' -- Leopold Mozart (Father of Wolfgang Mozart and the 'father of modern violin playing'.'
--Duffin 2007

"Those of us with a more delicate sense of hearing, such as the highly talented instrument maker Denis, can barely tolerate the temperament of equal steps."
--Isacoff 2001

Related Audio Tracks on Harmonic Secrets CD2:

Track 21. Huzam in E half-flat
Track 22. Huzam Melody in E half-flat -- Rhythm: 4/4 Sufi
Track 23. Huzam Taqasim in E half-flat by Adif

Huzam

Closely Related Maqamat: Sikah Arabi

Sikah			Hijaz			Rast		
E half-flat		F	G	Ab		B	C	D	E half-flat
Mi nuss-bemol		Fa	Sol	La bemol		Si	Do	Re	Mi nuss-be-mol
	3/4		1	1/2	1 1/2	1/2	1	3/4

Possible Descriptions: Sikah trichord on bottom; Hijaz pentachord on 3rd; Rast trichord on the 6th; Suznak maqam on 6th. The E half-flat in Huzam (like Rast) is frequently described as being very slightly sharper than the E half-flat in Bayyati.

The notes in Huzam are the same as the notes in Suznak, but the tonic is on E half-flat instead of on C.

The leading tone or "zahir" for this maqam is a D#, which is only 1/4 tone lower than the tonic on E half-flat.

The musical lore around maqam Huzam is rich and extensive and is commonly found in many styles of Arab music.

Tawfiq al-Sabbagh suggests that for changing the emotional flavor of this maqam to make it more melancholy it helps to raise the pitch of the D just a little bit. By looking at the next table called "Maqam Huzam as Reposition of Maqam Suznak on C" we see that the pitch of the 9:8 D is in fact somewhat sharp. And if we look at the Table "Maqam Sikah on E half-flat Based on 392.00 Hz ET G" which gives us another way to find the E half-flat tonic, we see that the 9:5 just D is even more sharp.

Al-Sabbagh also calls attention to the Hijaz jins and acknowledges the emotional power associated with using Hijaz Gharib in that location with its sharpened Ab and flattened B. Looking at the table we see that by using just intervals this has been achieved.

Comparing the intervals in Huzam with those in maqam Saba is revealing.
They differ only by quarter-tone degrees yet carry entirely different flavors.

Huzam Intervals:
    3/4   1   1/2   1 1/2   1/2   1   3/4

Saba Intervals:
    3/4   3/4   1/2   1 1/2   1/2   1   1/2

Maqam Huzam as Reposition of Maqam Suznak on C

Maqam Huzam can often be regarded as a reposition of maqam Suznak. Look at the chart to the right and you will understand this logic.

You see that the tonic for Huzam is the E half-flat or Just Major 3rd of Jins Rast in Maqam Suznak.

Huzam Tonic 2

Huzam Tonic 1

But that is not the only possible tonic.

There are many harmonious intervals defined by the justly intonated ratios and the 16:13 ratio which is 359.47 cents above the C may also be commonly used as the tonic for maqam Huzam. In that case the tonic is just a bit sharper than the ET quartertone at 350.00 cents above the C.

Approximate Interval	Approx. Note Names	Ratio of Interval	Exact Just Cents	Exact Just Hz	Nearest 12-note ET Cents	Nearest 24-note ET Cents	Nearest 24-note ET Hz
ET C	C - C	1:1	0.00	261.63	0	0	261.63
	C - C hs	25:24	70.67	272.53	100	50	269.30
	C - C#	19:18	93.60	276.16	100	100	277.18
ET Minor 2nd	C - C# or Db	2 to the 1/12th			100		277.18
Just Minor 2nd	C - Db	16:15	111.73	279.07	100	100	277.18
	C - D hf	13:12	138.57	283.43	100	150	285.31
	C - D hf	12:11	150.64	285.42	200	150	285.31
	C - D hf	11:10	165.00	287.79	200	150	285.31
Just Major 2nd Sm	C - D	10:9	182.40	290.70	200	200	293.66
ET Major 2nd	C - D	2 to the 1/6th			200		293.66
Just Major 2nd Lg	C - D	9:8	203.91	294.33	200	200	293.66
	C - D hs	8:7	231.17	299.01	200	250	302.27
	C - D hs	7:6	266.87	305.23	200	250	302.27
ET Minor 3rd	C - Eb	2 to the 1/4th			300		311.13
Just Minor 3rd	C - Eb	6:5	315.64	313.95	300	300	311.13
ET Qrtrtone	C - E hf	2 to the 1/4ths	350.00		300	350	320.25
	C - E hf	16:13	359.47	322.01	300	350	320.25
Just Major 3rd	C - E hf	5:4	386.31	327.03	400	350	329.63
ET Major 3rd	C - E	2 to the 1/3rd			400		329.63
	C - Fb	9:7	435.08	336.38	400	450	339.29
Just 4th	C - F	4:3	498.04	348.83	500	500	349.23
ET 4th	C - F	2 to the 5/12ths			500		349.23
	C - F#	11:8	551.32	359.74	600	550	359.47
Just Tritone	C - Gb	7:5	582.51	366.28	600	600	369.99
	C - Gb	10:7	617.49	373.76	600	600	369.99
ET 5th	C - G	2 to the 7/12ths			700		392.00
Just 5th	C - G	3:2	701.95	392.46	700	700	392.00
	C - G#	11:7	782.49	411.13	800	750	403.49
ET Minor 6th	C - Ab	2 to the 2/3rds			800		415.30
Just Minor 6th	C - Ab	8:5	813.69	418.61	800	800	415.30
	C - A hf	13:8	840.53	425.15	800	850	427.48
Just Major 6th	C - A	5:3	884.36	436.06	900	900	440.00
ET Major 6th	C - A	2 to the 3/4ths			900		440.00
	C - A#	12:7	933.13	448.51	900	950	452.90
	C - A#	7:4	968.83	457.85	1000	950	452.90
Just Minor 7th Sm	C - Bb	16:9	996.09	465.12	1000	1000	466.16
ET Minor 7th	C - Bb	2 to the 5/6ths			1000		466.16
Just Minor 7th Lg	C - Bb	9:5	1017.60	470.94	1000	1000	466.16
	C - B hf	11:6	1049.36	479.65	1000	1050	479.83
	C - B hf	13:7	1071.70	485.88	1100	1050	479.83
Just Major 7th	C - B	15:8	1088.27	490.57	1100	1050	479.83
ET Major 7th	C - B	2 to the 11/12ths			1100		493.88
	C - B	17:9	1101.04	494.19	1100	1100	493.88
	C - B	19:10	1111.20	497.10	1100	1100	493.88
	C - B#	125:64	1158.94	510.98	1100	1150	508.36
ET C	C - C	2:1	1200.00	523.26	1200	1200	523.25

Groupings (right side of table): Sikah, Sikah Alternative, Hijaz, Rast

Sikah

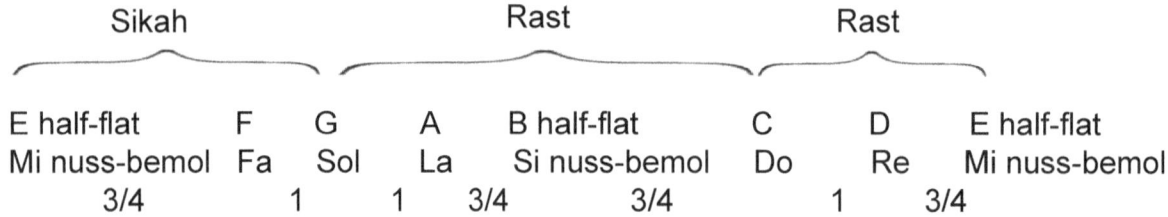

Sikah			Rast			Rast		
E half-flat	F	G	A	B half-flat	C	D		E half-flat
Mi nuss-bemol	Fa	Sol	La	Si nuss-bemol	Do	Re		Mi nuss-bemol
3/4	1	1	3/4	3/4	1	3/4		

Possible Descriptions: Sikah trichord on bottom; Rast tetrachord on 3rd; Rast trichord on 6th; Rast maqam on 6th. The E half-flat in Sikah (like Rast) is frequently described as being very slightly sharper than the E half-flat in Bayyati.

The notes in Sikah are the same as the notes in Rast, but the tonic is on E half-flat instead of on C.

The leading tone or "zahir" for this maqam is a D#, which is only 1/4 tone lower than the tonic on E half-flat.

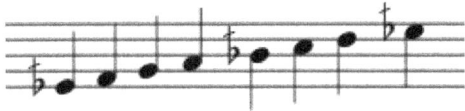

Related Audio Tracks on Harmonic Secrets CD2:

Track 24. Sikah in E half-flat
Track 25. Sikah Melody in E half-flat -- Rhythm: 8/8 Baladi
Track 26. Sikah Taqasim in E half-flat by Jihad

Maqam Sikah on E half-flat Based on 392.00 Hz ET G

When maqamat have their tonic (qarar) on a neutral tone (quartertone), it is more difficult to establish a set frequency for that tonic.

One option is to pick a note like G and use the ET frequency as a starting point. Then we must work both down and up the scale from there to find harmonious frequencies.

Approximate Interval	Approx. Note Names	Ratio of Interval	Exact Just Cents	Exact Just Hz	Nearest 12-note ET Cents	Nearest 24-note ET Cents	Nearest 24-note ET Hz
Tonic	E hf - E hf	1:1	0.00	326.67	0	0	329.63
Sm Minor 2nd	E hf - F hf	25:24	70.67	340.28	100	50	339.29
Sm Minor 2nd	E hf - F	19:18	93.60	344.82	100	100	349.23
ET Minor 2nd					100		
Minor 2nd	E hf - F	16:15	111.73	348.45	100	100	349.23
Lg Minor 2nd	E hf - F	13:12	138.57	353.89	100	150	359.46
Lg Minor 2nd	E hf - F#	12:11	150.64	356.37	200	150	
Sm Major 2nd	E hf - F#	11:10	165.00	359.33	200	150	
Sm Major 2nd	E hf - Gb	10:9	182.40	362.97	200	200	
Major 2nd	E hf - Gb	9:8	203.91	367.50	200	200	370.00
Lg Major 2nd	E hf - G hf	8:7	231.17	373.34	200	250	380.84
Lg Major 2nd	E hf - G hf	7:6	266.87	381.11	200	250	
ET Minor 3rd					300		392.00
Minor 3rd	E hf - G	6:5	315.64	392.00	300	300	392.00
Major 3rd	E hf - Ab	5:4	386.31	408.34	400	350	403.48
ET Major 3rd					400		415.31
Lg Major 3rd	E hf - Ab	9:7	435.08	420.00	400	450	427.47
4th	E hf - A	4:3	498.04	435.56	500	500	440.00
Sm Tritone	E hf - A#	11:8	551.32	449.17	600	550	452.90
Tritone	E hf - Bb	7:5	582.51	457.34	600	600	466.17
Lg Tritone	E hf - Bb	10:7	617.49	466.67	600	600	466.17
ET 5th					600		466.17
5th	E hf - B	3:2	701.95	490.00	700	700	493.89
Sm minor 6th	E hf - C	11:7	782.49	513.34	800	750	508.36
ET Minor 6th					800		523.26
Minor 6th	E hf - C	8:5	813.69	522.67	800	800	523.26
Lg Minor 6th	E hf - C#	13:8	840.53	530.84	800	850	538.59
Major 6th	E hf - C#	5:3	884.36	544.45	900	900	554.37
Lg Major 6th	E hf - Db	12:7	933.13	560.01	900	950	570.61
Sm Minor 7th	E hf - Db	7:4	968.83	571.67	1000	950	
Sm Minor 7th	E hf - D	16:9	996.09	580.75	1000	1000	587.33
ET Minor 7th							587.33
Minor 7th	E hf - D	9:5	1017.60	588.01	1000	1000	587.33
Lg Minor 7th	E hf - D#	11:6	1049.36	598.89	1000	1050	604.54
Sm Major 7th	E hf - D#	13:7	1071.70	606.67	1100	1050	
Sm Major 7th	E hf - Eb	15:8	1088.27	612.51	1100	1050	
Major 7th	E hf - Eb	17:9	1101.04	617.04	1100	1100	622.26
Lg Major 7th	E hf - Eb	19:10	1111.20	620.67	1100	1100	622.26
Lg Major 7th	E hf - Eb	125:64	1158.94	638.03	1100	1150	640.49
Octave	E hf - E hf	2:1	1200.00	653.34	1200	1200	659.26

Sikah bracket spans from Tonic through Lg Major 2nd (E hf - G hf, 7:6).
Rast bracket spans from Minor 3rd through Lg Major 6th (E hf - Db, 12:7), and continues from Sm Minor 7th through Octave.

Maqam Sikah as Transposition of Maqam Rast on C

Another option for establishing the E half-flat tonic frequency would be to use the ET frequency of C (the hidden or implied tonic of this family of maqamat) as a starting point as we did for maqam Huzam above.

Sikah Tonic 2 ⇨
Sikah Tonic 1 ⇨

Musicians may choose a lower E half-flat at times and a higher E half-flat at other times when modulations in and out of Rast are part of the composition.

The E half-flat tonic could be based on the same 16:13 ratio above the C which we saw as a possibility in Huzam, or it could be based on the slightly lower 11:9 ratio which gives us a third possibility! The choice of pitch of this tonic is very powerful and gives compositions in Sikah a deep power.

Approximate Interval	Approx. Note Names	Ratio of Interval	Exact Just Cents	Exact Just Hz	Nearest 12-note ET Cents	Nearest 24-note ET Cents	Nearest 24-note ET Hz
ET C	C - C	1:1	0.00	261.63	0	0	261.63
	C - C hs	25:24	70.67	272.53	100	50	269.30
	C - C#	19:18	93.60	276.16	100	100	277.18
ET Minor 2nd	C - C# or Db	2 to the 1/12th			100		277.18
Just Minor 2nd	C - Db	16:15	111.73	279.07	100	100	277.18
	C - D hf	13:12	138.57	283.43	100	150	285.31
	C - D hf	12:11	150.64	285.42	200	150	285.31
	C - D hf	11:10	165.00	287.79	200	150	285.31
Just Major 2nd Sm	C - D	10:9	182.40	290.70	200	200	293.66
ET Major 2nd	C - D	2 to the 1/6th			200		293.66
Just Major 2nd Lg	C - D	9:8	203.91	294.33	200	200	293.66
	C - D hs	8:7	231.17	299.01	200	250	302.27
	C - D hs	7:6	266.87	305.23	200	250	302.27
ET Minor 3rd	C - Eb	2 to the 1/4th			300		311.13
Just Minor 3rd	C - Eb	6:5	315.64	313.95	300	300	311.13
	C - E hf	11:9	347.40	319.77	300	350	320.25
ET Qrtrtone	C - E hf	2 to the 1/4ths	350.00		300	350	320.25
Just Major 3rd	C - E hf	5:4	386.31	327.03	400	350	329.63
ET Major 3rd	C - E	2 to the 1/3rd			400		329.63
	C - Fb	9:7	435.08	336.38	400	450	339.29
Just 4th	C - F	4:3	498.04	348.83	500	500	349.23
ET 4th	C - F	2 to the 5/12ths			500		349.23
	C - F#	11:8	551.32	359.74	600	550	359.47
Just Tritone	C - Gb	7:5	582.51	366.28	600	600	369.99
	C - Gb	10:7	617.49	373.76	600	600	369.99
ET 5th	C - G	2 to the 7/12ths			700		392.00
Just 5th	C - G	3:2	701.95	392.46	700	700	392.00
	C - G#	11:7	782.49	411.13	800	750	403.49
ET Minor 6th	C - Ab	2 to the 2/3rds			800		415.30
Just Minor 6th	C - Ab	8:5	813.69	418.61	800	800	415.30
	C - A hf	13:8	840.53	425.15	800	850	427.48
Just Major 6th	C - A	5:3	884.36	436.06	900	900	440.00
ET Major 6th	C - A	2 to the 3/4ths			900		440.00
	C - A#	12:7	933.13	448.51	900	950	452.90
	C - A#	7:4	968.83	457.85	1000	950	452.90
Just Minor 7th Sm	C - Bb	16:9	996.09	465.12	1000	1000	466.16
ET Minor 7th	C - Bb	2 to the 5/6ths			1000		466.16
Just Minor 7th Lg	C - Bb	9:5	1017.60	470.94	1000	1000	466.16
	C - B hf	11:6	1049.36	479.65	1000	1050	479.83
	C - B hf	13:7	1071.70	485.88	1100	1050	479.83
Just Major 7th	C - B	15:8	1088.27	490.57	1100	1050	479.83
ET Major 7th	C - B	2 to the 11/12ths			1100		493.88
	C - B	17:9	1101.04	494.19	1100	1100	493.88
	C - B	19:10	1111.20	497.10	1100	1100	493.88
	C - B#	125:64	1158.94	510.98	1100	1150	508.36
ET C	C - C	2:1	1200.00	523.26	1200	1200	523.25

Sikah (bracket covering middle section); Sikah Alternative (bracket to the right); Rast (bracket covering upper section); Rast (bracket lower).

F-Based Maqams
Jaharkah

Associated Moods: Strong and Straightforward.

The word Jaharkah means "fourth position" which refers to the fact that the F is the 4th note above the tonic in Rast, the most basic of all Arab maqamat.

Jaharkah

Closely Related Maqamat: Shahwar

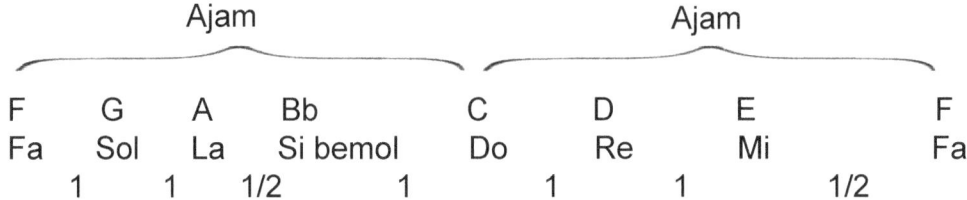

Possible Descriptions: Ajam or "Jaharka" pentachord on bottom; Ajam or "Jaharka" tetrachord on 5th.

In Western terms, Jaharka is "relative major" to the Nahawand on D (D minor scale).

Another, perhaps older, definition of maqam Jaharka requires a replacement of the E with an E half-flat which transforms the upper Ajam jins into Rast.

And some say that the 3rd note in Jaharkah is slightly flatter than the 3rd in Ajam. Since Ajam has become strongly associated with the ET major scale intervals, this is likely another way of saying "back to just intonation please!"

Related Audio Tracks on Harmonic Secrets CD2:

Track 27. Jaharkah in F
Track 28. Jaharkah Melody in F -- Rhythm: 4/4 Maqsum

It is not necessary to show just intonation interval charts for every maqam. Once you understand the choices available to you as a musician you can begin to refine your listening abilities and your musicianship and you will automatically begin to play truly harmonious intervals. There are many choices.
Different musicians from different backgrounds will make different choices.
The lower the number on the right side of the ratio, the more often the two sound waves will coincide and reinforce each other and the more harmonious the sound!

"In our modern tuning system, the deep, smooth pleasure of pentamerous harmony especially is sensibly compromised. The resultant sharpness of the major thirds is not enough to drive you crazy, but it is enough to make you restless, which is one of the reasons our music is restless."
-Mathieu 1997

"If a soprano, for example, sings the D# at the same pitch as the Eb, a sensitive ear will hear that it is out of tune, since the latter pitch should be somewhat higher than the former. -- Pier Francesco Tosi 1723"
--Duffin 2007

Transposed E half-flat--Based Maqamat

The most common place to transpose the E half-flat tonic is down a 4th to the B half-flat. The B half-flat is strategically located, as you will see below by reading about maqam Rahat el Arwah, between the G and D and can have it's pitch defined in more than one way.

With a tonic established on B half-flat musicians who have been improvising in the D maqamat have a wonderful place to settle which immediately creates a whole new, but calm and restful musical world.

It also now becomes musically very fun and inviting to explore all of the microtonal "quartertone" intervals which lie between the D and the G! With all that musical room to escape into below the D and finally come to rest on the B half-flat, the tastes of the hijaz, bayati, saba and rast ajnas which exist between the D and the G and which are contained in the maqamat called Rahat el Arwah, Iraq, Bastanikar and Farahnak all become a wonderful playground.

> "All I am suggesting is for string players to narrow the open strings a little more than they narrow them for ET. Then aim to play the major thirds fairly narrow and the minor thirds a little wide. Play the whole tones a little smaller than in ET... ...and make the diatonic semitones larger and the chromatic semitones smaller."
> --Duffin 2007

Related Audio Tracks on Harmonic Secrets CD2:

Track 29. Rahat el Arwah in B half-flat
Track 30. Rahat el Arwah Melody in B half-flat -- Rhythm: 9/8
Track 31. Rahat el Arwah Taqasim in B half-flat by Saadoun
Track 32. Rahat el Arwah Taqasim in B half-flat by Jihad

Rahat el Arwah (Huzam on B half-flat)

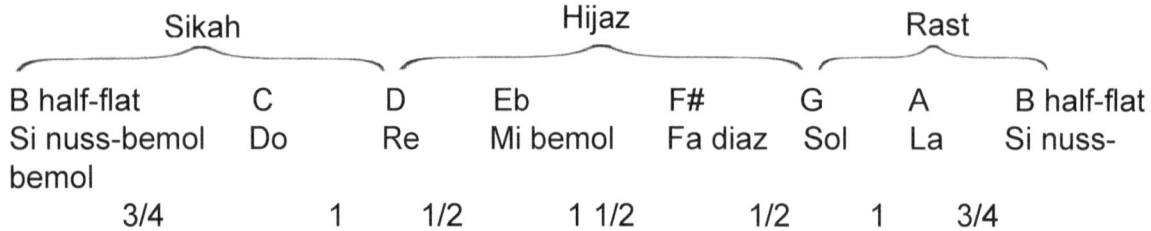

	Sikah			Hijaz			Rast	
B half-flat		C	D	Eb	F#	G	A	B half-flat
Si nuss-bemol		Do	Re	Mi bemol	Fa diaz	Sol	La	Si nuss-bemol
	3/4		1	1/2	1 1/2	1/2	1	3/4

Possible Descriptions: Sikah trichord on bottom; Hijaz pentachord on 3rd; Rast trichord on 6th; Suznak maqam on 6th.

This maqam is very extensively used. It is very common at the end of a D hijaz composition to move down and rest on the B half-flat. For Westerners it may feel like moving from a major scale to its relative minor. There is some kind of similarity in feeling.

The maqam Rahat el Arwah is extremely rich in justly intonated harmonic possibilities which are found extensively in Arabic music of many kinds. Holding the B half-flat tonic while moving to either the D or the G creates a deep magic. For a Westerner to learn to sing these approximately 1 3/4 step intervals with precision in just intonation takes some practice but is deeply rewarding. One enters a harmonic realm unknown in Western music.

And modulation from B half-flat to either G or D maqamat is an entryway into a huge musical playground of possibilities.

The pitch of the B half-flat tonic can be derived from one of two ways:
1) it can be amost exactly halfway between G and D
2) it can be the 3rd note of Rast on G
Studying the tables on the next two pages will illustrate these two possibilities.

Maqam Rahat al Arwah

Unless a musician is modulating out of Rast on G, he will generally find the tonic B half-flat at its quartertone position halfway between G and D. It so happens that there is a justly intonated interval with the ratio 11:9 which is 347 cents above the G. So this is how we define our pitch for the B half-flat tonic.

Because our instruments have fixed tunings for open strings we are constrained by those pitches for certain notes like G and D. As you can see by the table to the right, there are lovely "in-tune" just intervals extremely close to those "fixed-pitch" notes.

Notice, however, the strong magnetic pull exerted by the F# which, although it is part of the Hijaz jins, is also close to being a 5th above the B half-flat tonic. Although the 17:11 ratio gives us an F# which is very close to the ET F#, it will sound very out of tune if used above the B half-flat tonic in this maqam. The just 5th with the 3:2 ratio sounds so much better that muscians will be irresistably drawn to use it for the F# even though it is more than 10 cents flat. Of course this use aligns with the traditional flattening of the F# in Hijaz anyway.

But look at how many harmonious possibilities there are to choose from. Each musician can have his own favorite intervals and appreciative listeners will enjoy the perfection!

Approximate Interval	Approx Note Names	Ratio of Interval	Exact Just Cents	Exact Just Hz	Nearest 12-note ET Cents	Nearest 24-note ET Cents	Nearest 24-note ET Hz
Tonic	B hf - B hf	1:1	0.00	239.56	0	0	239.56
Sm Minor 2nd	B hf - C hf	25:24	70.67	249.54	100	50	246.58
Sm Minor 2nd	B hf - C	19:18	93.60	252.87	100	100	253.80
ET Minor 2nd	B hf - C				100	100	253.80
Minor 2nd	B hf - C	16:15	111.73	255.53	100	100	253.80
Lg Minor 2nd	B hf - C	13:12	138.57	259.52	100	150	261.24
Lg Minor 2nd	B hf - C	12:11	150.64	261.34	200	150	261.24
Sm Major 2nd	B hf - C#	11:10	165.00	263.52	200	150	261.24
Sm Major 2nd	B hf - Db	10:9	182.40	266.18	200	200	268.90
Major 2nd	B hf - Db	9:8	203.91	269.50	200	200	268.90
Lg Major 2nd	B hf - D hf	8:7	231.17	273.78	200	250	276.78
Lg Major 2nd	B hf - D hf	7:6	266.87	279.49	200	250	276.78
ET Minor 3rd					300		284.89
Minor 3rd	B hf - D hf	6:5	315.64	287.47	300	300	284.89
	B hf - D	11:9	347.41	292.80	300	350	293.23
Major 3rd	B hf - Eb	5:4	386.31	299.45	400	350	293.23
ET Major 3rd					400		301.83
Lg Major 3rd	B hf - Eb	9:7	435.08	308.00	400	450	310.67
4th	B hf - Eb	4:3	498.04	319.41	500	500	319.77
Sm Tritone	B hf - E hf	11:8	551.32	329.40	600	550	329.14
Tritone	B hf - F	7:5	582.51	335.38	600	600	338.79
Lg Tritone	B hf - F	10:7	617.49	342.23	600	600	338.79
ET 5th	B hf - F hs				700		358.93
5th	B hf - F#	3:2	701.95	359.34	700	700	358.93
	B hf - F#	17:11	753.64	370.23	700	750	369.45
	B hf - F#	14:9	764.92	372.65	800	750	369.45
Sm minor 6th	B hf - Gb	11:7	782.49	376.45	800	750	369.45
ET Minor 6th	B hf - G hf				800		380.28
Minor 6th	B hf - G	8:5	813.69	383.30	800	800	380.28
Lg Minor 6th	B hf - G	13:8	840.53	389.29	800	850	391.42
Major 6th	B hf - G#	5:3	884.36	399.27	900	900	402.89
Lg Major 6th	B hf - Ab	12:7	933.13	410.67	900	950	415.30
Sm Minor 7th	B hf - Ab	7:4	968.83	419.23	1000	950	414.70
Sm Minor7th	B hf - A hf	16:9	996.09	425.88	1000	1000	426.85
ET Minor 7th	B hf - A hf				1000		426.85
Minor 7th	B hf - A hf	9:5	1017.60	431.21	1000	1000	426.85
Lg Minor 7th	B hf - A	11:6	1049.36	439.19	1000	1050	439.35
Sm Major 7th	B hf - A	13:7	1071.70	444.87	1100	1050	439.35
Sm Major 7th	B hf - A hs	15:8	1088.27	449.18	1100	1050	439.35
Major 7th	B hf - A#	17:9	1101.04	452.50	1100	1100	452.23
Lg Major 7th	B hf - Bb	19:10	1111.20	455.16	1100	1100	452.23
Lg Major 7th	B hf - Bb	125:64	1158.94	467.89	1100	1150	465.48
Octave	B hf - B hf	2:1	1200.00	479.12	1200	1200	479.12

Bracketed groupings (right side of table): Sikah, Hijaz, Rast

Another option:
The B half-flat tonic is taken from the pitch of the "major 3rd" of maqam Yak-Gah, or Rast on G.

This happens extremely naturally if modulations from G Rast are part of the musical flow. After all, jins "Sikah" means "3rd position" above the main tonic.

So the table to the right offers the same intervals for playing maqam Rahat el Arwah as we saw on the previous page, but the pitches are somewhat different because we are choosing to define a different and sharper pitch for the B half-flat tonic.

The flow of improvisation or composition from maqam to maqam in Arabic music creates a living and changing context which determines, with the help of musical ears which are sensitive to pure, justly intonated intervals, the possibility of finding many different "in tune" pitches for the same note!

I know of an Arab violinist who claims to be able to play more than ten different E half-flats! Each one derives its pitch from the maqam from which it is born and in which it is musically cradled.

Maqam Rahat al Arwah as Reposition of tonic from within Maqam Suznak on G

Approximate Interval	Approx. Note Names	Ratio of Interval	Exact Just Cents	Exact Just Hz	Nearest 12-note ET Cents	Nearest 24-note ET Cents	Nearest 24-note ET Hz
ET G Silent Tonic Becomes 6th	G - G	1:1	0.00	196.00	0	0	196.00
Just Major 2nd Lg Becomes 7th	G - A	9:8	203.91	220.50	200	200	220.00
Just Major 3rd Becomes Tonic	G - B hf	5:4	386.31	245.00	400	350	239.91
ET Major 3rd	G - B	2 to the 1/3rd			400		246.94
	G - B	9:7	435.08	252.00	400	400	246.94
Just 4th Becomes 2nd	G - C	4:3	498.04	261.33	500	500	261.63
ET 4th	G - C	2 to the 5/12ths			500		261.63
Just Tritone	G - Db	7:5	582.51	274.40	600	600	277.18
ET 5th	G - D	2 to the 7/12ths			700		293.66
Just 5th Becomes 3rd	G - D	3:2	701.95	294.00	700	700	293.66
	G - D#	11:7	782.49	308.00	800	750	302.27
ET Minor 6th	G - D# or Eb	2 to the 2/3rds			800		311.13
Just Minor 6th Becomes 4th	G - Eb	8:5	813.69	313.60	800	800	311.13
	G - E hf	13:8	840.53	318.50	800	850	320.25
Just Major 6th	G - E	5:3	884.36	326.67	900	900	329.63
ET Major 6th	G - E	2 to the 3/4ths			900		329.63
Just Minor 7th Sm	G - Fb	16:9	996.09	348.44	1000	1000	349.23
ET Minor 7th	G - F	2 to the 5/6ths			1000		349.23
Just Minor 7th Lg	G - F	9:5	1017.60	352.80	1000	1000	349.23
	G - F hs	11:6	1049.36	359.33	1000	1050	359.47
	G - F hs	13:7	1071.70	364.00	1100	1050	359.47
Just Major 7th Becomes 5th	G - F hs	15:8	1088.27	367.50	1100	1050	359.47
ET Major 7th	G - F#	2 to the 11/12ths			1100		369.99
	G - F#	17:9	1101.04	370.22	1100	1100	369.99
	G - F#	19:10	1111.20	372.40	1100	1100	369.99
	G - Gb	125:64	1158.94	382.81	1100	1150	380.84
ET G Becomes 6th	G - G	2:1	1200.00	392.00	1200	1200	392.00
	G - G hs	25:24	1270.67	408.33	1300	1250	403.49
	G - G#	19:18	1293.60	413.78	1300	1300	415.31
ET Minor 2nd	G - G# or Ab	2 to the 1/12th			1300		415.31
Just Minor 2nd	G - Ab	16:15	1311.73	418.13	1300	1300	415.31
Just Major 2nd Sm	G - A	10:9	1382.40	435.55	1400	1400	440.00
ET Major 2nd	G - A	2 to the 1/6th	1400.00				440.00
Just Major 2nd Lg Becomes 7th	G - A	9:8	1403.91	440.00	1400	1400	440.00
	G - A hs	8:7	1431.17	448.00	1400	1450	452.90
	G - A hs	7:6	1466.87	457.33	1400	1450	452.90
ET Minor 3rd	G - Bb	2 to the 1/4th			1500		466.17
Just Minor 3rd	G - Bb	6:5	1515.64	470.40	1500	1500	466.17
	G - Bhf	11:9	1547.40	479.11	1500	1550	479.83
ET Qrtrtone	G - B hf	2 to the 1/4ths	1550.00		1600	1550	479.83
Just Major 3rd Becomes Tonic Octave	G - B hf	5:4	1586.31	490.00	1600	1550	479.83

Derived Maqams

The musician who has learned the previous ninteen maqamat will find that these additional modes described below are easy to master. They are created from those already covered.

Derived D-Based Maqams
Kurd Family

Shehnaz Kurdi

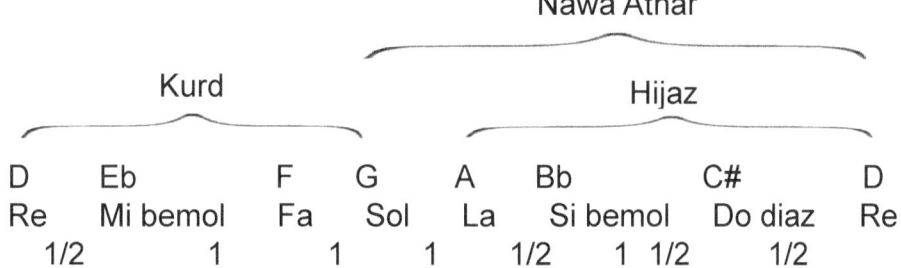

D	Eb	F	G	A	Bb	C#	D
Re	Mi bemol	Fa	Sol	La	Si bemol	Do diaz	Re
1/2	1	1	1	1/2	1 1/2	1/2	

Possible Descriptions: Kurd tetrachord on bottom; hijaz tetrachord on 5th; nawa athar pentachord on the 4th.

Zawqi Tarab

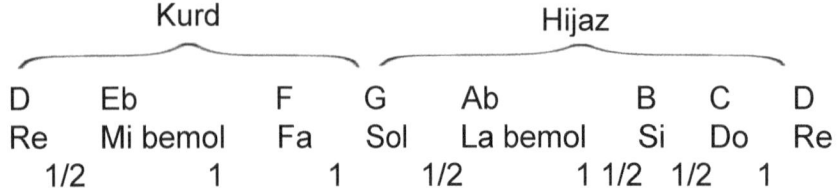

Possible Descriptions: Kurd tetrachord on bottom; hijaz pentachord on 4th. Similar to Shuri except for Eb instead of E half-flat.

Lami

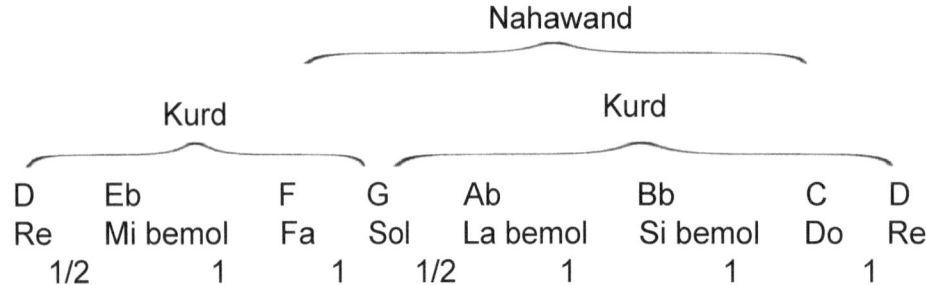

Possible Descriptions: Kurd tetrachord on bottom; nahawand pentachord on 3rd; kurd pentachord on 4th; ajam maqam on 2nd
This maqam is popular in Iraq.

Derived D-Based Maqams
Bayati Family

Mohayar

Closely Related Maqamat: Nahfat

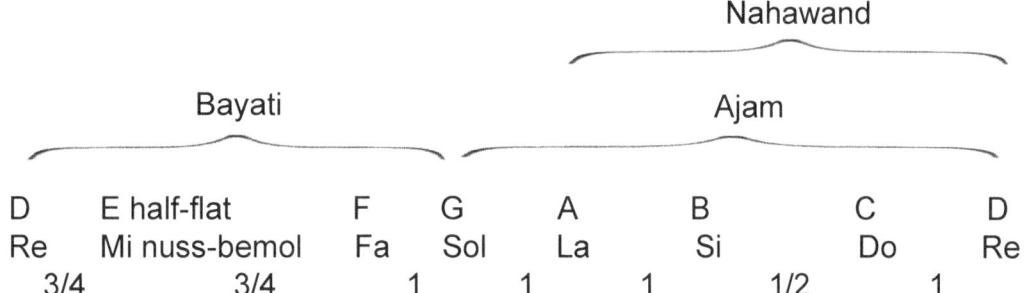

Possible Descriptions: Bayyati tetrachord on bottom; Nahawand tetrachord on 5th; Ajam pentachord on 4th.

This maqam usually opens at the top on the high D, emphasizing high notes in the second octave before finally descending through the lower octave to the lower D.

Shuri

Closely Related Maqamat: Bayati Araban, Ajem Murassa, Karjigar (Turkish)

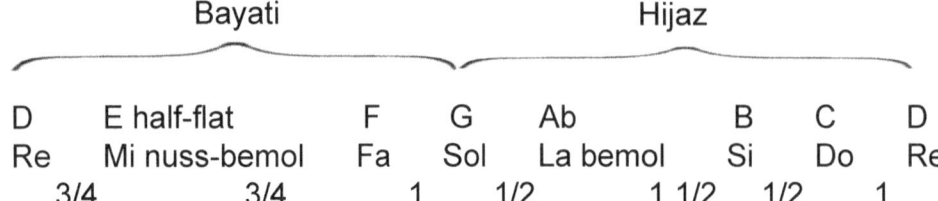

	Bayati				Hijaz			
D	E half-flat		F	G	Ab		B	C	D
Re	Mi nuss-bemol		Fa	Sol	La bemol		Si	Do	Re
	3/4	3/4		1	1/2	1 1/2	1/2	1

Possible Descriptions: Bayyati tetrachord on bottom; Hijaz pentachord on 4th. Used as a modulation and ornament inside of Bayyati.

Bayatayn

	Bayati				Bayati			
D	E half-flat		F	G	A half-flat		Bb	C	D
Re	Mi nuss-bemol		Fa	Sol	La nuss-bemol		Si bemol	Do	Re
	3/4	3/4		1	3/4	3/4		1	1

Possible Descriptions: Bayyati tetrachord on bottom; Bayati pentachord on 4th.

Used as a modulation and ornament inside of Bayyati.

Saba Zamzamah

Closely Related Maqamat: Saba Kurdi

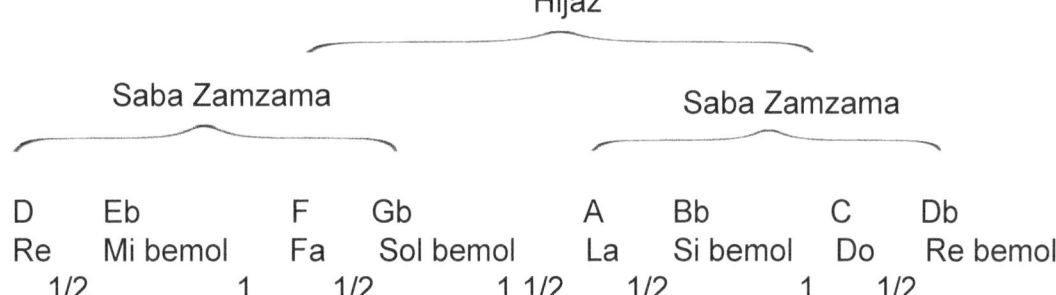

D	Eb	F	Gb	A	Bb	C	Db
Re	Mi bemol	Fa	Sol bemol	La	Si bemol	Do	Re bemol
1/2		1	1/2	1 1/2	1/2	1	1/2

Possible Descriptions: Kurd trichord on bottom; Saba Zamzama tetrachord on bottom; Hijaz tetrachord on 3rd; Shehnaz maqam on 3rd; Saba Zamzama tetrachord on 5th.

This version of Saba can be played on equal-tempered instruments.

Saba Najdi

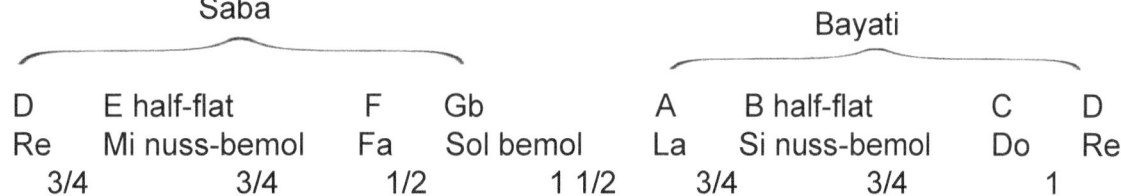

D	E half-flat	F	Gb	A	B half-flat	C	D
Re	Mi nuss-bemol	Fa	Sol bemol	La	Si nuss-bemol	Do	Re
3/4	3/4	1/2	1 1/2	3/4	3/4	1	

Possible Descriptions: Saba tetrachord on bottom; Bayati tetrachord on 5th.

Saba Busalik

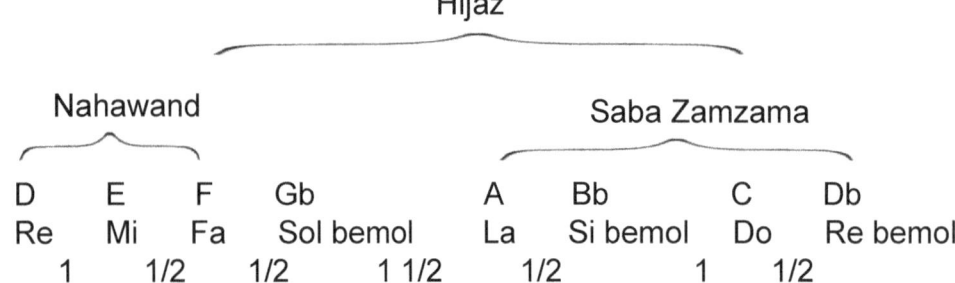

D	E	F	Gb	A	Bb	C	Db
Re	Mi	Fa	Sol bemol	La	Si bemol	Do	Re bemol
1	1/2	1/2	1 1/2	1/2	1	1/2	

Possible Descriptions: Nahawand trichord on bottom; Hijaz pentachord on 3rd; Shehnaz maqam on 3rd. Saba Zamzama tetrachord on 5th.

This version of Saba can be played on equal-tempered instruments. Frequently heard in Greek rebetika music.

Sabr Jadid

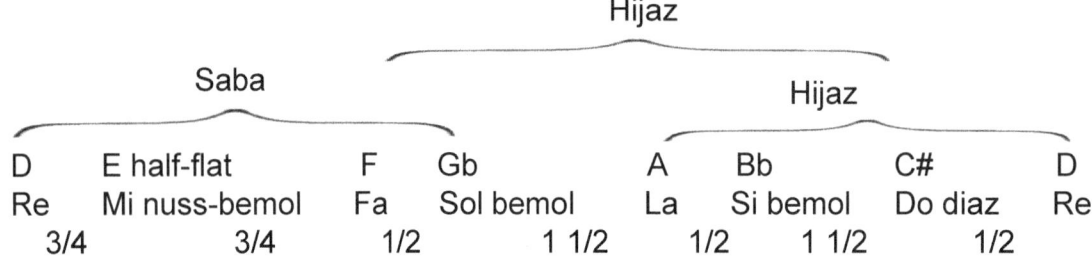

D	E half-flat	F	Gb	A	Bb	C#	D
Re	Mi nuss-bemol	Fa	Sol bemol	La	Si bemol	Do diaz	Re
3/4	3/4	1/2	1 1/2	1/2	1 1/2	1/2	

Possible Descriptions: Saba tetrachord on bottom; Hijaz tetrachord on 3rd; Hijaz tetrachord on 5th.

Derived C-Based Maqams
Nahawand Family

Nahawand Kabir

Closely Related: Dorian Mode

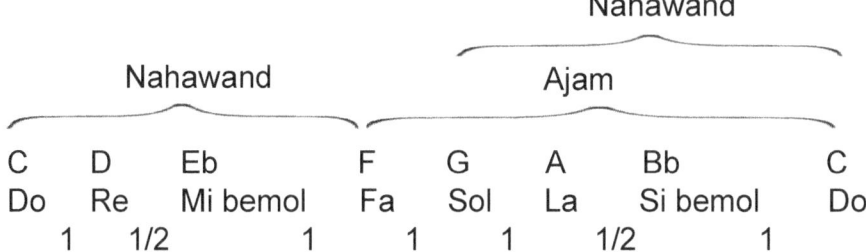

C	D	Eb		F	G	A	Bb		C
Do	Re	Mi bemol		Fa	Sol	La	Si bemol		Do
	1	1/2	1		1	1	1/2	1	

Possible Descriptions: Nahawand tetrachord on bottom; Ajam (Jaharkah) pentachord on 4th; Nahawand tetrachord on 5th.

Nahawand Murassa

Closely Related Maqamat: Nahawand Rumi

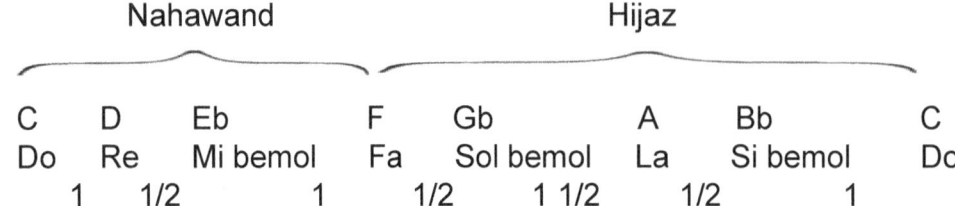

C	D	Eb	F	Gb	A	Bb	C
Do	Re	Mi bemol	Fa	Sol bemol	La	Si bemol	Do
1	1/2	1	1/2	1 1/2	1/2	1	

Possible Descriptions: Nahawand tetrachord on bottom; Hijaz tetrachord on 4th.
If the 2nd, the D, were 1/4 step lower this would be maqam shuri transposed down from D to C.

"In 1835 professional string players still differentiated sharps and flats unless they had to perform with a fixed pitch instrument."
 --Duffin 2007

Derived C-Based Maqams
Rast Family

Mahur

Closely Related Maqamat: Kirdan

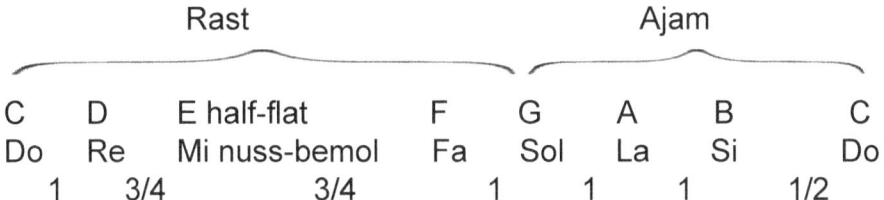

C	D	E half-flat	F	G	A	B	C
Do	Re	Mi nuss-bemol	Fa	Sol	La	Si	Do
1	3/4	3/4	1	1	1	1/2	

Possible descriptions: Rast pentachord on bottom; Ajam tetrachord on the 5th. Some say to flatten the E half-flat and the B by an 1/8th of a tone. We can interpret this as a move toward just intonation.

Suzdilar

Closely Related Maqamat: Suzdil 'Ara

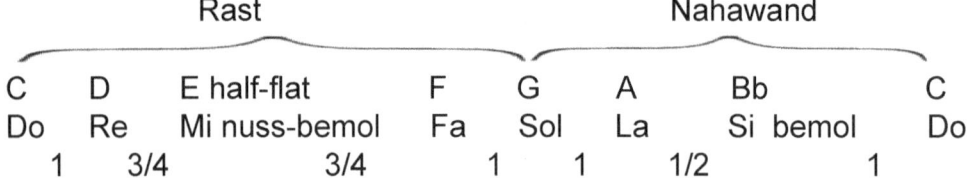

	Rast				Nahawand			
C	D	E half-flat	F	G	A	Bb		C
Do	Re	Mi nuss-bemol	Fa	Sol	La	Si bemol		Do
1	3/4	3/4	1	1	1/2	1		

Possible Descriptions: Rast pentachord on bottom; Nahawand tetrachord on 5th. Used as ornament in Rast.

Associated Moods: Soft and tender joy.

Nerz Rast

Closely Related Maqamat: Nayruz

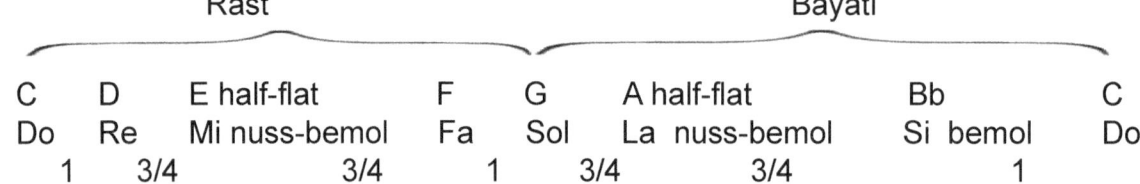

	Rast				Bayati			
C	D	E half-flat	F	G	A half-flat	Bb		C
Do	Re	Mi nuss-bemol	Fa	Sol	La nuss-bemol	Si bemol		Do
1	3/4	3/4	1	3/4	3/4	1		

Possible Descriptions: Rast pentachord on bottom; Bayyati tetrachord on 5th. Used as ornament in Rast.

Rast Beshayer

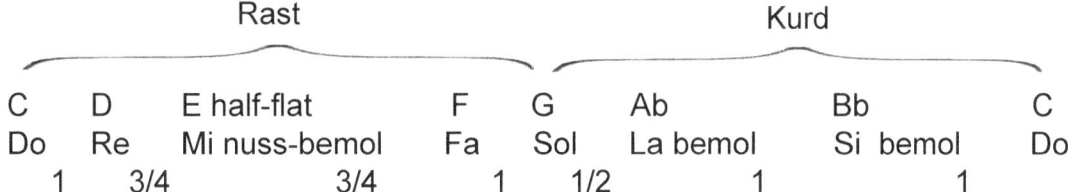

	Rast				Kurd		
C	D	E half-flat	F	G	Ab	Bb	C
Do	Re	Mi nuss-bemol	Fa	Sol	La bemol	Si bemol	Do
1	3/4	3/4	1	1/2	1	1	

Possible Descriptions: Rast pentachord on bottom; Kurd tetrachord on 5th; Nahawand tetrachord on 4th.
Used as ornament in Rast.

Dalanshin

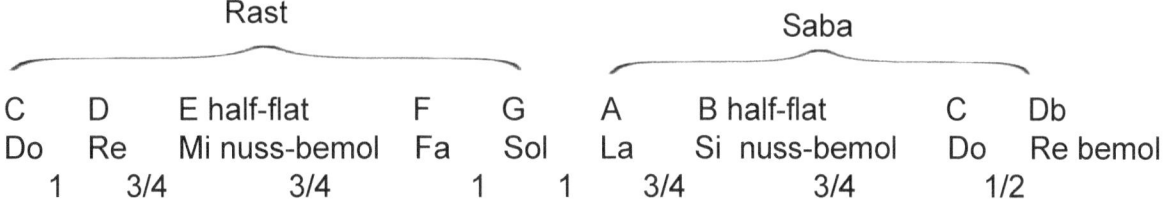

	Rast					Saba			
C	D	E half-flat	F	G	A	B half-flat	C	Db	
Do	Re	Mi nuss-bemol	Fa	Sol	La	Si nuss-bemol	Do	Re bemol	
1	3/4	3/4	1	1	3/4	3/4	1/2		

Possible Descriptions: Rast pentachord on bottom; Saba tetrachord on 6th. Ghammaz on 6th. Modulate into this by moving from the high C to the Db and then down to the A. Improvise in A Saba for a while and then move back to Rast by starting on the G and walking up through A, B half-flat to C.
Used as very exotic ornament in Rast.

Derived C-Based Maqams
Nawa Athar Family

Nakriz

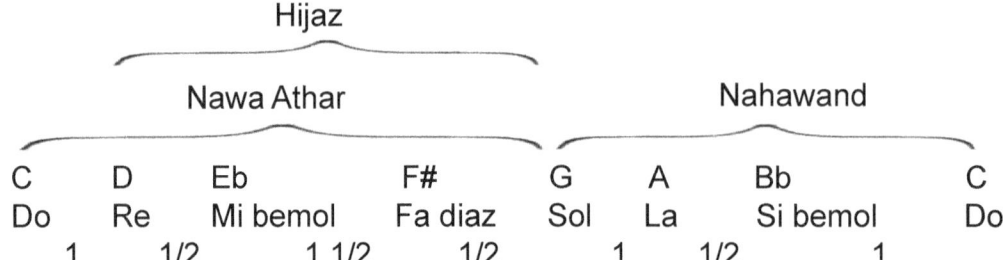

C	D	Eb		F#	G	A	Bb	C
Do	Re	Mi bemol		Fa diaz	Sol	La	Si bemol	Do
	1	1/2	1 1/2	1/2	1	1/2		1

Possible Descriptions: Nawa Athar pentachord on bottom; Hijaz tetrachord on 2nd; Nahawand tetrachord on 5nd.

Common in central mountain Greek tsamika-style dance music with clarinet lead. 2nd (Re) is heard as sub-dominant or ghammaz. It is frequently used in melodies as if it were the tonic. This turns out to be temporary as the tune finally resolves back to the 1st (Do).

Basandidah

C	D	Eb		F#	G	A	B half flat	C
Do	Re	Mi bemol		Fa diaz	Sol	La	Si nuss bemol	Do
	1	1/2	1 1/2	1/2	1	3/4		3/4

Possible Descriptions: Nawa Athar pentachord on bottom; Hijaz tetrachord on 2nd; Rast tetrachord on the 5th.

Derived Bb-Based Maqams
Ajam Family

Shawq Afza

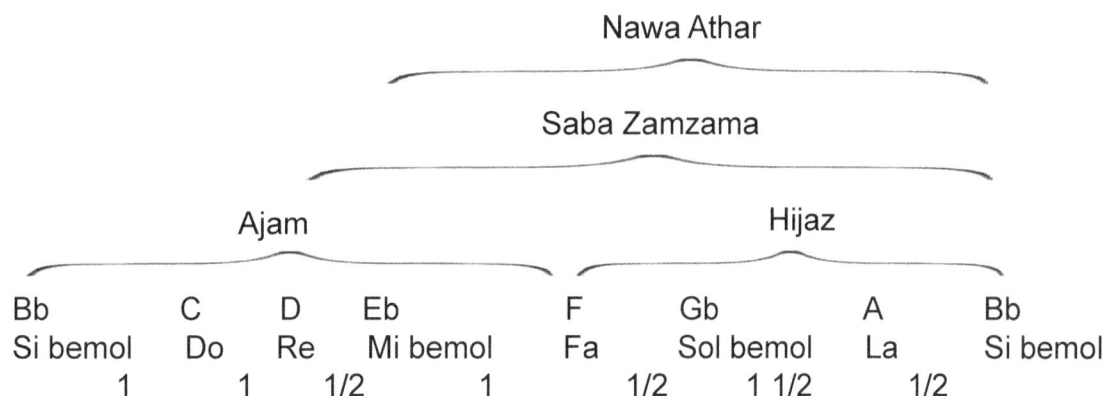

	Ajam				Hijaz		
Bb	C	D	Eb	F	Gb	A	Bb
Si bemol	Do	Re	Mi bemol	Fa	Sol bemol	La	Si bemol
1		1	1/2	1	1/2	1 1/2	1/2

(Brackets above: Saba Zamzama spans Eb–A; Nawa Athar spans F–Bb)

Possible Descriptions: Ajam or "Jaharka" pentachord on bottom; Hijaz tetrachord on 5th; Nawa Athar pentachord on 4th; maqam Saba Zamzama on 3rd. And if the Eb is raised to E half-flat then maqam Saba appears on the 3rd. This is an acceptable substitution within Shawq Afza.

The option of using jins hijaz on the 5th is a common pattern. Rast becomes Suznak with this change and Nahawand 1 becomes Nahawand 2 with this same change.

Shawqi Awir

Closely Related Maqamat: Tarz Jadid

	Nahawand						
Ajam				Nahawand			
Bb	C	D	Eb	F	G	Ab	Bb
Si bemol	Do	Re	Mi bemol	Fa	Sol	La bemol	Si bemol
1	1	1/2	1	1	1/2	1	

Possible Descriptions: Ajam or "Jaharka" pentachord on bottom; Nahawand tetrachord on 5th (ghammaz on 5th); Nahawand maqam on 2nd (if ghammaz is placed on 2nd, then maqam Shawqi Awir becomes maqam Tarz Jadid.)

"The majority of musicians think that these two notes, Ab and G#, should not be rendered by the same key and that if this is done for the convenience of instrument manufacture, the ear suffers for it... ...there is a small distance from F# to Gb and instruments on which the same key renders both sounds are false. --Philippe Marc Antoine Geslin -1825"
    --Duffin 2007

Derived E half-flat-Based Maqams
Sikah Family

Awshar

Closely Related Maqamat: Sha'ar, Mayah, Wajh 'ardibar

Sikah			Nahawand			Rast		
E half-flat	F	G	A	Bb		C	D	E half-flat
Mi nuss-bemol	Fa	Sol	La	Si bemol		Do	Re	Mi nuss-be-mol
3/4	1	1	1/2		1		1	3/4

Possible Descriptions: Sikah trichord on bottom; Nahawand tetrachord on 3rd; Rast trichord on 6th.

Ramal

Sikah			Bayati			Rast		
E half-flat	F	G	A half-flat		Bb	C	D	E half-flat
Mi nuss-bemol	Fa	Sol	La nuss-bemol		Si bemol	Do	Re	Mi nuss-bemol
3/4	1	3/4	3/4		1		1	3/4

Possible Descriptions: Sikah trichord on bottom; Bayati tetrachord on 3rd; Rast trichord on 6th.

Derived F-Based Maqams
Jaharkah Family

Jaharkah Arabi

Closely Related Maqamat: Najdi

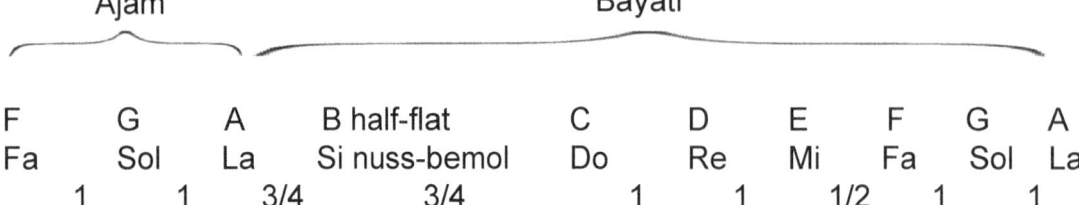

	Ajam			Bayati					
F	G	A	B half-flat	C	D	E	F	G	A
Fa	Sol	La	Si nuss-bemol	Do	Re	Mi	Fa	Sol	La
1	1	3/4	3/4	1	1	1/2	1	1	

Possible Descriptions: Ajam trichord on bottom; Bayti maqam on 3rd.

Jaharka Turki (Shehnaz on F)

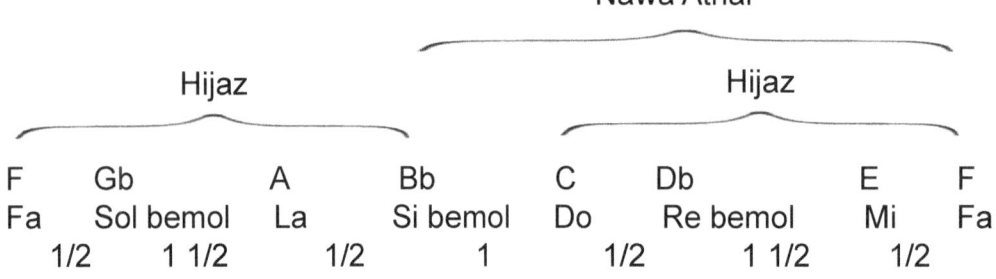

	Hijaz			Nawa Athar / Hijaz			
F	Gb	A	Bb	C	Db	E	F
Fa	Sol bemol	La	Si bemol	Do	Re bemol	Mi	Fa
1/2	1 1/2	1/2	1	1/2	1 1/2	1/2	

Possible Descriptions: Hijaz pentachord on bottom; Hijaz tetrachord on 5th. The upper Hijaz tetrachord can also be replaced by a Rast tetrachord.

Derived Transposed D--Based Maqamat
Transposed to C

Zanjaran (Hijaz on C with Ajam)

Closely Related Maqamat: Zingaran, Zankulah, Zankhala

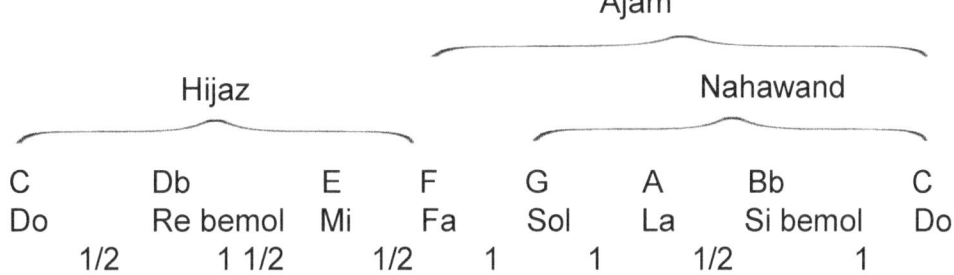

	Hijaz				Ajam		
						Nahawand	
C	Db	E	F	G	A	Bb	C
Do	Re bemol	Mi	Fa	Sol	La	Si bemol	Do
1/2		1 1/2	1/2	1	1	1/2	1

Possible Descriptions: Hijaz tetrachord on bottom; Ajam pentachord on 4th; Nahawand tetrachord on 5th.

Hijaz Kar Kurd (Kurd on C)

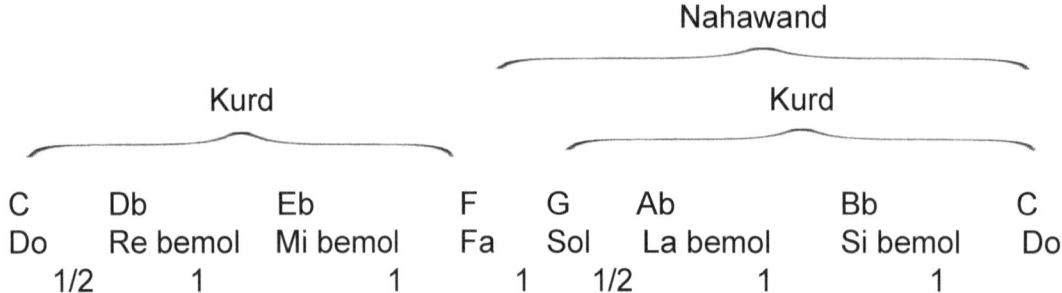

	Kurd				Nahawand		Kurd	
C	Db	Eb	F	G	Ab		Bb	C
Do	Re bemol	Mi bemol	Fa	Sol	La bemol		Si bemol	Do
	1/2	1	1	1	1/2		1	1

Possible Descriptions: Kurd tetrachord on bottom; Nahawand pentachord on 4th; Kurd tetrachord on 5th.
Associated Moods: Lightly romantic.
Tawfiq al-Sabbagh suggests that for maximum ecstatic effect the Db and Eb should not be played with too low a pitch. By looking at the table for jins Athar Kar Kurd we verify that we have 16:15, 13:12, 12:11 or 11:10 to choose from for the Db, and the 11:9 as well as the 6:5 for the Eb.

Tarz Nawin (Kurd on C with Hijaz)

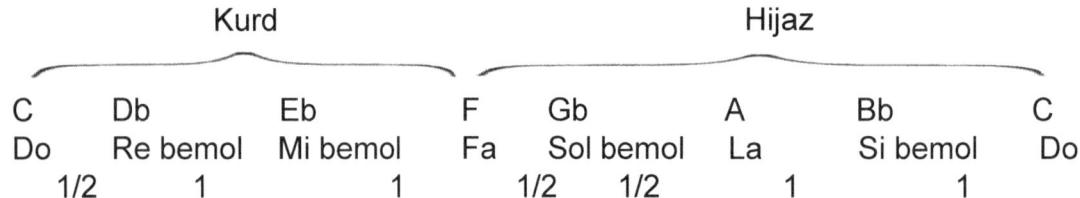

	Kurd				Hijaz			
C	Db	Eb	F	Gb	A		Bb	C
Do	Re bemol	Mi bemol	Fa	Sol bemol	La		Si bemol	Do
	1/2	1	1	1/2	1/2		1	1

Possible Descriptions: Kurd tetrachord on bottom; Hijaz pentachord on 4th.

Derived Transposed D-Based Maqamat
Transposed to G

Shad Araban (Shehnaz on G)

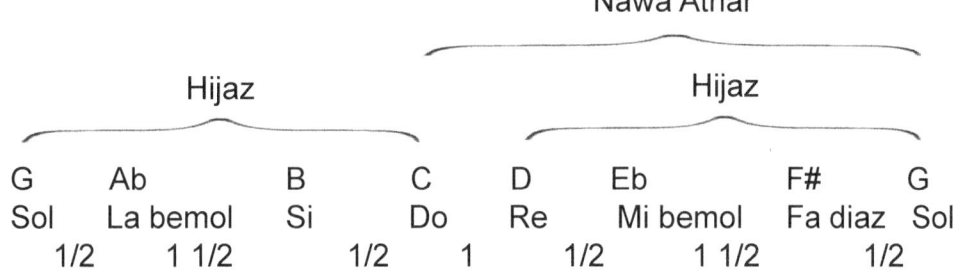

Possible Descriptions: Hijaz tertrachord on bottom; Hijaz tetrachord on 5th; Nawa Athar pentachord on the 4th.

Sikah Balady (Shehnaz on G with the "old intervals")

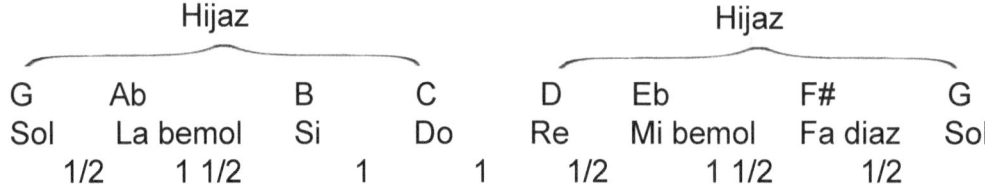

Possible Descriptions: Hijaz tetrachord on bottom; Hijaz tetrachord on 5th.

Sikah Balady follows the pattern of Hijaz Gharib (Old Hijaz) in that only the justly intonated intervals are used. In other words the 1 1/2 step intervals in both hijaz tetrachords are shrunk so that the Ab and Eb are augmented or sharpened and the B and F# are diminished or flattened.

The word "sikah" calls this "quartertone" emphasis to mind. Since sikah is the name of the E half-flat note in the Arabic musical scale, loose use of this term always brings to mind the fact that the ET notes are not called for. Also in maqam Sikah the very first interval from E half-flat to F is a "3/4 step" so again the word "sikah" references non-ET intervals and harmonies. The term "sikah" is commonly used in musicians' language to mean quartertones as in "Si Sikah" meaning "B half-flat."

Sikah Baladi is a common folk maqam in Egypt.

Derived Transposed D-Based Maqamat
Transposed to A

Suzidil (Shehnaz on A)

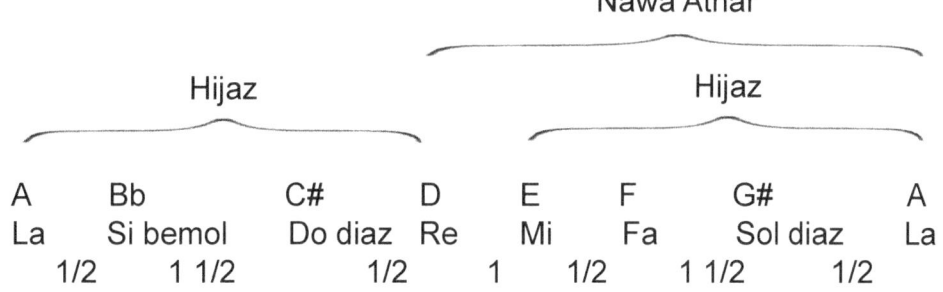

Possible Descriptions: Hijaz tetrachord on bottom; Hijaz tetrachord on 5th; Nawa Athar pentachord on the 4th.

Shawki Tarab (Kurd on A with Saba)

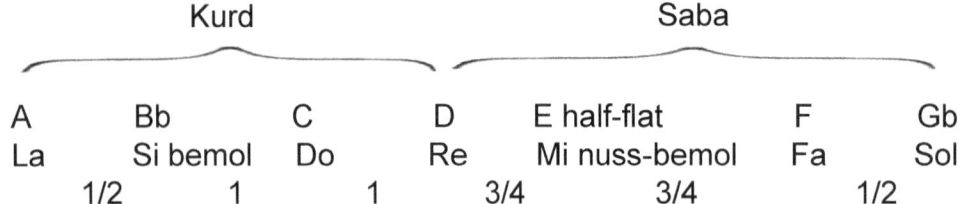

A	Bb	C	D	E half-flat	F	Gb
La	Si bemol	Do	Re	Mi nuss-bemol	Fa	Sol
	1/2	1	1	3/4	3/4	1/2

Possible Descriptions: Kurd tetrachord on bottom; Saba tetrachord on 4th.

Busalik Ushayran (Bayati on A)

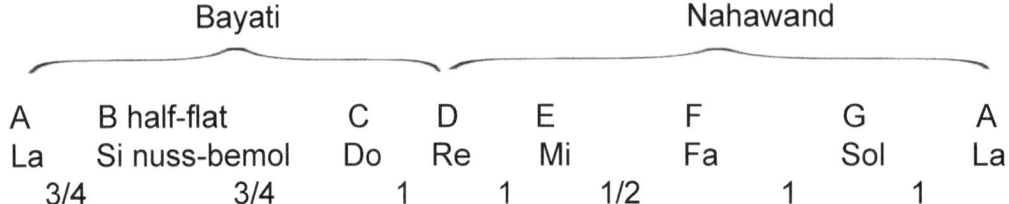

A	B half-flat	C	D	E	F	G	A
La	Si nuss-bemol	Do	Re	Mi	Fa	Sol	La
3/4	3/4	1	1	1/2	1	1	

Possible Descriptions: Bayyati tetrachord on bottom; Nahawand (Buselik) pentachord on 4th.

Nuhuft (Huseyni on A)

Closely Related Maqamat: Huseyni Ushayran

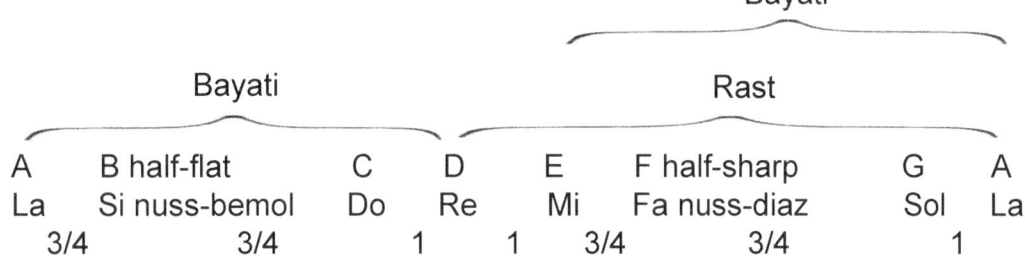

A	B half-flat	C	D	E	F half-sharp	G	A
La	Si nuss-bemol	Do	Re	Mi	Fa nuss-diaz	Sol	La
3/4		3/4	1	1	3/4	3/4	1

Possible Descriptions: Bayyati tetrachord on bottom; Bayyati tetrachord on 5th; Rast pentachord on 4th. An alternate form of this maqam uses Ajam instead of Rast on the 4th which makes it a transposition of Mohayar..

Hijazi Ushayran (Shuri on A)

Bayati | Hijaz

A	B half-flat	C	D	Eb	F#	G	A
La	Si nuss-bemol	Do	Re	Mi bemol	Fa diaz	Sol	La
3/4		3/4	1	1/2	1 1/2	1/2	1

Possible Descriptions: Bayyati tetrachord on bottom; Hijaz pentachord on 4th.

Bayati Ushayran (Bayatayn on A)

	Bayati				Bayati			
A	B half-flat	C	D	E half-flat	F		G	A
La	Si nuss-bemol	Do	Re	Mi nuss-bemol	Fa		Sol	La
3/4	3/4	1	3/4	3/4		1		1

Possible Descriptions: Bayyati tetrachord on bottom; Bayyati pentachord on 4th.

"If the musical quality of all the tones is precisely the same, there seems to be no ground for understanding how each different key should have a different character. Hermann von Helmholz -1863"
  --Duffin 2007

Derived Transposed D-Based Maqamat
Transposed to E

Qatar (Saba Zamzamah on E)

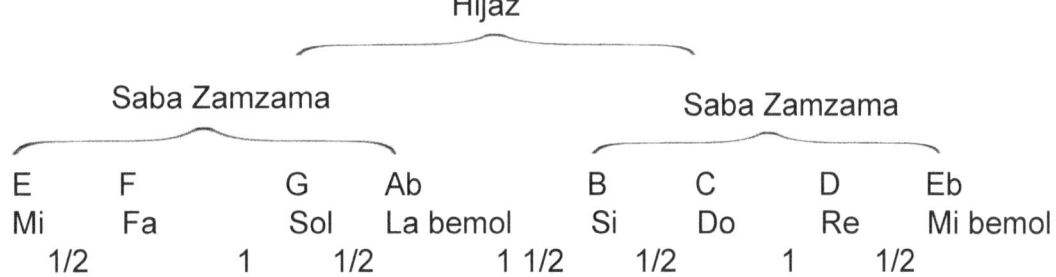

E	F		G	Ab	B	C	D	Eb
Mi	Fa		Sol	La bemol	Si	Do	Re	Mi bemol
1/2		1		1/2	1 1/2	1/2	1	1/2

Possible Descriptions: Kurd trichord on bottom; Saba Zamzama tetrachord on bottom; Hijaz tetrachord on 3rd; Shehnaz maqam on 3rd; Saba Zamzama tetrachord on 5th.

Derived Transposed C--Based Maqamat
Transposed to G

Farahfaza (Nahawand 1 on G)

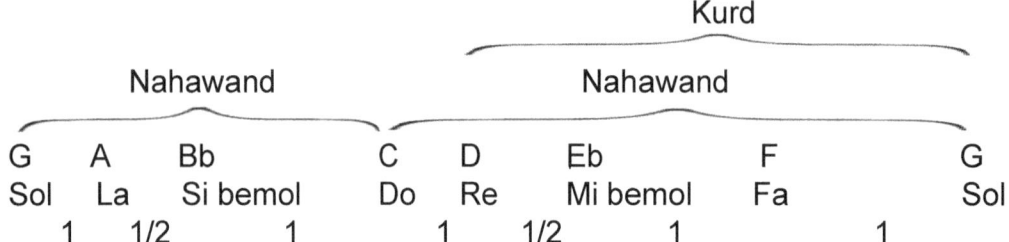

G	A	Bb	C	D	Eb	F	G
Sol	La	Si bemol	Do	Re	Mi bemol	Fa	Sol
1	1/2	1	1	1/2	1	1	

Possible Descriptions: Nahawand tetrachord on bottom; Nahawand pentachord on 4th; Kurd tetrachord on 5th. Equivalent to "G minor" in the West.

Associated Moods: Festive, joyful.

Sultani Yaka (Nahawand 2 on G)

Closely Related Maqamat: Rahat Faza

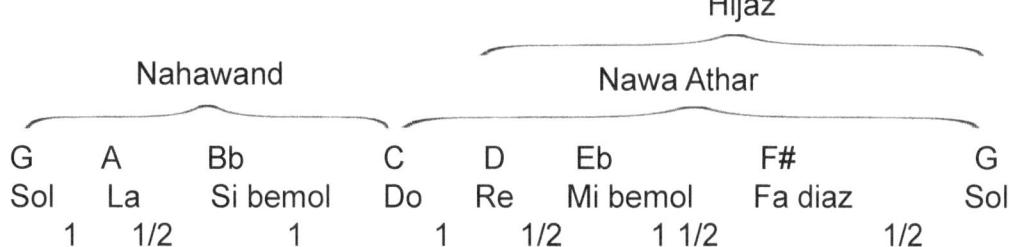

| | | Hijaz | |
| | Nahawand | Nawa Athar | |

G	A	Bb	C	D	Eb	F#	G
Sol	La	Si bemol	Do	Re	Mi bemol	Fa diaz	Sol
1	1/2	1	1	1/2	1 1/2	1/2	

Possible Descriptions: Nahawand tetrachord on bottom; Nawa Athar pentachord on 4th; Hijaz tetrachord on 5th. Equivalent to "G harmonic minor" in the West.

Dilkashidah (Nahawand on G with Bayati)

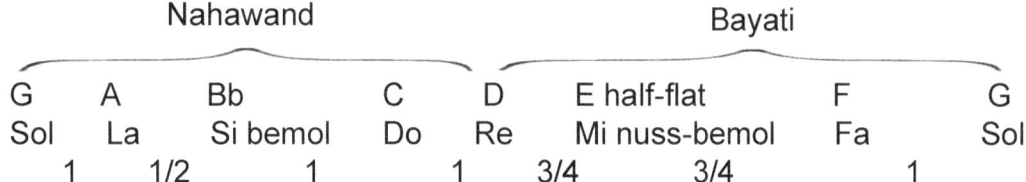

| | Nahawand | | | | Bayati | | |
G	A	Bb	C	D	E half-flat	F	G
Sol	La	Si bemol	Do	Re	Mi nuss-bemol	Fa	Sol
1	1/2	1	1	3/4	3/4	1	

Possible Descriptions: Nahawand pentachord on bottom; Bayati tetrachord on 5th.

Yak-Gah (Rast on G) (Rast Nawa)

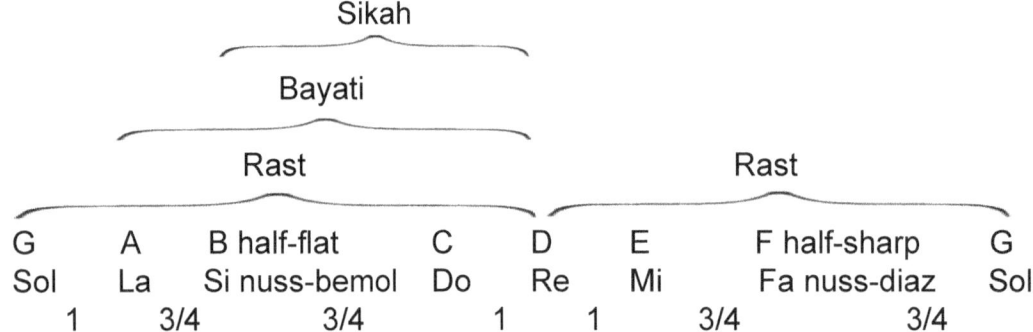

Possible Descriptions: Rast pentachord on bottom; Rast tetrachord on 5th; Bayyati tetrachord on the 2nd; Sikah trichord on the 3rd.

This maqam contains the most fundamental sequence of notes in the Arabic scales. Transpositions aside, most "quartertone" maqamat are born from this sequence.

A musician who tunes his instrument to the just intervals in Yak-Gah will find himself to be fundamentally in tune across a large range of fundamental maqamat.

The Rast jins on the 5th may sometimes appear as jins Ajam which can make this maqam a transposition of Mahur.

Associated Moods: Same as Rast: elegant, soaring, deep-rooted, romantic, spiritual, everything is contained here.

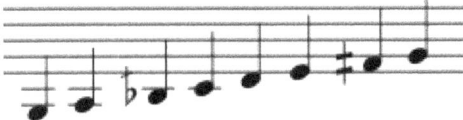

Yekah (Nayruz on G)

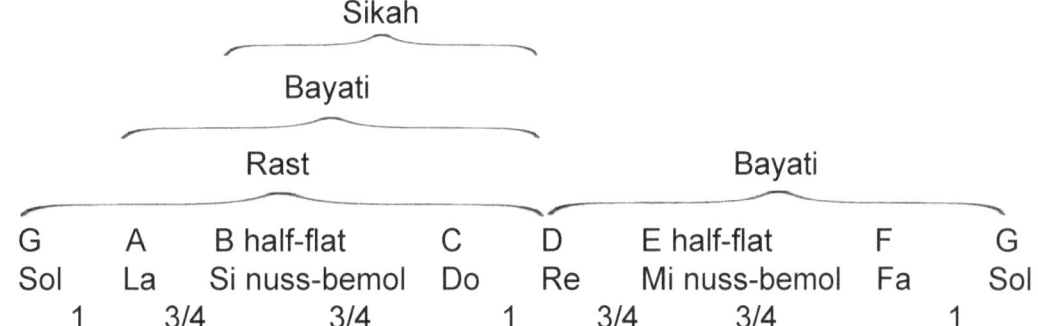

Possible Descriptions: Rast pentachord on bottom; Bayati tetrachord on 5th.

Derived Transposed C-Based Maqamat
   Transposed to E

Busalik (Nahawand on E)

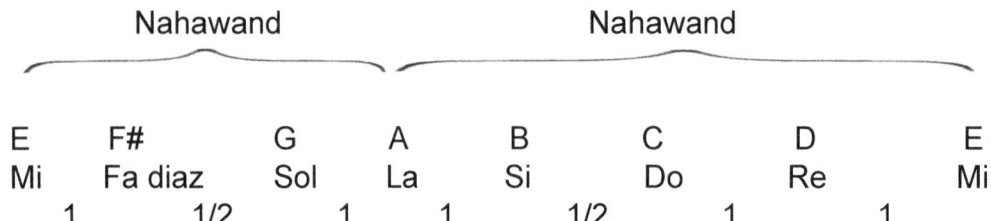

Nahawand				Nahawand			
E	F#	G	A	B	C	D	E
Mi	Fa diaz	Sol	La	Si	Do	Re	Mi
1	1/2	1	1	1/2	1	1	

Possible Descriptions: Nahawand tetrachord on bottom; Nahawand pentachord on 4th.
Like other forms of Nahawand, the top jins may evolve from Nahawand to Nawa Athar with its Hijaz interval. Both forms may also be called "E minor" in the West.

Some say that the third note in Busalik is slightly flatter than the Nahawand 3rd. Choosing the just minor 3rd described by the 7/6 ratio is some 35 cents flatter than the ET minor 3rd and 50 cents flatter than the usual just minor 3rd and it can be very sultry and pleasing to the ear.

Busalik is primarily a Turkish maqam.

Shiar (Nahawand on E with Bayati)

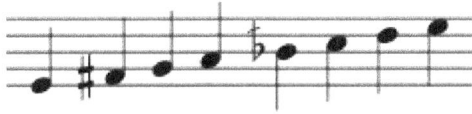

	Nahawand				Bayati			
E	F#	G	A	B half-flat		C	D	E
Mi	Fa diaz	Sol	La	Si nuss-bemol		Do	Re	Mi
1		1/2	1	3/4	3/4		1	1

Possible Descriptions: Nahawand tetrachord on bottom; Bayati pentachord on 4th.

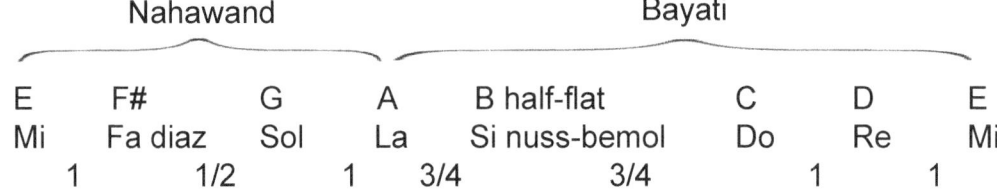

"An equal temperament, however, cannot subsist, or else we would no longer have any key characteristics. - Pietro Lichtenthal -1826"
        --Duffin 2007

Derived Transposed C-Based Maqamat
Transposed to D

Nahawand Kurdi (Nahawand on D)

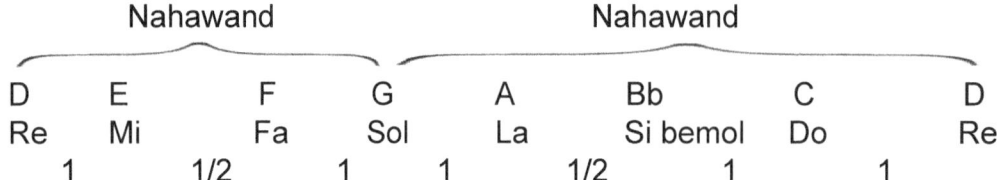

Possible Descriptions: Nahawand tetrachord on bottom; Nahawand pentachord on 4th.

Like other forms of Nahawand, the top jins may evolve from Nahawand to Nawa Athar with its Hijaz interval. Both forms may also be called "D minor" in the West.

Ushaq Masri (Nahawand on D with Bayati)

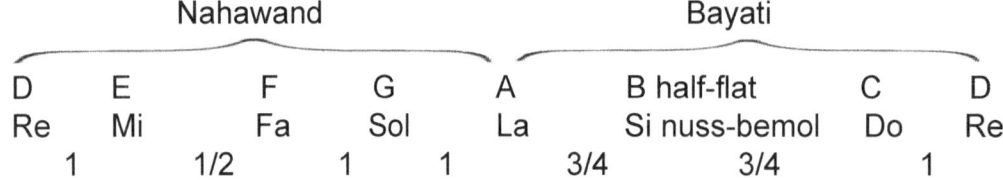

Possible Descriptions: Nahawand pentachord on bottom; Bayati tetrachord on 5th.

Nishaburk (Nayruz on D)

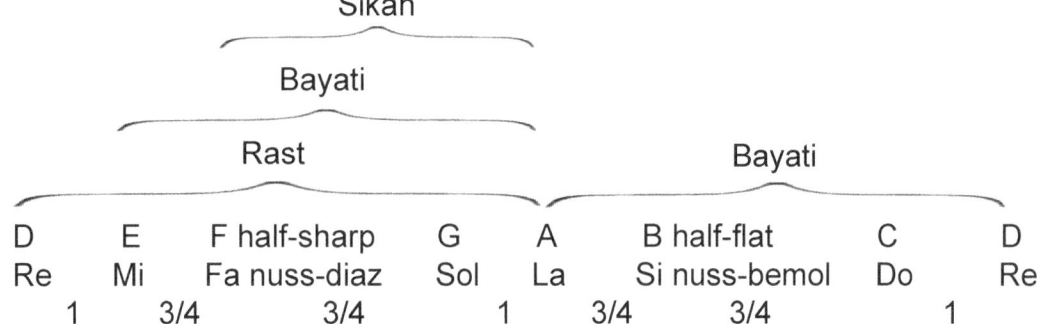

D	E	F half-sharp	G	A	B half-flat	C	D
Re	Mi	Fa nuss-diaz	Sol	La	Si nuss-bemol	Do	Re
1	3/4	3/4	1	3/4	3/4	1	

Bracketing: Rast (D–G), Bayati (E–A), Sikah (F half-sharp–A), Bayati (A–D).

Possible Descriptions: Rast pentachord on bottom; Bayati tetrachord on 5th.

Hisar (Nawa Athar on D)

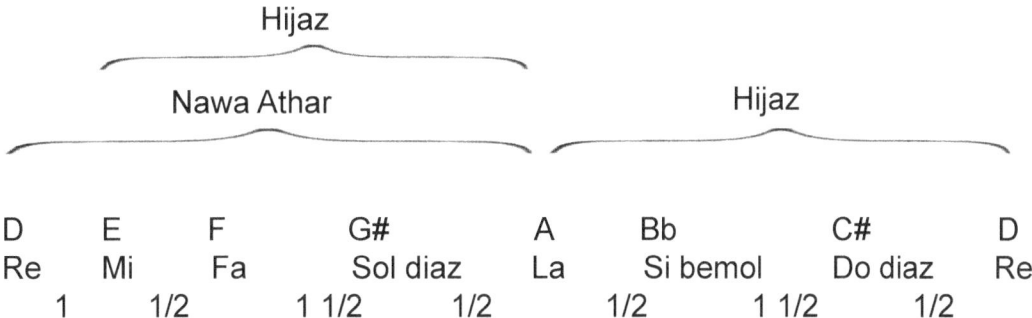

D	E	F	G#	A	Bb	C#	D
Re	Mi	Fa	Sol diaz	La	Si bemol	Do diaz	Re
1	1/2	1 1/2	1/2	1/2	1 1/2	1/2	

Bracketing: Nawa Athar (D–A), Hijaz (E–A), Hijaz (A–D).

Possible Descriptions: Nawa Athar pentachord on bottom; Hijaz tetrachord on 2nd; Hijaz tetrachord on the 5th.

Derived Transposed C-Based Maqamat
Transposed to Db

Midmi (C Hijaz Kar 2nd becomes Tonic on Db)

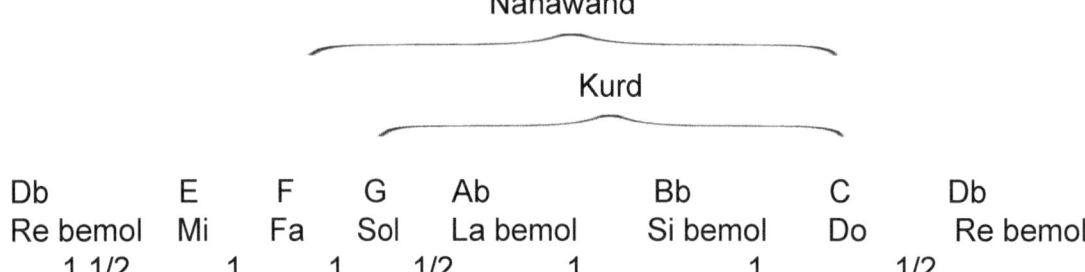

Db	E	F	G	Ab	Bb	C	Db
Re bemol	Mi	Fa	Sol	La bemol	Si bemol	Do	Re bemol
1 1/2		1	1	1/2	1	1	1/2

Possible Descriptions: Hijaz fragment on bottom; Nahawand pentachord on 3rd: Kurd tetrachord on 4th.

This is an Iraqi maqam which follows its own unique pattern.

Derived Transposed F--Based Maqamat
Transposed to D

Zirgulah (Jaharka on D)

	Ajam				Ajam		
D	E	F#	G	A	B	C#	D
Re	Mi	Fa diaz	Sol	La	Si	Do diaz	Re
1	1	1/2	1	1	1	1/2	

Possible Descriptions: Ajam or "Jaharka" pentachord on bottom; Ajam or "Jaharka" tetrachord on 5th.

Just as in maqam Jaharka, some would replace the upper Ajam jins with Rast. This would change the C to a C half-sharp.

Derived Transposed Bb--Based Maqamat
  Transposed to D

Nishabur (Ajam on D with Nahawand)

	Ajam			Nahawand			
D	E	F#	G	A	Bb	C	D
Re	Mi	Fa diaz	Sol	La	Si bemol	Do	Re
1	1	1/2	1	1/2	1	1	

Possible Descriptions: Ajam tetrachord on bottom; Nahawand pentachord on 4th.

Derived Transposed Bb-Based Maqamat
 Transposed to C

Ajam on C

Closely Related: C major

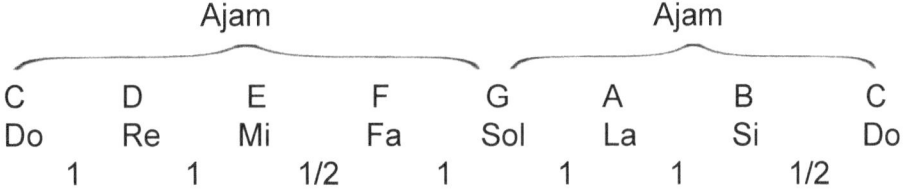

	Ajam				Ajam		
C	D	E	F	G	A	B	C
Do	Re	Mi	Fa	Sol	La	Si	Do
1	1	1/2	1	1	1	1/2	

Possible Descriptions: Ajam pentachord on bottom; Ajam tetrachord on 5th; Nahawand maqam on 6th; Ajam is "relative major" to the Nahawand on A (A minor scale).

Maqam Ajam on C

Approximate Interval	Approx. Note Names	Ratio of Interval	Exact Just Cents	Exact Just Hz	Nearest 12-note ET Cents	Nearest 24-note ET Cents	Nearest 24-note ET Hz
ET Tonic on C	C - C	1:1	0.00	261.63	0	0	261.63
	C - C hs	25:24	70.67	272.53	100	50	269.30
	C - C#	19/18	93.60	276.16	100	100	277.18
ET Minor 2nd	C - C# or Db	2 to the 1/12th			100		277.18
Just Minor 2nd	C - Db	16:15	111.73	279.07	100	100	277.18
	C - D hf	13:12	138.57	283.43	100	150	285.31
	C - D hf	12:11	150.64	285.42	200	150	285.31
	C - D hf	11:10	165.00	287.79	200	150	285.31
Just Major 2nd Sm	C - D	10:9	182.40	290.70	200	200	293.66
ET Major 2nd	C - D	2 to the 1/6th			200		293.66
Just Major 2nd Lg	C - D	9:8	203.91	294.33	200	200	293.66
	C - D hs	8:7	231.17	299.01	200	250	302.27
	C - D hs	7:6	266.87	305.23	200	250	302.27
ET Minor 3rd	C - Eb	2 to the 1/4th			300		311.13
Just Minor 3rd	C - Eb	6:5	315.64	313.95	300	300	311.13
	C - E hf	11:9	347.40	319.77	300	350	320.25
ET Qrtrtone	C - E hf	2 to the 1/4ths	350.00		300	350	320.25
Just Major 3rd	C - E hf	5:4	386.31	327.03	400	350	329.63
ET Major 3rd	C - E	2 to the 1/3rd			400		329.63
Just Major 3rd Lg	C - E	19:15	409.24	331.40	400	400	329.63
	C - Fb	9:7	435.08	336.38	400	450	339.29
Just 4th	C - F	4:3	498.04	348.83	500	500	349.23
ET 4th	C - F	2 to the 5/12ths			500		349.23
	C - F#	11:8	551.32	359.74	600	550	359.47
Just Tritone	C - Gb	7:5	582.51	366.28	600	600	369.99
	C - Gb	10:7	617.49	373.76	600	600	369.99
ET 5th	C - G	2 to the 7/12ths			700		392.00
Just 5th	C - G	3:2	701.95	392.46	700	700	392.00
	C - G#	11:7	782.49	411.13	800	750	403.49
ET Minor 6th	C - Ab	2 to the 2/3rds			800		415.30
Just Minor 6th	C - Ab	8:5	813.69	418.61	800	800	415.30
	C - A hf	13:8	840.53	425.15	800	850	427.48
Just Major 6th	C - A	5:3	884.36	436.06	900	900	440.00
ET Major 6th	C - A	2 to the 3/4ths			900		440.00
	C - A#	12:7	933.13	448.51	900	950	452.90
	C - A#	7:4	968.83	457.85	1000	950	452.90
Just Minor 7th Sm	C - Bb	16:9	996.09	465.12	1000	1000	466.16
ET Minor 7th	C - Bb	2 to the 5/6ths			1000		466.16
Just Minor 7th Lg	C - Bb	9:5	1017.60	470.94	1000	1000	466.16
	C - B hf	11:6	1049.36	479.65	1000	1050	479.83
	C - B hf	13:7	1071.70	485.88	1100	1050	479.83
Just Major 7th	C - B	15:8	1088.27	490.57	1100	1050	479.83
ET Major 7th	C - B	2 to the 11/12ths			1100		493.88
	C - B	17:9	1101.04	494.19	1100	1100	493.88
	C - B	19:10	1111.20	497.10	1100	1100	493.88
	C - B#	125:64	1158.94	510.98	1100	1150	508.36
ET Octave	C - C	2:1	1200.00	523.26	1200	1200	523.25

Suznal (Shawq Afza on C)

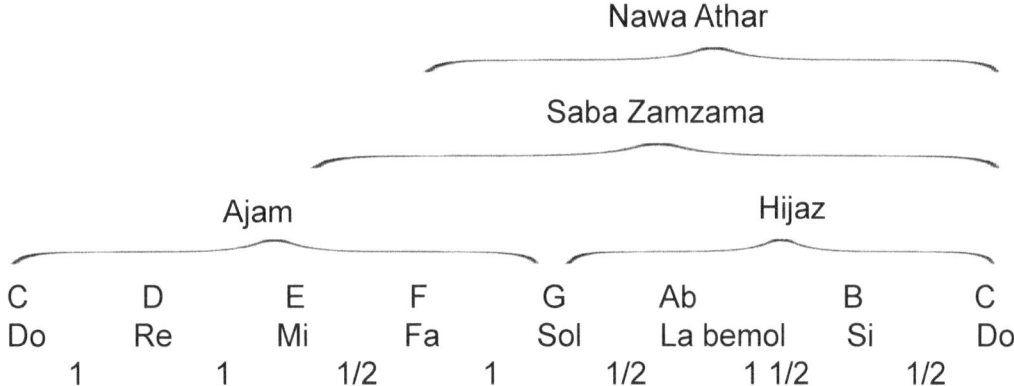

C	D	E	F	G	Ab	B	C
Do	Re	Mi	Fa	Sol	La bemol	Si	Do
1	1	1/2	1	1/2	1 1/2	1/2	

Possible Descriptions: Ajam pentachord on bottom; Hijaz tetrachord on 5th; Nawa Athar pentachord on 4th; maqam Saba Zamzama on 3rd.

Panjigah (Shawqi Awir on C)

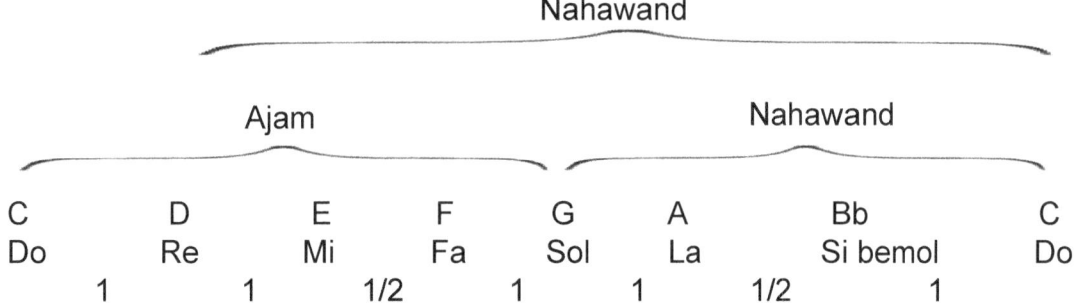

C	D	E	F	G	A	Bb	C
Do	Re	Mi	Fa	Sol	La	Si bemol	Do
1	1	1/2	1	1	1/2	1	

Possible Descriptions: Ajam pentachord on bottom; Nahawand tetrachord on 5th; Nahawand maqam on 2nd.

Derived Transposed E half-flat--Based Maqamat
Transposed to B half-flat

Bastanikar (Huzam on B half-flat with Saba)

Closely Related Maqamat: Taz Nuin

	Sikah				Saba			
B half-flat		C	D	E half-flat		F	Gb	A	B half-flat
Si nuss-bemol		Do	Re	Mi nuss-bemol		Fa	Sol bemol	La	Si nuss-bemol
3/4		1	3/4	3/4		1/2	1 1/2	3/4

Possible Descriptions: Sikah trichord on bottom; Saba pentachord on 3rd.

The quartertone mystique of numerous 3/4 step intervals is exquisitely available in this maqam.

Irak (Huzam on B half-flat with Bayati)

      Sikah   Bayati

B half-flat	C	D	E half-flat	F	G	A	B half-flat
Si nuss-bemol	Do	Re	Mi nuss-bemol	Fa	Sol	La	Si nuss-bemol
3/4	1	3/4	3/4	1	1	3/4	

Possible Descriptions: Sikah trichord on bottom. Bayyati pentachord on 3rd.

Farahnak (Sikah on B half-flat)

      Sikah   Rast

B half-flat	C	D	E	F half-sharp	G	A	B half-flat
Si nuss-bemol	Do	Re	Mi	Fa nuss-diaz	Sol	La	Si nuss-bemol
3/4	1	1	3/4	3/4	1	3/4	

Possible Descriptions: Sikah trichord on bottom. Rast pentachord on 3rd; Rast maqam on 6th.

Unusual C-Based Ajnas and Maqams
Sazkar and Zawil Family

Jins Sazkar on C

Approximate Interval	Approx. Note Names	Ratio of Interval	Exact Just Cents	Exact Just Hz	Nearest 12-note ET Cents	Nearest 24-note ET Cents	Nearest 24-note ET Hz
ET Tonic on C	C - C	1:1	0.00	261.63	0	0	261.63
	C - C hs	25:24	70.67	272.53	100	50	269.30
	C - C#	19:18	93.60	276.16	100	100	277.18
ET Minor 2nd	C - C# or Db	2 to the 1/12th			100		277.18
Just Minor 2nd	C - Db	16:15	111.73	279.07	100	100	277.18
	C - D hf	13:12	138.57	283.43	100	150	285.31
	C - D hf	12:11	150.64	285.42	200	150	285.31
	C - D hf	11:10	165.00	287.79	200	150	285.31
Just Major 2nd Sm	C - D	10:9	182.40	290.70	200	200	293.66
ET Major 2nd	C - D	2 to the 1/6th			200		293.66
Just Major 2nd Lg	C - D	9:8	203.91	294.33	200	200	293.66
	C - D hs	8:7	231.17	299.01	200	250	302.27
	C - D hs	7:6	266.87	305.23	200	250	302.27
ET Minor 3rd	C - Eb	2 to the 1/4th			300		311.13
Just Minor 3rd	C - Eb	6:5	315.64	313.95	300	300	311.13
	C - E hf	11:9	347.40	319.77	300	350	320.25
ET Qrtrtone	C - E hf	2 to the 1/4ths	350.00		300	350	320.25
Just Major 3rd	C - E hf	5:4	386.31	327.03	400	350	329.63
ET Major 3rd	C - E	2 to the 1/3rd			400		329.63
	C - Fb	9:7	435.08	336.38	400	450	339.29
Just 4th	C - F	4:3	498.04	348.83	500	500	349.23

Rast Kabir

	Sazkar				Nahawand		
C	D#	E half-flat	F	G	A	Bb	C
Do	Re diaz	Mi nuss-bemol	Fa	Sol	La	Si bemol	Do
5/4	1/4	3/4	1	1	1/2	1	

Possible Descriptions: Sazkar tetrachord on bottom; Nahawand tetrachord on 5th.

Sazkar

	Sazkar				Rast		
C	D#	E half-flat	F	G	A	B half-flat	C
Do	Re diaz	Mi nuss-bemol	Fa	Sol	La	Si nuss bemol	Do
5/4	1/4	3/4	1	1	3/4	3/4	

Possible Descriptions: Sazkar tetrachord on bottom; Rast tetrachord on 5th.

Jins Zawil on C

Approximate Interval	Approx. Note Names	Ratio of Interval	Exact Just Cents	Exact Just Hz	Nearest 12-note ET Cents	Nearest 24-note ET Cents	Nearest 24-note ET Hz
ET Tonic on C	C - C	1:1	0.00	261.63	0	0	261.63
	C - C hs	25:24	70.67	272.53	100	50	269.30
	C - C#	19/18	93.60	276.16	100	100	277.18
ET Minor 2nd	C - C# or Db	2 to the 1/12th			100		277.18
Just Minor 2nd	C - Db	16:15	111.73	279.07	100	100	277.18
	C - D hf	13:12	138.57	283.43	100	150	285.31
	C - D hf	12:11	150.64	285.42	200	150	285.31
	C - D hf	11:10	165.00	287.79	200	150	285.31
Just Major 2nd Sm	C - D	10:9	182.40	290.70	200	200	293.66
ET Major 2nd	C - D	2 to the 1/6th			200		293.66
Just Major 2nd Lg	C - D	9:8	203.91	294.33	200	200	293.66
	C - D hs	8:7	231.17	299.01	200	250	302.27
	C - D hs	7/6	266.87	305.23	200	250	302.27
ET Minor 3rd	C - Eb	2 to the 1/4th			300		311.13
Just Minor 3rd	C - Eb	6:5	315.64	313.95	300	300	311.13
	C - E hf	11:9	347.40	319.77	300	350	320.25
ET Qrtrtone	C - E hf	2 to the 1/4ths	350.00		300	350	320.25
Just Major 3rd	C - E hf	5:4	386.31	327.03	400	350	329.63
ET Major 3rd	C - E	2 to the 1/3rd			400		329.63
	C - E	19:15	409.24	331.40	400	400	329.63
	C - Fb	9:7	435.08	336.38	400	450	339.29
Just 4th	C - F	4:3	498.04	348.83	500	500	349.23
ET 4th	C - F	2 to the 5/12ths			500		349.23
	C - F#	11:8	551.32	359.74	600	550	359.47

Zawil

```
         Zawil                                    Nahawand
⎯⎯⎯⎯⎯⎯⎯⎯⎯⎯⎯⎯⎯⎯⎯⎯⎯⎯⎯⎯⎯⎯⎯⎯         ⎯⎯⎯⎯⎯⎯⎯⎯⎯⎯⎯⎯⎯⎯⎯⎯⎯⎯⎯⎯⎯⎯⎯⎯
C    D      E half-flat      F#       G    A     Bb          C
Do   Re     Mi nuss-bemol    Fa diaz  Sol  La    Si bemol    Do
     1      3/4              5/4      1/2  1     1/2         1
```

Possible Descriptions: Zawil tetrachord on bottom; Nahawand tetrachord on 5th.

Rast Jadid

Closely Related Maqamat: Rahawi, Pesendide

```
         Zawil                                    Rast
⎯⎯⎯⎯⎯⎯⎯⎯⎯⎯⎯⎯⎯⎯⎯⎯⎯⎯⎯⎯⎯⎯⎯⎯         ⎯⎯⎯⎯⎯⎯⎯⎯⎯⎯⎯⎯⎯⎯⎯⎯⎯⎯⎯⎯⎯⎯⎯⎯
C    D      E half-flat      F#       G    A     B half flat    C
Do   Re     Mi nuss-bemol    Fa diaz  Sol  La    Si nuss bemol  Do
     1      3/4              5/4      1/2  1     3/4            3/4
```

Possible Descriptions: Zawil tetrachord on bottom; Rast tetrachord on 5th.

Unusual E half-flat-Based Ajnas and Maqams
Mustaar and Mukhalaf

Jins Mustaar on E half-flat

Approximate Interval	Approx. Note Names	Ratio of Interval	Exact Just Cents	Exact Just Hz	Nearest 12-note ET Cents	Nearest 24-note ET Cents	Nearest 24-note ET Hz
Tonic	E hf - E hf	1:1	0.00	326.67	0	0	329.63
Sm Minor 2nd	E hf - F hf	25:24	70.67	340.28	100	50	339.29
Sm Minor 2nd	E hf - F	19:18	93.60	344.82	100	100	349.23
ET Minor 2nd					100		
Minor 2nd	E hf - F	16:15	111.73	348.45	100	100	349.23
Lg Minor 2nd	E hf - F	13:12	138.57	353.89	100	150	359.46
Lg Minor 2nd	E hf - F	12:11	150.64	356.37	200	150	
Sm Major 2nd	E hf - F	11:10	165.00	359.33	200	150	
Sm Major 2nd	E hf - F	10:9	182.40	362.97	200	200	
Major 2nd	E hf - F#	9:8	203.91	367.50	200	200	370.00
Lg Major 2nd	E hf - F#	8:7	231.17	373.34	200	250	380.84
Lg Major 2nd	E hf - G hf	7:6	266.87	381.11	200	250	
ET Minor 3rd					300		392.00
Minor 3rd	E hf - G	6:5	315.64	392.00	300	300	392.00

Mustaar

Mustaar		Nahawand			Rast		
E half-flat	F#	G	A	Bb	C	D	E half-flat
Mi nuss-bemol	Fa diaz	Sol	La	Si bemol	Do	Re	Mi nuss-bemol
1 1/4		1/2	1	1/2	1	1	3/4

Possible Descriptions: Mustaar trichord on bottom; Nahawand tetrachord on 3rd; Rast trichord on 6th. This maqam is popular in Iraq.

Mukhalaf

E half-flat	F	Gb	A half-flat	A
Mi nuss-bemol	Fa	Sol bemol	La nuss bemol	La
3/4	1/2	5/4	1/4	

Possible Descriptions: This five note maqam is popular in Iraq.

Unusual B half-flat-Based Maqams
Awj Ara Family

Jins Awj Ara on B half-flat

Approximate Interval	Approx. Note Names	Ratio of Interval	Exact Just Cents	Exact Just Hz	Nearest 12-note ET Cents	Nearest 24-note ET Cents	Nearest 24-note ET Hz
Tonic	B hf - B hf	1:1	0.00	239.56	0	0	239.56
Sm Minor 2nd	B hf - C hf	25:24	70.67	249.54	100	50	246.58
Sm Minor 2nd	B hf - C	19:18	93.60	252.87	100	100	253.80
ET Minor 2nd	B hf - C				100	100	253.80
Minor 2nd	B hf - C	16:15	111.73	255.53	100	100	253.80
Lg Minor 2nd	B hf - C	13:12	138.57	259.52	100	150	261.24
Lg Minor 2nd	B hf - C	12:11	150.64	261.34	200	150	261.24
Sm Major 2nd	B hf - C#	11:10	165.00	263.52	200	150	261.24
Sm Major 2nd	B hf - Db	10:9	182.40	266.18	200	200	268.90
Major 2nd	B hf - Db	9:8	203.91	269..50	200	200	268.90
Lg Major 2nd	B hf - D hf	8:7	231.17	273.78	200	250	276.78
Lg Major 2nd	B hf - D hf	7:6	266.87	279.49	200	250	276.78
ET Minor 3rd					300		284.89
Minor 3rd	B hf - D hf	6:5	315.64	287.47	300	300	284.89
	B hf - D	11:9	347.41	292.80	300	350	293.23
Major 3rd	B hf - D#	5:4	386.31	299.45	400	350	293.23
ET Major 3rd					400		301.83
Lg Major 3rd	B hf - D#	9:7	435.08	308.00	400	450	310.67
4th	B hf - E hf	4:3	498.04	319.41	500	500	319.77

Awj Ara

Closely Related Maqamat: Rawnaq Numa

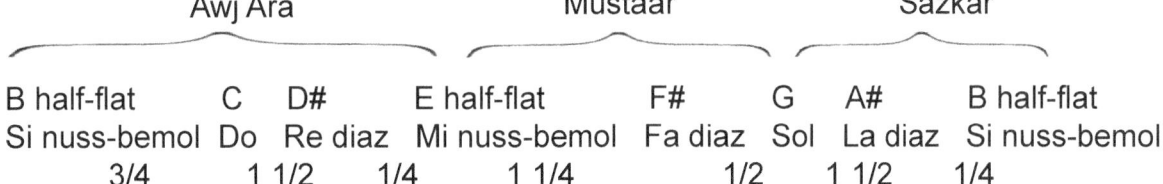

	Awj Ara			Mustaar			Sazkar	
B half-flat	C	D#	E half-flat	F#	G	A#	B half-flat	
Si nuss-bemol	Do	Re diaz	Mi nuss-bemol	Fa diaz	Sol	La diaz	Si nuss-bemol	
3/4	1 1/2	1/4	1 1/4	1/2	1 1/2	1/4		

Possible Descriptions: Awj Ara tetrachord on bottom; Mustaar trichord on 4th; Sazkar trichord on 6th.

If you're looking for something exotic, try this one!

Maqam Awj Ara on B half-flat

Approximate Interval	Approx. Note Names	Ratio of Interval	Exact Just Cents	Exact Just Hz	Nearest 12-note ET Cents	Nearest 24-note ET Cents	Nearest 24-note ET Hz
Tonic	B hf - B hf	1:1	0.00	239.56	0	0	239.56
Sm Minor 2nd	B hf - C hf	25:24	70.67	249.54	100	50	246.58
Sm Minor 2nd	B hf - C	19:18	93.60	252.87	100	100	253.80
ET Minor 2nd	B hf - C				100	100	253.80
Minor 2nd	B hf - C	16:15	111.73	255.53	100	100	253.80
Lg Minor 2nd	B hf - C	13:12	138.57	259.52	100	150	261.24
Lg Minor 2nd	B hf - C	12:11	150.64	261.34	200	150	261.24
Sm Major 2nd	B hf - C#	11:10	165.00	263.52	200	150	261.24
Sm Major 2nd	B hf - Db	10:9	182.40	266.18	200	200	268.90
Major 2nd	B hf - Db	9:8	203.91	269..50	200	200	268.90
Lg Major 2nd	B hf - D hf	8:7	231.17	273.78	200	250	276.78
Lg Major 2nd	B hf - D hf	7:6	266.87	279.49	200	250	276.78
ET Minor 3rd					300		284.89
Minor 3rd	B hf - D hf	6:5	315.64	287.47	300	300	284.89
	B hf - D	11:9	347.41	292.80	300	350	293.23
Major 3rd	B hf - D#	5:4	386.31	299.45	400	350	293.23
ET Major 3rd					400		301.83
Lg Major 3rd	B hf - D#	9:7	435.08	308.00	400	450	310.67
4th	B hf - E hf	4:3	498.04	319.41	500	500	319.77
Sm Tritone	B hf - E hf	11:8	551.32	329.40	600	550	329.14
Tritone	B hf - F	7:5	582.51	335.38	600	600	338.79
Lg Tritone	B hf - F	10:7	617.49	342.23	600	600	338.79
ET 5th	B hf - F hs				700		358.93
5th	B hf - F#	3:2	701.95	359.34	700	700	358.93
	B hf - F#	17:11	753.64	370.23	700	750	369.45
	B hf - F#	14:9	764.92	372.65	800	750	369.45
Sm minor 6th	B hf - Gb	11:7	782.49	376.45	800	750	369.45
ET Minor 6th	B hf - G hf				800		380.28
Minor 6th	B hf - G	8:5	813.69	383.30	800	800	380.28
Lg Minor 6th	B hf - G	13:8	840.53	389.29	800	850	391.42
Major 6th	B hf - G#	5:3	884.36	399.27	900	900	402.89
Lg Major 6th	B hf - Ab	12:7	933.13	410.67	900	950	415.30
Sm Minor 7th	B hf - Ab	7:4	968.83	419.23	1000	950	414.70
Sm Minor7th	B hf - A hf	16:9	996.09	425.88	1000	1000	426.85
ET Minor 7th	B hf - A hf				1000		426.85
Minor 7th	B hf - A hf	9:5	1017.60	431.21	1000	1000	426.85
Lg Minor 7th	B hf - A	11:6	1049.36	439.19	1000	1050	439.35
Sm Major 7th	B hf - A	13:7	1071.70	444.87	1100	1050	439.35
Sm Major 7th	B hf - A hs	15:8	1088.27	449.18	1100	1050	439.35
Major 7th	B hf - A#	17:9	1101.04	452.50	1100	1100	452.23
Lg Major 7th	B hf - A#	19:10	1111.20	455.16	1100	1100	452.23
Lg Major 7th	B hf - A#	125:64	1158.94	467.89	1100	1150	465.48
Octave	B hf - B hf	2:1	1200.00	479.12	1200	1200	479.12
Octave above C	B hf - C	12:11	1350.64	522.68	1300	1350	522.48
Octave above D	B hf - D	11:9	1547.41	585.59	1500	1550	586.47

Awj Ara: Tonic through 4th
Mustaar: Sm Tritone through Lg Minor 6th
Sazkar: Major 6th through Octave above D

Table A: Note Names of Basic Arabic scale

G:	Sol	Ramal Tuti or Jawab Nawa
F:	Fa	Mahuran
E half-flat:	Mi nuss-bemol	Buzrak
D:	Re	Muhayyar
C:	Do	Kirdan or Mahur
B half-flat:	Si nuss-bemol	Awj
A:	La	Husayni
G:	Sol	Nawa
F:	Fa	Jaharka
E half-flat:	Mi nuss-bemol	Sikah
D:	Re	Dukah
C:	Do	Rast (Old Name = Yakah)
B half-flat:	Si nuss-bemol	'Iraq
A:	La	Ushayran
G:	Sol	Yakah (Old Name = Nuhuft)

Note: these names are not always known by modern musicians.

These note names do not necessarily correlate with maqam names but it is possible to see obvious relationships.

Some of these words are originally Persian while others are Arabic. The presence of the Persian words doesn't mean that the scales used in contemporary Persian music are related to maqamat. Persian, Afghani, Pakistani and Hindu music scales have more similarity to each other than to the Arabic and Turkish scale system being taught in this book. It should also be noted that this book presents scales primarily from the Arabic way of teaching rather than the Turkish. But there is a great deal of overlap.

Table B: Names of Expanded 24-note Arabic Scale

G:	Sol	Ramal Tuti or Jawab Nawa
--		
Gb/F#	Sol bemol/Fa diaz	Jawab Hijaz
--		
F:	Fa	Mahuran
--		
E:	Mi	Jawab Busalik or Husayni Shadd
E half-flat:	Mi nuss-bemol	Buzurk
Eb	Mi bemol	Sinbulah
--		
D:	Re	Muhayyar
--		
Db/C#	Re bemol/ Do diaz	Shahnaz
--		
C:	Do	Kirdan or Mahur
--		
B	Si	Nuhuft or Mahur
B half-flat:	Si nuss-bemol	Awj
Bb	Si bemol	Ajam
--		
A:	La	Husayni
--		
Ab/G#	La bemol/Sol diaz	Hisar
--		
G:	Sol	Nawa
--		
Gb/F#	Sol bemol/Fa diaz	Hijaz
--		
F:	Fa	Jaharkah
--		
E	Mi	Busalik
E half-flat:	Mi nuss-bemol	Sikah
Eb/D#	Mi bemol/Re Diaz	Kurd
--		
D:	Re	Dukah
--		
Db/C#	Re bemol/ Do diaz	Zirkulah
--		
C:	Do	Rast
--		
B	Si	Kawasht
B half-flat:	Si nuss-bemol	Iraq
Bb	Si bemol	Ajam Ushayran
--		
A:	La	Ushayran
--		
Ab/G#	La bemol/Sol diaz	Qarar Hisar
--		
G:	Sol	Yakah

Note: the double hyphen "--" indicates the presence of another possible quartertone pitch for which the words "nim" (lower) and "tik" (higher) would be used before the nearest note name to provide a label.

Table C: Most Useful Fifty-Eight Just Notes in 1 Octave
Tonic G: = 196 Hz for tuning (Standard Equal Tempered Pitch for G)

Note		Just Hz	Just Cents	Just Ratio	=Decimal
G:		**392.00**	**1200.00**	**2/1**	**= 2.000000**
Gb		374.18	1119.46	21/11	= 1.909091
Gb		372.40	1111.20	19/10	= 1.900000
Gb		370.22	1101.04	17/9	= 1.888888
F#		**367.50**	**1088.27**	**15/8**	**= 1.875000**
F hs		364.00	1071.70	13/7	= 1.857143
F hs		359.33	1049.36	11/6	= 1.833333
F hs		356.36	1035.00	20/11	= 1.818182
F		**352.80**	**1017.60**	**9/5**	**= 1.800000**
F		348.44	996.09	16/9	= 1.777778
F hf		343.00	968.82	7/4	= 1.750000
F hf		338.54	946.19	19/11	= 1.727273
F hf		336.00	933.13	12/7	= 1.714285
E		333.20	918.64	17/10	= 1.700000
E	(also called a high E hf)	**326.67**	**884.36**	**5/3**	**= 1.666667**
E hf		320.73	852.59	18/11	= 1.636364
E hf		318.50	840.53	13/8	= 1.625000
E hf		316.61	830.25	21/13	= 1.615385
Eb		**313.60**	**813.69**	**8/5**	**= 1.600000**
D#		310.33	795.56	19/12	= 1.583333
D#		308.00	782.49	11/7	= 1.571428
D hs		304.89	764.92	14/9	= 1.555555
D hs		302.91	753.64	17/11	= 1.545455
D		**294.00**	**701.95**	**3/2**	**= 1.500000**
D hf		286.46	656.98	19/13	= 1.461538
D hf		685.09	648.68	16/11	= 1.454545
D hf		283.11	636.62	13/9	= 1.444444
Db		280.00	617.49	10/7	= 1.428571
C#		**274.40**	**582.51**	**7/5**	**= 1.400000**
C hs		269.50	551.32	11/8	= 1.375000
C hs		267.27	536.95	15/11	= 1.363636
C		**261.33**	**498.05**	**4/3**	**= 1.333333**
C hf		257.25	470.78	21/16	= 1.312500
C hf		254.80	454.21	13/10	= 1.300000
C hf		252.00	435.08	9/7	= 1.285714
B		249.45	417.51	14/11	= 1.272727
B		248.27	409.24	19/15	= 1.266666
B		247.58	404.44	24/19	= 1.263157
B	(also called a high B hf)	**245.00**	**386.31**	**5/4**	**= 1.250000**
B hf		242.12	365.82	21/17	= 1.235294
B hf		241.23	359.47	16/13	= 1.230769
B hf		**239.56**	**347.41**	**11/9**	**= 1.222222**
B hf		238.00	336.13	17/14	= 1.214285
Bb		**235.20**	**315.64**	**6/5**	**= 1.200000**
Bb		232.75	297.51	19/16	= 1.187500
A#		231.64	289.21	13/11	= 1.181818
A hs		228.67	266.87	7/6	= 1.166666
A hs		226.15	247.74	15/13	= 1.153846
A hs		224.00	231.17	8/7	= 1.142857
A		**220.50**	**203.91**	**9/8**	**= 1.125000**
A		217.78	182.40	10/9	= 1.111111
A hf		215.60	165.00	11/10	= 1.100000
A hf		212.33	138.57	13/12	= 1.083333
A hf		211.08	128.30	14/13	= 1.076923
Ab		210.00	119.44	15/14	= 1.071428
Ab		**209.07**	**111.73**	**16/15**	**= 1.066667**
Ab		208.25	104.95	17/16	= 1.062500
G#		206.89	93.60	19/18	= 1.055555
G:		**196.00**	**0**	**1/1**	**= 1.000000**

Essential Notes in Table C

With the 16 just notes highlighted in **Bold Print** in Table C, we have the notes we need for the following ajnas, or tetrachords. With these building blocks we can create all the essential maqamat. Once this is thoroughly understood, the entire maqam system suddenly reveals itself to be extremely elegant and quite simple.

Formed on D Tonic:
  Jins Hijaz
  Jins Kurd
  Jins Bayat
  Jins Saba
  Jins Saba Zamazama

Formed on both C and G Tonics:
  Jins Rast
  Jins Nahawand
  Jins Nawa Athar
  Jins Athar Kurd

Formed on Bb Tonic:
  Jins Ajem

Formed on both E half-flat and B half-flat Tonics
  Jins Sikah

> *"Arab theory books stress that Arab and Western instruments differ because the latter confine the musician to a specific tuning system. Arab instruments, on the other hand, such as the fretless ud, leave the musician free to play the Western scale of half-steps or the Arab scale of quarter-steps. They also allow the musician to tune his notes as he wishes. Thus we find that most modern theorists introduce the quarter-tone system in their works but do not mention the concept of equal temperament. When presenting the quarter-tone scale, most theorists are not refuting the existence of the Pythagorean third of 81/64 or the just third of 5/4 in Arab music, in part, because most Arab instruments do not confine performers to any one tuning system. Musicians are free to respond to a variety of acoustical issues and artistic urges..."*
> --Forster 2010

Study of the harmonic divisions of fretted musical instruments or instruments with multiple moveable bridges produces a vast number of ratios essential for these tunings.
27/22, 32/27, 81/64, 81/68, 256/243 are some of these ratios.

Inverse Symmetry

Note the inverse symetry of these Just Internvals as measured in Cents:
Tonic on G

Note	Just Hz	Just Cents	Just Ratio	=Decimal
The minor 2nd: **Ab** is the exact inverse of The major 7th: **F#**	209.07 367.50	111.73 1088.27	16/15 15/8	= 1.066667 = 1.875000

(1200 Cents - 111.73 Cents = 1088.27 Cents)

| The major 2nd: **A** is the exact inverse of The minor 7th: **F** | 217.78 352.80 | 182.40 1017.60 | 10/9 9/5 | = 1.111111 = 1.800000 |

(1200 Cents - 182.40 Cents = 1017.60 Cents)

| The minor 3rd: **Bb** is the exact inverse of The major 6th: **E** (also called a high E hf) | 235.20 326.67 | 315.64 884.36 | 6/5 5/3 | = 1.200000 = 1.666667 |

(1200 Cents - 315.64 Cents = 884.36 Cents)

| The major 3rd: **B** (also called a high B hf) is the exact inverse of The minor 6th: **Eb** | 245.00 313.60 | 386.31 813.69 | 5/4 8/5 | = 1.250000 = 1.600000 |

(1200 Cents - 386.31 Cents = 813.69 Cents)

| The 4th: **C** is the exact inverse of The 5th: **D** | 261.33 294.00 | 498.05 701.95 | 4/3 3/2 | = 1.333333 = 1.500000 |

(1200 Cents - 498.05 Cents = 701.95 Cents)

We also note that a Just Minor 3rd plus a Just Major 3rd equals a Just 5th:
315.64 + 386.31 = 701.95

...and that:
an Octave minus a Just Major 6th
plus
an Octave minus a Just Minor 7th
equals a Just 4th...
1200 - 884.35 = 315.65
1200 - 1017.5 = 182.40

498.05

We realize that we are right in the middle of musical magic... Some real harmonies are happening here that we don't want to miss out on!

Measuring Frequency
Note that these inverse relationships are not reflected in pitch change as measured in Hz:
Remember that wave frequencies increase as pitch rises.
So although:
The number of Hz from the low G to the D (the 5th) = 98.00
And the number of Hz from the D (the 5th) to the high G also = 98.00

...because of this compacting of wavelengths as pitch rises,
The number of Cents from the low G to the D (the 5th) = 701.95
The number of Cents from the D (the 5th) to the high G = 498.05

So although we see the inverse mathematical symmetry in Cents, we do not see it in Hz:

The minor 2nd:
Ab   209.07   111.73   16/15 = 1.066667
is the exact inverse of
The major 7th:
F#   367.50   1088.27   15/8 = 1.875000

The pitch change up from the lower G to the minor 2nd = 13.07 Hz
(111.73 Hz - 196.00 Hz = 13.07 Hz)
The pitch change down from the higher G to the major 7th = 24.5 Hz
(392 Hz - 367.50 Hz = 24.5 Hz)

Tastes of Other Ancient World Music Traditions

Iraqi Maqam Names and Classification

Iraqi music uses maqamat which are somewhat different from those used in Egypt, Syria, Lebanon and Jordan. Because they are speakers of Arabic they are not considered to be a distinct culture. But any student of Iraqi maqamat will find these differences. In this book no serious attempt is made to classify and describe these Iraqi maqamat. But the following classification system is offered. More commonality with Persian music exists both in structure and instrumentation. The hammered dulcimer known as Santur is used in Iraq as it is in Persia.

The Five Iraqi Fusul:
fasl al-bayat and its maqamat: bayat, nari, tahir, mahmudi, sikah, mukhalaf, hililawi
fasl al-hijaz and its maqamat: hijaz diwan, quriyat, 'uraybun 'ajam, ibrahimi, hadidi
fasl al-rast and its maqamat: rast, mansuri, hijaz shaytani, juburi, khanabat
fasl al-nawa and its maqamat: nawa, miskin, 'ajam 'ashiran, panjikah, rashdi
fasl al-husayni and its maqamat: husayni, dasht, urfah, arwah, awj, hakimi, saba

Chinese Music

To provide a window into ancient indigenous Chinese musical tradition we can take a quick look at the "guqin" (or "qin"), a highly revered musical instrument. This instrument's history goes back around 5000 years, and writings about it have been preserved from 3000 years ago. The oldest actual instruments which has been found in archeological sites date back 2500 years. Mythology supposes that legendary figures of China's pre-history — Fuxi, Shennong and Huang Di, the "Yellow Emperor" — were involved in its creation.

The Guqin has a musical scale based on "just" intervals. The dots on its soundboard indicate the notes reflected by these interval ratios: $9/8, 7/6, 6/5, 5/4, 4/3, 7/5, 3/2, 8/5, 5/3, 7/4, 9/5, 11/6, 15/8$.

In 1977, a recording by one of the best qin players of the 20th century was chosen to be included in the Voyager Golden Record, a gold-plated LP recording containing music from around the world, which was sent into outer space by NASA on the Voyager 1 and Voyager 2 spacecrafts. It is the longest excerpt included on the disc. The reason to select a work played on this specific instrument is because the tonal structure of the instrument, its musical scale, is derived from fundamental physical laws related to vibration and overtones, representing the intellectual capacity of human beings on this subject.

Persian Music

Persian musical culture traces its history back to the end of the Sassanian period, around the 5th century AD. A musician from the court of Chosroes II named Barbod, from the early 7th century, is credited with organizing modes into seven major categories, each of which contained thirty modes represented by 360 melody maps called "dastan."

After the Arab Islam expansion, which began in Persia in AD 642, Persian musicians found themselves in a position to make major contributions during the next centuries when Damascus and then Baghdad became the major capitals. Persian musical contributions to the Arabic Music Tradition of Maqamat is very large. The names of many maqamat and Arabic note names are Persian in origin. Since its probable invention during the Qajar period, 1787-1925, the "dastgah" concept has become important in classifying Persian musical modes, to a large extent supplanting the much older maqam categories. For this reason current Persian musical structures rarely match Arabic ones and there is sometimes confusion regarding roots and origins from these two closely connected but basically linguistically unrelated cultures.

Here is a list of the twelve dastgāhs:
Dastgāh-e Šur
Dastgāh-e Abuatā
Dastgāh-e Dašti
Dastgāh-e Bayāt-e Tork
Dastgāh-e Afšari
Dastgāh-e Segāh
Dastgāh-e Čahārgāh
Dastgāh-e Homāyun
Dastgāh-e Bayāt-e Esfahān
Dastgāh-e Navā
Dastgāh-e Māhur
Dastgāh-e Rāst (Rāst-Panjgāh)

The pieces which make up the repertoire of classical Persian music are called "radif". These are melody models which serve as the basis for improvisation.

Traditional Persian music of course includes "just" notes in its modes. Recently identified for comparison with equal-tempered intervals, for example, we have the following notes identified by Farhat:

1. Semi-tone or minor 2nd ca. 90 cents.   19:18
2. Small neutral tone ca. 135 cents.   13:12
3. Large neutral tone ca. 160 cents.   11:10
4. Whole-tone or major 2nd ca. 204 cents.   9:8
5. Plus-tone ca. 270 cents.   7:6

In 1860 the first western-style music school was founded with the aim of creating an imperial military band, Persian music was increasingly influenced by western ideas. As a result, a number of ideas were introduced that were new to Persian music.

1. The concept of fixed pitch, the major-minor key system, scales etc.

2. Playing accurately from notation with a consequent separation of the roles of performer and composer.

3. Clarity of melodic and rhythmic forms in contrast to the melodically ornate and rhythmically free Persian classical tradition.

4. The systematic use of harmony.

5. The introduction of new instruments, only some of which were capable of producing the intervals used in Persian music.

6. Western conservatoire-type pedagogical methods. Traditionally Persian music had been taught one-on-one from master to student.

"In Indian music, musicians improvise on a given raga, and never modulate to a different raga. In Persian music, however, musicians improvise on a collection of modes, which requires them to modulate to different modes." --Forster 2010

"There is no doubt that Ibn Sina (980-1037) accurately comprehended and recorded the distinctive intonational characteristics of Persian music. His entire work is a living testament to the enduring significance of the 17-tone scale and 13-limit ratios." --Forster 2010

Music of India

The Hindustani music of Northern India and the Carnatic music of Southern India can both be traced back to Vedic times around 1000 BC. Written Sanskrit sources describing these traditions go back 2500 years. Persian influences were also incorporated during the 13th and 14th centuries AD.

The sample table of intervals below, based on an earlier table first published in 1963 by Professor Sambamurthi, was published in 2006 by Wolfgang von Schweinitz. These scales derived from just intonation are at the heart of the underlying beauty of classical Indian music. I have abbreviated the table considerably so as not to add too much complexity.

The Classical Indian Just Intonation Tuning System
with 22 SRUTI-s defining the 7 SWARA-s of Hindu Classical Music
combining the three different kinds of SRUTI which are understood as
PRAM ANA ("measuring" or "standard") SRUTI = Syntonic Comma (81/80) = 21.5 cents
NYUNA ("deficient") SRUTI = Minor Chroma (25/24) = 70.7 cents
PURNA ("fullfilling") SRUTI = Pythagorean Limma (256/243) = 90.2 cents

Note	Sa	ri	ri	ri	ri	ri	Ri	Ri	ga	ga	ga	Ga	Ga
Ratio	1:1	25:24	21:20	256:243	135:128	16:15	10:9	9:8	7:6	32:27	6:5	5:4	81:64
Cents	0	70.7	84.5	90.2	92.2	111.7	182.4	203.9	266.9	294.1	315.6	386.3	407.8

Carnatic Names: Ekasruti   Trisruti   Suddha Gandhara.   Antara
                  Rishabha   Risbabha   Kamal Sadharana Ga Gandhara

Hindustani Names: Kamal   Suddha   Ati-komal   Suddha

Note	ma	ma	Ma	Ma	Ma	Ma	Pa	dha	dha	dha	dha	Dha	Dha
Ratio	4:3	27:20	45:32	64:45	729:512	10:7	3:2	25:16	128:81	405:256	8:5	5:3	27:16
Cents	498.0	519.6	590.2	609.8	611.7	617.5	702.0	772.7	792.2	794.1	813.7	884.4	905.9

Carnatic Names: Suddha   Prati   Chyuta Panchama   Ekasruti   Trisruti
                  Madhyama   Madhyama   Madhyama   Dhaivata   Dhaivata

Hindustani Names: Suddha   Tivra   Panchama   Ati-komal   Suddha

Note	ni	ni	ni	Ni	Ni	Ni	Sa
Ratio	7:4	16:9	9:5	15:8	243:128	40:21	2:1
Cents	968.8	996.1	1017.6	1088.3	1109.8	1115.5	1200

Carnatic Names: Suddha Nishada.   Kakali   Shadja
                           Komal Kaisiki Nishada   Nishada

Hindustani Names: Ati-komal   Suddha   Shadja

"Quartertones" or, more precisely, "exactly harmonious microtonal intervals" are called "srutis" in the Indian music tradition.

"My initial fascination with pure tunings stems from my interest in North Indian classical music, which I began singing and studying in 1978... Singing Indian ragas while accompanying myself on the tamboura, a resonant Indian string instrument, awakened my ears to the beauty of just intonation. As I became more familiar with the intonation of the Indian ragas, the compromises of equal temperament, the tuning used on the modern piano, sounded increasingly "out of tune" to my newly sensitive hearing. I began exploring the application of just intonation to the piano and these two musical worlds came together for me, opening the door to a new musical universe."

--Michael Harrison Website

Music of Turkey

It seems Turks learned maqam-based music from the Arabs in the 12th century when they descended to Anatolia and the Near East from Central Asia. The Turkish musicians who then performed and composed during the long, 400-year Ottoman reign (1517-1917 CE), made immense contributions to this same, originally Arabic and Persian system of maqamat. Turkish "makamlar" sometimes have different names than the Arab maqamat equivalents, but have obviously evolved from the same underlying musical system. Since Turkish language and culture is unrelated at its roots to both Arab and Persian cultures there are frequent confusions again about certain origins.

Earlier forms of Turkish music, although mentioned by Chinese writers, could not be so easily preserved. Early Turkish tribes such as the Huns and Uygurs were nomadic peoples without a commonly used writing system.

But any student of Arabic music is immediately aware of the vast repertoire of Turkish music and theory. Makamlar (plural for makam in Turkish) are extensive and highly organized. Since teaching methods for Westerners evolved around the beginning of the 20th century, Turkish musicians created a system of 53 intervals per octave based on nine equal divisions (komas) per whole tone. This system actually enables a much closer approximation to the real just intervals than does the 24-note equal-tempered system adopted in Cairo by the Arabs as a response to the need to teach their music to Westerners.

"When we examine the First Ud Tuning in the context of Safi Al_Din's (d. 1294) 84 Melodic Modes, the origins of modern Turkish music come to light. ...when we examine the Second Ud Tuning of Safi Al_Din's 84 Melodic Modes...the origins of modern Arabian music come to light." --Forster 2010

Music of Greece

Pythagoras is credited with associating musical scale intervals with numeric ratios. He may have gotten this idea from Babylonian culture. The ancient Greek modes are learned by students of Western music today although obviously the ancient Greek intervals were not equally tempered. So it does not make sense to think that a Greek mode played on a modern ET piano really reflects the sounds of the ancient intervals.

Ptolemy is credited with having produced the most advanced ancient Greek music theory and he recognized the intrinsic beauty of what he called the "Tense Diatonic" which has evolved into the justly-intonated major scale which, since it underlies the modern equal-tempered major scale, remains one of the most popular scales used in the world today.

Modern Greek music of the 20th century was tremendously influenced by the Anatolian Greeks who left Greek cities in the East upon the creation of the modern Turkish state. This rembetika music contained the just intervals of the Turkish and Arabic maqam system and the Greek "dromos" or modes which are associated with this music contained the just intervals commonly called "quartertones." Greeks preferred to leave out the details of this musical history because of their unpleasant associations with the long Turkish occupation. However, I was pleased to notice during my most recent visit to Greek music venues on the island of Rhodes in 2008 that the Rembetika orchestras were bringing the Turkish saz, with its quartertone frets, back into use.

Greek Orthodox psaltic tradition, as well as its Gregorian counterpart, preserves musical chanting styles which have some of their roots in the ancient Middle East. Greek musicologists from relatively modern times such as Chrysanthos of Madytos (ca. 1770 - ca. 1840), who was responsible for a reform of the notation of Byzantine Greek ecclesiastical music, found it necessary to create scales with 64 notes per octave in order to analyze the traditional Byzantine musical intervals.

Musical Instruments

Fretless Stringed Instruments

Fretless stringed intstruments yield all possible pitches depending on finger positioning. All maqamat can be easily played.

Plucked: Oud
Bowed: Rebab, Kamenje, Violin, Cello, Bass

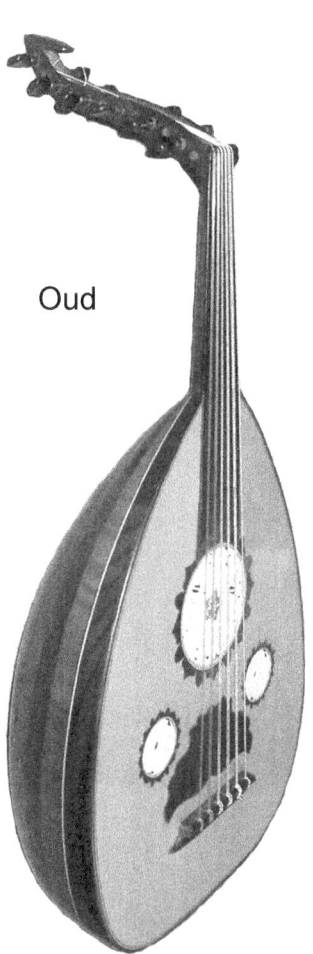

Oud

The large body of the oud enables low and mid-range notes, as well as high notes, to reverberate and sustain their pitches as they are plucked. This makes the oud an ideal instrument for hearing harmonic intervals as the ringing of successive notes overlap their sound waves. Hence the oud player becomes sensitized to the harmonic quality of intervals between the notes played. The oud thus becomes an ideal instrument for performance in just intonation.

There are six theories on the origin of al-'ud: One says it is originally Sumerian, the second is Persian, the third is Egyptian, the fourth is Arian, the fifth is Jewish and the sixth is Akkadian of ancient Iraq.

The word 'Ud comes from the Arabic word for wood. Pictures of 'Ud-like instruments have been discovered in the ruins of ancient Egypt and Mesopotamia. Persians and Indians played it in ancient times. However, it was the Arabs (during the Abbasid Era), who perfected the 'Ud, called it so and passed it on to the West."

The bowed string instruments are ideal for hearing justly intonated harmonic intervals for the same reasons which apply to the oud. In addition to this, they are ideal for generating harmonic overtones as the continuous friction from the bow excites the strings to generate them.

Eastern musicians, by using alternations of firm and light touches with the left hand on the strings can become very adept at generating simultaneous just intervals generated by friction against two strings at once which simultaneously stimulating the production of overtone pitches. This creates a marvelous and sometimes very complex and "other-worldly" mix of musical frequencies.

The human voice, as evidenced by the now-famous Central Asian "throat singers," can also become adept at creating overtone frequencies.

Cello

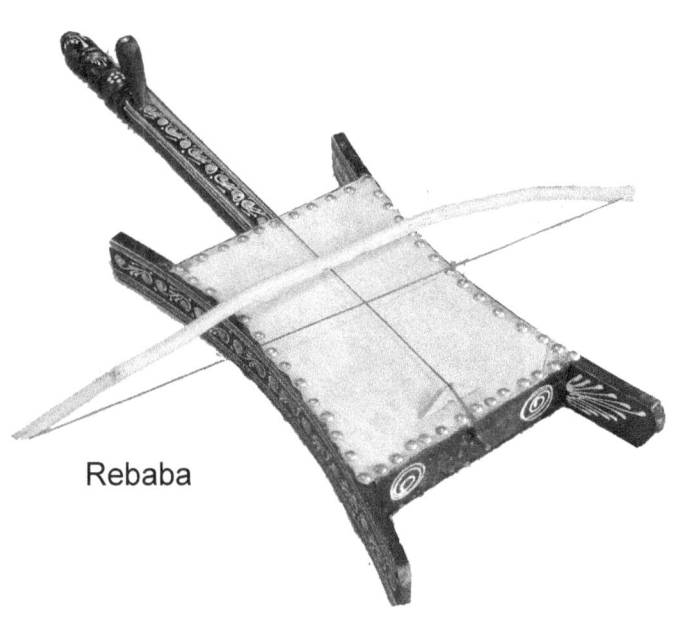

Rebaba

"Quartertone" Fretted Stringed Instruments

Plucked: Arabic Buzuk, Turkish Saz, Baglama, Tamboura
Bowed: Turkish Yayli Tambour

Fretted stringed instruments yield specific "quartertone" pitches. They commonly have 18 frets per octave instead of the 12 commonly found on equal-tempered instruments. The common notes such as E half-flat, B half-flat, F half-sharp and A half-flat become available but other quartertones remain unplayable. It is only possible to play these instruments in certain pre-defined keys.

Other Fretted Stringed Instruments

Plucked: Guitars, Banjoes, Bouzoukia, Mandolins, Balalaikas, etc

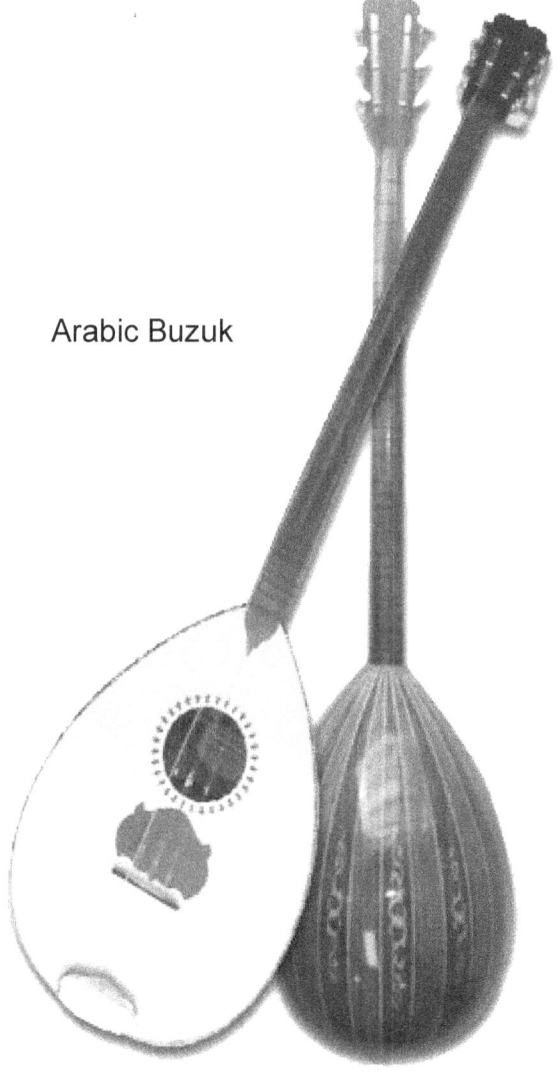

Arabic Buzuk

With 12 frets per octave, positioned for equal-tempered intervals, it is not easily possible to play maqamat which include "quartertones." It is possible to bend the pitch of notes by pushing the string sideways. This raises the pitch but cannot lower the pitch. Nevertheless, the signature sound of electric rock 'n roll guitar playing involves bending notes. Musicians, as they develop their ear for harmony, will of course naturally bend light guage "slinky" electric guitar strings into just positions. This may be why this style of playing has become so popular. It sounds really good! And when electronic distortion is added, the bandwidth of pitches generated is widened so that justly intonated pitches are accidentally included. And that sounds good too! The magic qualities of just intonation are re-creating themselves even without the musicians being conscious of what is going on!

Zithers

"Four theories are available to us by Arab and European scholars on the origin of al-qanoon: One states that al-qanoon is originally Greek, the other indicates that it has originated in ancient Egypt, the third says it has originated from a rectangular musical instrument used in ancient Assyria which had parallel strings on top of a sound box, and the fourth theory states that qanoon is originally Indian.

There has been various theories in regard to the origin of the word qanoon as well. However, the oldest recorded usage of the word qanoon as a chrodophone instrument was during the Abbasid era around the 10th century. It was mentioned in the stories of One Thousand and one Nights." Qanoon means "canon" or "law" and the tuning of the qanoon is frequently, for better or for worse, regarded as the standard to which all other members of the band must tune.

Plucked Zithers: Arabic Qanun, Turkish Kanun

The strings on these instruments have 5 to 9 moveable bridges, or mandrels, under them. By flipping these up and down, quartertone (or even finer) pitches can be set.

"The vast majority of the Arabic qanun players today employ minimal tuning systems, quite often four working levers per string course, that change the pitch roughly by quarter-tone increments. Although on such instruments some of the levers are set in places that may suit certain common modes, the format as a whole continues to reflect the popular paradigm of equal temperament and to render certain intervals blatantly out of tune. The same applies to the buzuq, which as generally played in Arab world, uses a minimal system of basically stationary frets arranged in terms of half-steps with a few neutral steps on certain typical degrees. Obviously, such intonational inadequacies are becoming more striking with the recent proliferation and increasing prominence of keyboard instruments." --Racy 2003

Arabic Qanoon

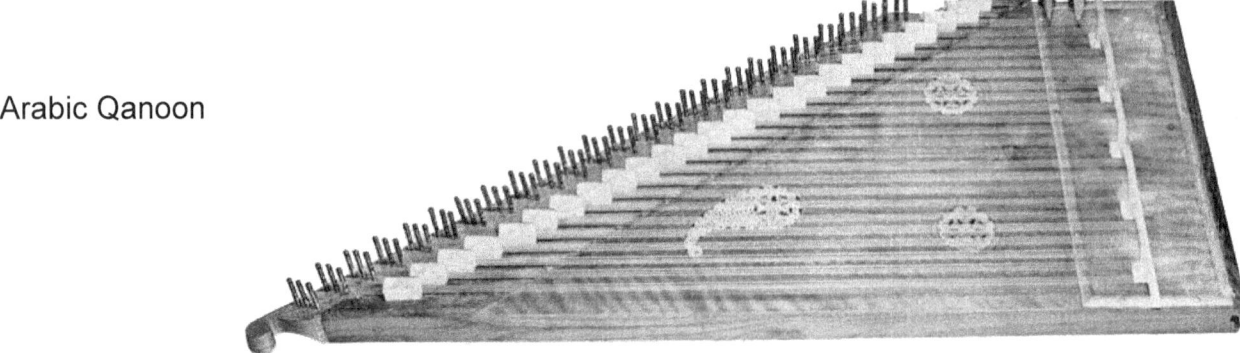

Hammered Zithers: Santur

Not common in Arabic or Turkish music except in Iraq. Common notes such as E half-flat and B half-flat are available on these instruments and they are used in maqam music.

Wind Instruments

Flutes: Arabic Nay, Turkish Ney
Reed: Arabic Mizmar, Mijwiz, Narghoul, Turkish Zurna, Clarinet, Accordion

The holes in the Nay are drilled to yield specific "quartertone" pitches. The common notes such as E half-flat and B half-flat become available but other quartertones and many halftones including E natural and B natural can only be played by "half-holing" (partially covering an open hole with part of a finger.) There is also considerable bending of note pitches possible through the use of mouth technique alone (embouchure.) Since it is difficult to play these instruments outside of certain pre-defined keys, instruments of different lengths are available.

The Clarinet is used in Turkey and pitch control is accomplished through mouth technique alone (embouchure.)

Accordions are a recent import into the Arab world and extra banks of reeds are added with common notes such as E half-flat and B half-flat included.

Arabic Nay

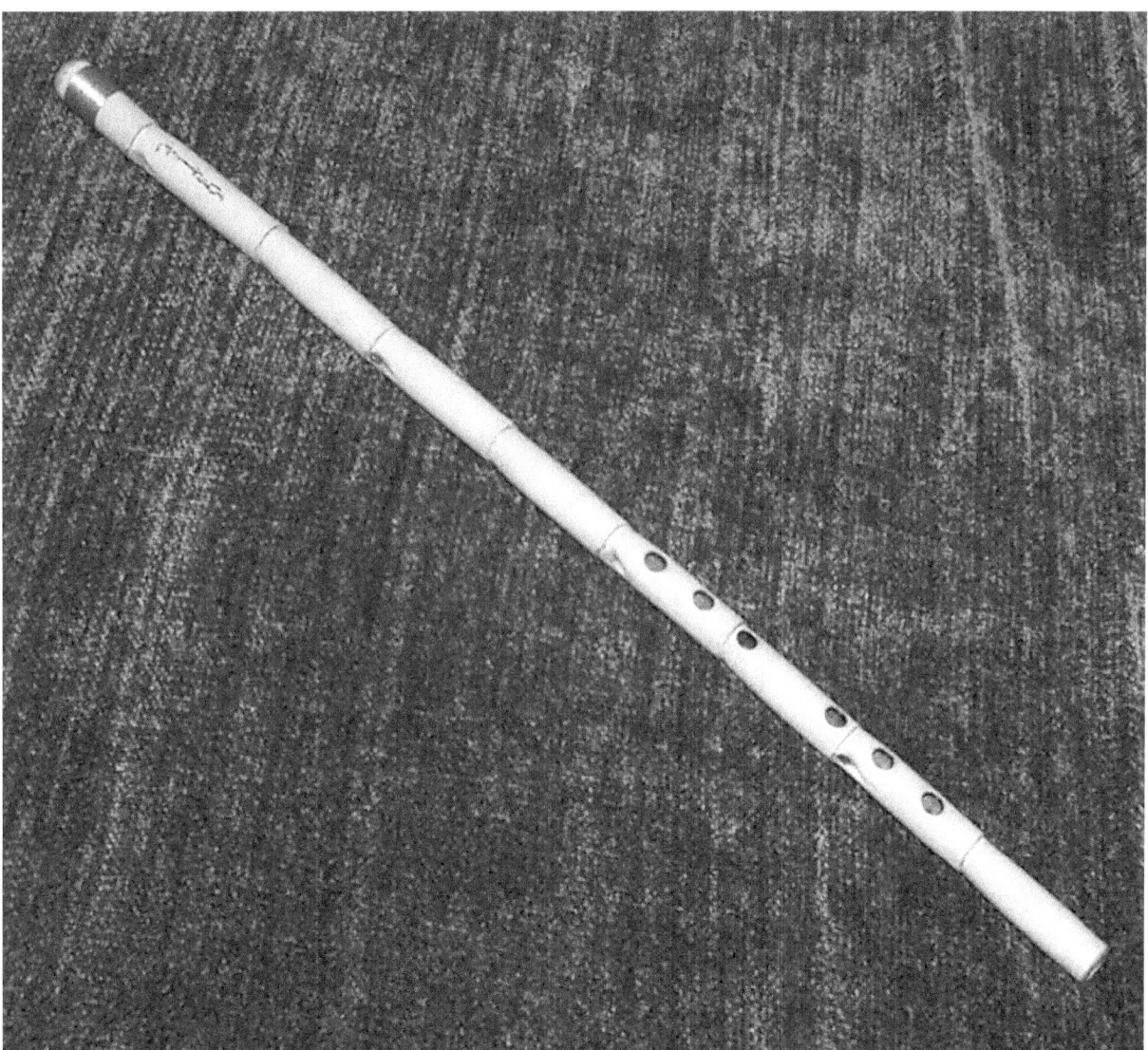

Other Wind Instruments

The Human Voice: The Ultimate Wind Instrument
The Trombone and the Trumpet

"Singers obviously have complete flexibility to place the notes wherever they want, and are not even constrained by the fixed pitches of open strings. Wind players should be able to make most of these pitch adjustments as well. Clearly, the trombone is completely flexible. Trumpet players constantly adjust their valve tuning slides as they play. With other instruments, like flute and oboe, for example, it may be more difficult, but players are adept at shading the pitch one way or another (by fingering, breath or embouchure). The music will sound so good in "harmonic intonation" that the players will find a way to make it happen."
--Duffin 2007

Flutes and Oboes: Open-Holed
If the holes are drilled for equal-tempered intervals it is necessary to use combinations of "half-holing" (partially covering an open hole with part of a finger) and embouchure (mouth positions) in order to achieve quartertone pitches.

Flutes and Oboes: Keyed
It is very difficult to achieve quartertone pitches on these instruments unless it is a reed instrument which can easily yield mouth and breath controlled pitch bends.

Keyboards

Accoustic Pianos: It is not possible to play maqamat which include "quartertones."

Electronic Keyboards
Notes such as E half-flat, B half-flat, A half-flat, F half-sharp can quite easily be programmed into these keyboards and many pre-programmed models are available so that all maqamat can be played.

For a long list of electronic keyboards with microtonal tuning capacity, go to:
http://www.h-pi.com/gm.html
To help automate microtonal keyboard setups there is a device called a TBX1 which offers a tuning resolution of 0.01 cents. The ability to work with both cents and ratios makes it even more attractive to microtonal musicians at large.

"Do not be afraid to be out of tune with the piano. It is the piano that is out of tune.
Pablo Casals -1972" --Duffin 2007

Glossary of Terms

Ajnas (singular: jins)
    Arabic word meaning "basic maqam building blocks" or sequences of notes. Translated as "tetrachords" or "trichords" or "pentachords."

Amal
    Arabic word meaning "the work." The creative process brought by a musician to building a musical improvisation.

Bemol
    French word imported into modern Arabic: "flat."

Diaz or Diese
    French word imported into modern Arabic: "sharp."

Dulab
    An introductory musical melody which is specific to a particular maqam.

Ghammaz (has two meanings in music)
    Arabic word literally meaning "the wink of an eye."
    This term is used to label delicate musical decorations.
    Also means the 2nd most prominent note in a maqam: usually the 5th but sometimes the 4th or 3rd note.

Half-flat
    A note played somewhere between the pitch of the "natural," above, and the "flat," below.

Half-sharp
    A note played somewhere between the pitch of the "sharp," above, and the "natural," below.

Interval
    Musicians frequently talk about intervals such as "5ths," meaning the 5th note in the scale. More strictly speaking, "harmonic intervals" are based on dividing musical intervals such as a whole octave into equal parts. A "harmonic 5th," for example, results from just such a division. However, since specific notes in a scale don't always fall on pitches defined by strict harmonic theory, the student should be aware that terms like the "2nd," "3rd," "4th," etc, can simply refer to the number of a note in a particular scale. When intervals are used to describe pitch differences less than a whole step, terms such as "half-step," "three-quarter-step," "quarter-step" or "quarter-tone" arise.

Jins
    A building block of 3 or 4 or 5 notes which can be assembled with other Ajnas (Jins plural) to create a maqam. The lower jins may be called al-jusa and the upper jins may be called al-fara. Commonly translated as Tetrachord (or Trichord or Pentachord). The plural of Jins is Ajnas.

Koma
An interval defined in Pythagorian musical theory but commonly used in Turkish maqam teaching literature to mean an increment of pitch equal to one-ninth of a whole step. Very precise pitch descriptions can be made using this term.

Mabda
Usual starting note of a maqam.

Maqam
An Arabic or Turkish musical scale or mode. In older traditions, learning to perform and improvise in a particular maqam meant learning a whole world of standardized embellishments and phrases, beginnings and endings which are specific to a given maqam. Given the depth of each maqam, very few artists could manage to master more than a few in one lifetime. Specific emotions are typically associated with each maqam. English plural: "maqams." Arabic plural: "maqamat." Turkish spelling: "makam" and "makamlar" (plurral).
Maqam names frequently reflect geographic locations and towns and landscapes, tribal identities or scalar note positions from Maqam Rast or other Arabic music note names.

Markaz
A note which can be a resting place in the middle of a maqam.

Modulate
To change from on maqam to another. Sometimes the tonic, or "home base" note, remains the same during modulations and sometimes it changes.

Nuss Bemol
Half flat.

Nuss Diaz
Half sharp.

Penta-chord
A sequence of 5 notes which form a building block or "jins" in a maqam.

Qafla
A traditional ending musical flourish for a particular maqam.

Qarar
Tonic note or Home Key of a maqam.

Quartertone
Pitches approximately halfway between the equal-tempered notes. Equal tempered notes are all defined by either "whole-step" or "half-step" intervals. "Three-quarter-step" intervals create what we are calling "quartertones."

Reboton
    Half flat.

Shakhsiyyah
    A traditional opening musical flourish for a particular maqam.

Sikah
    Half flat. This term, although becoming common, is based on the Arabic note name for E half-flat. It is now becoming common to use it to refer to any half-flat. "Si sikah," for example, can refer to "B half-flat."

Solfege
    European syllables, Do Re Mi Fa Sol La Si, used to name notes in a scale. Unlike note names A B C D E F G, Do is portable and can be assigned to be the tonic of a scale at any absolute pitch. The note names in Indian music, Sa Re Ga Ma Pa Da Ni are roughly equivalent to Solfege syllables.

Taqasim
    Improvisation performed in Arabic music. Turkish spelling: "taksim" or "taxim."

Tetra-chord
    A sequence of 4 notes which form a building block or "jins" in a maqam. The term "tetra-chord" is used generically to refer to any sequence of 3, 4 or 5 notes.

Tonic
    The "home base" note of a maqam or scale.

Transpose
    To move the "tonic" of a scale from one pitch to another. This can be done to accomodate the range of a singer's voice, in which case the whole framework of maqamat becomes portable. Or it can be done by designating a new "tonic" for a particular maqam so that it can interplay with other maqamat in pleasing ways.

Tri-chord
    A sequence of 3 notes which form a building block or "jins" in a maqam.

Equal-tempered
    The scale which has become familiar in Europe and the Western world: 12 notes composed of equal "half-steps" which make up an octave.

Zaghrafa
    Musical ornamentations or decorations.

Zahir
    Leading tone of a maqam. Usually a step below the Qarar.

Acknowledgements

I would like to acknowledge the many teachers who have helped me with maqam study. They include Haig Manoukian, George Lammam, Faruk Tekbilek, Simon Shaheen, J A Racy, Nabil Azzam, Joe Zeytoonian, Naser Musa, Rachid Halihal, Chakib Hilali as well as many others who have taken the time to hang out with me in the music stores, music schools and personal homes in Cairo, Aleppo, Amman and many other places in the Arab world. Kadri Srour and Naser on Mhmd Ali Street are among these. Very special acknowledgement must go to Scott Marcus. His doctoral dissertation, "Arab Music Theory in the Modern Period" is a treasure of detailed information. The Arabic note name tables are also from his work. Jesse Manno and James Hoskins, dear musician friends in Boulder, Colorado have shared in the fascination of maqam study.

I would like to invite my teachers, as well as other teachers and students, to make corrections and additions to this work.

Maqamat vary from region to region. The ones in this book are reflective of what is popular in Egypt, Jordan, Palestine, Syria and Lebanon. I have not attempted to focus on the Iraqi maqam system nor on Turkish makamlar.

Very special thanks go to Jihad Ibrahim from Amman, Jordan, Saadoun Al Bayati from Baghdad, Iraq, and Atef Abd elHameed from Cairo, Egypt, for offering me the opportunities to record their oud playing and present them as part of the teaching materials which accompany this book on cd's.

Many Thanks to Eva Soltes for gifting me a Residency at Harrison House in Joshua Tree, CA, for time and space for recording and mixing those cd's.

Cameron Powers
cameron@rmi.net
303-449-4196

Cameron Powers -- Biography

Fascination with Peruvian Indian peoples encountered on mountaineering expeditions led Cameron to spend 8 years going to and from Andean villages back in the 1960's and 70's. He immediately discovered the value of learning to play their music with them as an easy aid to bonding in trust and friendship.

Cameron graduated with BA in Anthropology and Linguistics, University of Colorado, Boulder, with an emphasis on the study of Quechua, the language of the Incas.

Cameron also received a fellowship to attend a two-month intensive immersion program in Quechua at Cornell University. It was there that he began to realize the value of being a musician as well as a linguist.

Cameron also received a scholarship to work on a Doctoral program in Linguistics at the University of California, Berkeley. He continued to study the Inca language and began studies of the Tibetan language.

In 1973 Cameron lived in Greece with the Papanastassiou family and studied Greek language and Greek music.

Returning to Boulder, Colorado, Cameron performed Greek music and began the study of Arabic music with various local bands: "The Silk Route," "The Boulder Bouzouki Band," "Solspice," and "Sherefe."

He created Musical Instruments, built Houses, and helped produce a Spanish Language Teaching Program in Boulder while raising his children.

Cameron has a long association with Middle Eastern Music Camp which takes place every summer in Mendocino, California.

After the events in New York on 9/11, a pall was cast on his role as an American musician playing Middle Eastern Music. "Terrorism" had somehow entered the music. Gigs were cancelled; people became nervous about producing Middle Eastern Music-oriented shows.

Knowing full well from his travels in the Middle East and from his extensive chain of friendships with Middle Eastern musicians that there is a warm reception available to anyone, including Americans, who wish to travel the Middle East, he realized the importance of continuing his "musical missions."

Now back from additional travels in Iraq, Egypt, Jordan, Lebanon, Syria and Palestine, he is working to help American people understand the Arab psyche.

The 501c3 non-profit organization, Musical Missions of Peace, has been built around his international work. Through the Musical Ambassador programs founded by Musical Missions of Peace help has been provided to other American musicians who have traveled and performed in Iran, Iraqi Kurdistan and Indonesia. Through the Iraqi Refugee program support has also been provided for Iraqi refugee musicians in Syria to facilitate the teaching of traditional Iraqi music to young Iraqi children.

Bibliography

A Study of Persian Musical Literature from 1000 to 1500 AD -- by Fallahzadeh
Doctoral Dissertation: Uppsala University in Sweden
2005

Al-Dalil al-Musiqi al-Amm: fi Atrab al-Angham
(General Musical Guide into the Most Ecstatic Modes)
Tawfiq al-Sabbagh, Syria
(Translatiions Found in AJ Racy's "Making Music in the Arab World:
The Culture and Artistry of Tarab")
1950

Anatomy of an Octave
http://www.kylegann.com/Octave.html
Current Online Source

Ancient Natural Harmony, Maqams and Just Intonation
http://www.innernationals.com/microtonal.html
Current Online Source

Arab Music - Part One
A J Racy
http://trumpet.sdsu.edu/M151/Arab_Music1.html
1983

Arab Music Theory in the Modern Period
Scott Marcus -- Doctoral Dissertation
1989

Azerbaijan Mugams
http://www.mugam.com/ingl/inglinfo.htm
Current Online Source

Byzantine Music: Parameters of Traditional Psaltiki
Georgios K. Michalakis
2008
http://gfax.ch/literature/Byzantine%20Music--Parameters%20of%20Traditional%20Psaltiki.pdf

Cents to Frequencies Ratios Conversions
http://www.sengpielaudio.com/calculator-centsratio.htm
Current Online Source

Frequencies for equal-tempered scale
http://www.phy.mtu.edu/~suits/notefreqs.html
Current Online Source

Harmonic Experience: Tonal Harmony from its Natural Origins to its Modern Expression
W. A. Mathieu
1997

Historical Worldview of Early Ethnomusicologist: An East-West Encounter in Cairo, 1932.
Ethnomusicology and Modern Music History. Racy, Ali J.
eds. Blum, Stephen & Bohlman, Philip V. & Daniel M. Neuman.
(University of Illinois Press.)
1993

History and Periods of Turkish Music
by Çetin Körükçü
http://www.turkishmusicportal.org/history.php?id=1&lang2=en
Current Online Source

History of Music and Musical Instruments
by Wafaa' Salman
Institute of Near Eastern & African Studies
1997

How Equal Temperament Ruined Harmony: And Why You Should Care
Ross W. Duffin
2007

Intervention And Reform Of Arab Music In 1932 And Beyond.
Conference on Music in the world of Islam. (Roanoke, VA.)
Thomas, Anne. 2007

Kitab al-Musiqa al-Kabir
Abu Nasr al-Farabi
c. 900 AD

La Musique Arabe
Baron Rodolphe D'Erlinger
Volume 5
1949

Making Music in the Arab World: The Culture and Artistry of Tarab.
(Cambridge: Cambridge University Press.) Racy, Ali.J. 2003.

Microtonally Tuneable Electronic Keyboards
http://www.h-pi.com/gm.html

Mikha'il Mishaqa: virtual founder of the twenty-four equal quartertone scale
Journal of the American Oriental Society, by Shireen Maalouf
Oct-Dec, 2003

Musical Mathematics: On the Art and Science of Acoustic Instruments
Cris Forster
2010

Music in Contemporary Cairo: A Comparative Overview
Asian Music 13 (1): 4-26 (University of Texas Press.) Racy, Ali J.
1981

Music in Egypt: Experiencing Music, Expressing Culture
Scott Marcus
2007

Music in Pure Intonation by Michael Harrison
http://michaelharrison.com/web/pure_intonation.htm#top

Music of India
http://en.wikipedia.org/wiki/Music_of_India
Current Online Source

Musical Aesthetics in Present-Day Cairo
Ethnomusicology 26 (3): 391-406.
(University of Illinois Press on behalf of Society for Ethnomusicology.) Racy, Ali J.
1982

Musical changes and commercial recordings in Egypt, 1904-1932
(University of Illinois.) Racy, Ali J.
1977

Notes from Chris Mohr -- Private Transmission
2010

On the Sensations of Tone
Hermann Helmholtz
1885

Recording Industry and Egyptian Traditional Music: 1904-1932
Ethnomusicology. 20(1): 23-48. (USA: University of Illinois.) Racy, Ali J.
1976

Science & Music
Sir James Jeans
1937

Solfege: Alternative theories of origin -- Arab
François de Mesgnien Meninski in his Thesaurus Linguarum Orientalum (1680)
http://en.wikipedia.org/wiki/Solfège
Current Online Source

Temperament: How Music Became a Battleground
for the Great Minds of Western Civilization
Stuart Isacoff
2001

The Classical Indian Just Intonation Tuning System with 22 SRUTI's
defining the 7 SWARA's of Hindu Classical Music
Wolfgang von Schweinitz
http://gfax.ch/literature/TheClassicalIndianJustIntonationTuningSystem.pdf
2006

The Dastgāh Concept in Persian Music,
by Farhat, Hormoz
Cambridge Studies in Ethnomusicology, Cambridge University Press
http://theoryofmusic.wordpress.com/2008/06/09/essentials-of-persian-music-part-1/
http://theoryofmusic.wordpress.com/2008/06/09/essentials-of-persian-music-part-2/
http://theoryofmusic.wordpress.com/2008/06/09/essentials-of-persian-music-part-3/
1990

The Maqam Book - A Doorway to Arab Scales and Modes
David Muallem
2010

The Music of the Arabs
Habib Hassan Touma
1996

The Oud: The King of Arabic Instruments
Abdoun, Seifed-Din Shehadeh
1996, Irbid, Jordan

Traditional Chinese Instrument: The Guqin
http://en.wikipedia.org/wiki/Guqin
Current Online Source

Turkish & Arab Makams
ΘΕΡΙΑ & ΑΚΤΥΛΟΘΕΣΙΑ ΓΙΑ ΟΥΤΙ
(Music Theory For Oud)
Βαγγέλης Κατσούλας
(Vangelis Katsoulas)
http://gfax.ch/literature/TurkishArabMakamMaqamOudRight-Handed.pdf
Current Online Source

Iraqi Maqam Blogspot
http://iraqimaqam.blogspot.com/
Current Online Source

Other Books by Cameron Powers

Arabic Musical Scales
*Basic Maqam Teachings
with 2 Audio CDs*

*Enter the Exotic World
of Quartertone Scales*

Designed for both the beginner and the professional musician, Arabic Musical Scales is the ultimate guide to 45 of the most popular Maqams

$34.95 +shipping & handling
with 2 audio CDs

"Excellent book. I would highly recommend the CDs that are sold separately as well. They are very well done. Very informational and also have improvised demonstrations of the scales so you can hear each scale in a musical setting."

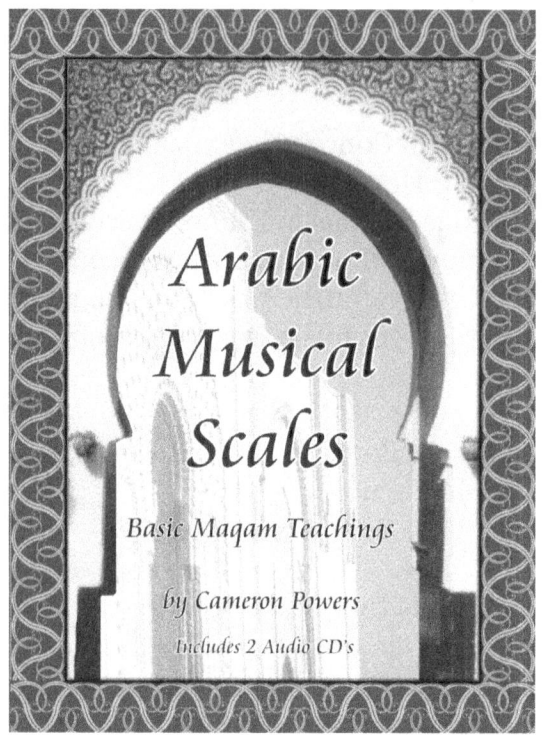

"All I have to say is 'WOW'!

You just put together what I was looking for, a concise yet comprehensive material for someone like me to study and get on with my ultimate passion, Arabic music!"

"I bought your CDs and book of basic maqam techniques. It was a wonderful surprise... it put everything I was looking for in my hands with no effort!"

"Your book on Middle Eastern scales has been invaluable to me. I lead a Middle Eastern musical ensemble but I'm the only Arab in the group, so your book has been the standard by which I teach my musicians. It really is a great book."

Singing in Baghdad
A Musical Mission of Peace
Second Edition
Author: Cameron Powers

Price: $16.95 + shiipping & handling

The story of events leading up to and including a journey to Baghdad, Iraq made at the same time as the US Marines were entering the city in the spring of 2003. The success of this journey illustrates the capacity of the Iraqi people to distinguish love-based invasions from fear-based invasions. The story told in Singing in Baghdad illustrates the possibility of expanding cross-cultural musical study and performance into a new kind of people-to-people international diplomacy.

"I have had the good fortune of reading two of Cameron's books. Just like his and Kristina's visionary simplicity in connecting with peoples our culture habitually misconstrues, they are replete with profound insights. It is not often that I get entirely new perspectives on how our world is shaped through culture. Cameron's works are chock full of them. For example, so many Americans take the oppression of women in the Middle East as a given, without ever imagining that below the head scarf, the veil or the burka there is a human being and a feminine expression of Life that deserves to be discovered before it is summarily and casually dismissed under the reductive epithet "oppressed." Cameron's books speak of the amazing power of feminine presence in the Middle East, a feminine enchantment that, in the United States, people hardly have an inkling of, much less deep, experiential appreciation for. To read Cameron's books is to feast upon delicious new territories of the heart, it inspires taking the next flight to the Middle East so that we ourselves might become a little bit more roundly human.

I recommend Cameron as someone who is an expression of the change our world inspires. When you meet him, you realize that he is the change wherever he is, always ready to sing and travel widely with spirited gentleness into the landscape of the human heart. And all of his words lead toward that knowing that there is a realm which is fully human that we can dwell in together in a way that words can't express – but a voice, a drum or an oud can... And that is the disarming genius that Cameron expounds; rather than taking us through more thought processes about how we might think ourselves into having a different perception of other, Cameron takes us directly into ecstatic song, directly into shared ecstasy which, once shared, radically softens the very sense of other and opens us to mutual discovery through the bliss that inhabits our core and is yearning for release and connection. He is not out in the world resisting fear; he is out in the world inviting fear directly to the party and the feast which always awaits us in the communion of hearts.

Cameron's vision of turning the "missionary efforts" of the West inside out is brilliant: rather than sending Western young men and women out to the far corners of the Earth to spread Jesus and Tupperware, Cameron has a vision of sending young men and women out to learn songs, wisdom and culture from global inhabitants. When I think of that, I am astounded by its brilliance: nothing to teach, nothing to propagandize – simply the willingness to learn from others a new way of being human together." -- Olivier Tryba

Spiritual Traveler: Journeys Beyond Fear

Musicians have long held many of the keys to cross-cultural journeying as a spiritual path. Along the way many things are learned. In this book we find many clues about Arab-world people and the beauties of their ancient ways. With fear removed from our perceptions, we find a way paved for endless cross-cultural love affairs.

Price: $16.95 + shiipping & handling

"I've recently returned to this book to take in its inspiration all over again. Cameron writes with infectious love and warmth that will fill your heart. In a world with serious conflict and pain, this work is encouragement to keep reaching out and connecting. It should be read at least once every year." -- Wendy Moffat

"This book is not a polished piece of writing, but it is a heartfelt, sympathetic, and eye-opening look into the world of Islam, from the standpoint of a traveler and entertainer. He has discovered the way into the hearts of foreigners through music, and thereby shares with us a look at Islamic culture from the inside. He points out that any of us could do what he does, simply by learning a few bars of a popular song, and then singing or playing it - it's an automatic door-opener."

The books listed above can be ordered from:
www.gldesignpub.com
or
E-Mail: distrib@gldesignpub.com
or
Write to:
GL Design Publishing
1930 Central Ave -- Suite E
Boulder, CO 80301   USA

www.ingramcontent.com/pod-product-compliance
Lightning Source LLC
Chambersburg PA
CBHW082121230426
43671CB00015B/2763